Information Technology

Information Technology

S.L. SAH

GYAN PUBLISHING HOUSE
NEW DELHI-110002

Information Technology
(Communication Systems)

ISBN : 81-212-0601-4

Published in 1999 in India by
Gyan Publishing House
5, Ansari Road
New Delhi-110002

Laser Type Setting at: K Computer Services

Printed at Mehra Offset Press, New Delhi

Dedicated to the Scientists, Engineers, Programers, Organizations and Institutions which are engaged in Information Technology

Contents

List of Tables

Preface

The developed countries have long ago realised that information is power and have invested substantially in research in this area. Within the last three decades they have developed a host of innovative equipment for storage, processing and dissemination of information. As information became a marketable product the commercial houses and big computer companies also produced computers, information related products and machines in competition with each other. The world has become the market for the new equipment and products like computers, optical discs, CD-ROMs, VDTs, modular charging desks, modems, microform readers, word processors, disk drivers, printers, facsimile transmitters, etc.

If we look at the last 30 years of information technology (IT) which is the synthesis of computers and communication, we will find that every 18 months, practically there has been a new breakthrough in technology. Such breakthroughs have had two dramatic impacts. The first is the continuous fall in prices and the second is the continuous increase in the number crunching capacities of computers as well as increase in versatility.

A lot of information is available on tap today and perhaps it will be much cheaper to build CD-ROM libraries of technical literature than subscribing to the journals themselves. It is estimated that India imports about Rs. 150 crore worth of information every year. Of these Rs. 35 crore worth of information is of bibliographic nature containing indices and abstracts. The culture of sharing information and using technology for information sharing is growing. Technological breakthroughs may further expedite the process.

Presently communication systems are dedicated to bring the world people close together. Through Research and Development engineers are continually enhancing the capability and efficiency of communication networks. This includes such advanced services as broad-band communications, corporate networks and the highly intelligent Global System for Mobile Communications (GSM).

The vital role played by communication infrastructure in steering Indian business towards global competitiveness cannot be ignored. The seed of liberalisation sown in the early 90s in the telecom sector have today blossomed into a multicrore industry spanning a range of services, making possible the dream of being in touch any time, anywhere.

The arrival of such networking technologies as ATMS, Fast Ethernet, Frame Relay, Internet, switched networks, ISDN, etc. promise to transform the way we work. Already the mother of all networks, the Internet, has begun influencing our business and lifestyle.

In this digital age, it is hard to segregate computers and communication technologies into clear watertight compartments. As the line between them is getting blurred, a whole new wonderful world is opening up before us, be it video conferencing, digital broadcasting or multimedia. While it is crucial for corporate India to adapt to the fast-paced changes in technology and services, access to information about these new developments is limited. This coming together of computers and communications has led to the development of IT. If IT is the brain of hi-tech industry, telecom is the heart.

The National Telecom Policy of 1994 is a landmark document which has created the environment for a quantum jump in the growth of IT in India. While the world average of computers is 25 for every thousand people, it is 0.7 in India. While the world average of telephone density is 10 telephones for every 100 people, it is less than one per 100 people in India. But the policy environment and technological breakthroughs that are taking place in India will help us grow rapidly.

In 1994-95, the Indian IT industry posted a revenue of Rs. 6823.40 crore with a growth rate of 44 per cent. In the last five years, this industry has recorded a CAGR (Compound Annual Growth Rate) of 26 per cent, which is roughly double the growth rate of developed countries. The telecom sector posted a revenue of Rs. 15000 crore in the year 1994-95. The growth in terms of direct exchange lines has been in the range of 17 to 18 per cent whereas the overall growth of telecom the world over is estimated at 9 to 16 per cent.

The reach and power of telecom and IT outpace politics and defy geographical boundaries. World Wide Web spans across time and space to put cybersurfers in contact with each other. IT has taken over our lives, having even permeated activities which require imagination and sensitivity. For the print media, the National Informatics Centre (NIC) has set up a satellite data broadcasting facility that has the potential of propelling the country to the very frontiers of IT. It has over 700 micro-earth station nodes, connecting the national capital, state capitals and district headquarters to one another. It is also connected to over 200 International Networks in 160 countries. It can transmit newspaper pages on TV screens together with photographs and even sound bytes or video clips in computer–communication mode. The receiving equipment is a low-cost receiver only very Small Aperature Terminal (RO-VSAT). Government is keen to expand the NIC network from 520 districts to 6300 development blocks. The Electronic Data Interchange (EDI) format has been successful in achieving "information transparency".

Internet is one of technology's greatest democracies, permitting the passage of all kinds of information criss-crossing with full freedom. Through this channel, millions of scholars, scientists, businessmen, libraries, journalists, artists and software developers are woven into a global village.

Today India is the sixth largest exporters of computer software in the world. It could become the second largest exporter in the world in a few years. If things go smoothly, India could end up as the world's leading exporter within a decade.

There are nearly 200,000 IT professionals in India today. It is today possible to operate a computer in any part of the world by sitting in India. And providing software solutions to the world has become India's competitive advantage. The software export sector is growing at the rate of 64 per cent. India is exporting software to 75 countries, out of which some 28 are totally dependent on India. India's largest market is the USA, with Japan being the second largest.

This book covers the development of computers and communication systems in India and abroad. New frontiers of IT have been described elaborately. One chapter in information theory has been included so that the reader will have better understanding about signal detection and processing in presence of noise. To make the book interesting the "News in Focus" and glossary of technical words are included in the appendix. Addresses of vendors will help the customers to get the required items and information easily.

This book will be helpful in generating innovative ideas in the field of IT. It will be very suitable for students, engineers, scientists, planners, and others who are interested to know about the new horizons in IT.

The author will be grateful for comments and criticism which might help to improve the latter edition of this book.

Some of the material of this book has been taken from the books and the papers published in different journals. I am thankful to all of them who have contributed to the development of this book.

RISHIKESH **S.L. SAH**

1.10.1998

1

Information Theory

Man is a communicator of information. It is characteristic of man to communicate information to other men. This capability of communication of very complex ideas from man to man has led to our present state of civilisation.

The history of civilisation is the history of improved means of communication of information. Only during the last few decades has this fact been theorised and information defined in such a way that quantities of information can be measured. As C.E. Shannon has stated that information can be treated very much like a physical quantity such as mass or energy. It has been suggested that, like thermodynamics, information theory will always remain conceptual and guiding rather than definitive. There is one major achievement of information theory which must not be overlooked : researchers in many different disciplines have found that this theory can be applied to their work. Because of this, the theory has helped in the process of cross-fertilisation of ideas from one discipline to another. It provides a common language and definable quantities, for use in many different fields of endeavour. Progress in research often follows from the application of techniques and theories which were originated in one field to another, related field.

In 1953, Daniel Bell predicted that information would succeed the raw materials, natural resources and energy as a commodity. The increasing complexity and competition in the global market, the vast uncontrolled information explosion, just-in-time delivery systems, and socio-economic and cultural changes are already proving that the world is now getting tuned to the information era. It has taken many decades to realise that the new wealth is neither money nor power but information and knowledge.

Historical Development

Information theory is concerned with the basic limitations of various methods of communication. The earliest forms of communication evolved by living creatures were probably tactile and visual. Although sound was used for communication between creatures at various levels of evolution, only man has had the capacity to produce more than an elementary form of phonetics.

Modern work on the theory of information and its transmission can be said to have started with the study of frequency modulation by Carson in 1922. In 1924, Nyquist showed that a definite minimum bandwidth is required for a given rate of transmission of information. In 1928, Hartley suggested that the transmission of a definite quantity of information required a definite bandwidth and time product. Gabor later elaborated this concept, while Tuller added the phenomenon of noise to Hartley's work.

The modern theory of information is based largely on the theories of Shannon. The basic principle adopted is that any message which has a high probability of occurrence conveys little information. Most information is conveyed by the least likely messages. Thus, information theory is based on probability. Meaningful messages can appear by sheer chance. By making use of tables of probabilities of various words and symbols, it is possible to construct in various languages, sentences and paragraphs which approximate very closely the appearance of the natural language and yet which are quite meaningless.

The classical paper of Shannon gave a precise mathematical definition for the intuitive notion of information. In terms of this definition it was possible to define precisely the notion of a communication channel and its capacity.

By a communication channel we mean an apparatus for signalling from one point to another. The abstracted properties of a channel are : (a) a finite set of signals that may be transmitted, (b) a set of signals that may be received, (c) the probability of the reception of any particular signal when the signal transmitted is specified. A simple telegraph system is a concrete example. The transmitted signals are long pulse, a short pulse and a pause. If there is no noise in the wire, the received signals are identical with the transmitted signals. If there is noise in the wire, the received signals will be mutilations of the transmitted signals, and the conditional probability of the received signals will depend on the statistical characteristics of the noise present.

General Communication System

Information must be conveyed from a source to a destination. There are imperfections in all methods of conveying information, and these introduce the possibility of misunderstanding.

At the information source, a selection is made of one or more of the permissible messages which the system is capable of handling. The message can take various forms in communication system, i.e. :

1. A simple function of time, e.g., a particular sinusoidal frequency.
2. A more complex function of time and one other variable, e.g., an amplitude modulation sinusoid.
3. A sequence pattern in which time has importance, e.g., morse code.
4. A function of time and two other variables, e.g., a television signal.
5. Several simultaneous functions, each of time and one other variable, e.g., stereo sound signals.
6. Several simultaneous functions, each of time and of several other variables, e.g., colour television signals.
7. Messages consisting of combinations of the above, e.g., a television signal with accompanying sound.

Basically, information theory at present is limited to a consideration of discrete signals, e.g., to signals which can have only certain restricted values of amplitude (such as pulse signals). When continuously variable signals have to be considered, it is necessary to reduce them theoretically to equivalent quantized signals.

The message controls the transmitter to produce a signal suitable for transmission over the channel. The channel carries the signal from transmitter to receiver, and it can take the form of wires, electromagnetic radiation, fibre optic, etc. At the receiver the signal is usually reconverted into the form of the original message, and then it is passed on to the destination, which might be either a human recipient or a machine. No practical system conveys information without some distortion. Signal distortion and interfering noise occur on all practical communication systems. The object of information theory is to provide methods for studying and discussing such effects. Fig. 1.1 shows the general communication system.

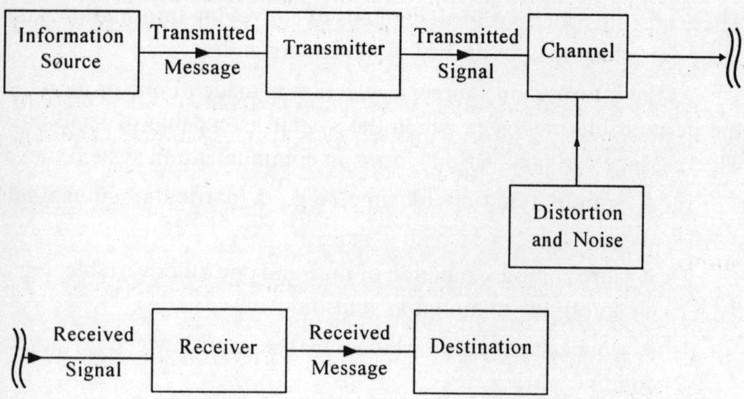

Fig.1.1. General Communication System.

In order to study the communication of information it is necessary to consider and to devise measures for the following aspects :

1. Quantity of information.
2. The maximum quantity of information which can be passed over a channel.
3. The efficiency of the coding process.
4. The effects of distortion and of interfering noise.
5. The degree of discreteness.

Signals of all kinds have a discrete nature and they differ mainly in degree of discreteness. It is not possible to consider discrete signals fully without a careful study of noise. Information is communicated by means of symbols. The symbols can be visual or aural. It can be said that information theory deals with nominal data. That is, the interest is often in symbols or labels rather than in physical quantities which can be measured with an instrument.

When a source of information is producing a sequence of symbols at the rate of Q symbols per second, then it can be said that information is being produced at a certain rate. The maximum speed of transmission of information which can be achieved is always limited by the nature of communication channel. Any given channel is capable of transmitting a certain number of bits of information per second. The distortion of signals produced by the characteristics of transmission lines places a severe limitation on the speed of transmission of information. In the 1920s, Nyquist and Kupfmuller both stated that in order to carry signals at a given rate, a telegraph circuit must have a certain bandwidth. Hartley showed that maximum rate of transmitting information should be proportional to the system bandwidth.

Mathematics of Communication

A general communication system consists of five elements: an information source, the transmitter, the channel, the receiver and the destination. It is convenient to use a logarithmic measure of information. If a device has n possible position, it can store $\log_b n$ units of information. The choice of the base b amounts to a choice of unit, since $\log_b n = \log_b c . \log_c n$. The base 2 unit is called the binary digits or bits. A group of m relays or flip-flop circuits have 2^m possible sets of positions, and can therefore store $\log_2 2^m = m$ bits.

If it is possible to distinguish reliably M different signal functions of duration T on a channel, then the channel can transmit $\log_2 M$ bits in time T. The rate of transmission is then $\log_2 \frac{M}{T}$. The channel capacity C may be defined as : $C = \lim_{T\to\infty} \frac{\log_2 M}{T}$ ...(1)

If a function f(t) contains no frequencies higher than WHz, it is completely determined by giving its ordinates at a series of points spaced $\frac{1}{2W}$ second a-part.

Let F(*w*) be the spectrum of *f(t)*, then

$$f(t) = \frac{1}{2\pi}\int_{-\infty}^{\infty} F(w)e^{jwt}\,dw \qquad ...(2)$$

or

$$f(t) = \frac{1}{2\pi}\int_{-2\pi w}^{+2\pi w} F(w) \qquad ...(3)$$

Since F(*w*) is assumed zero outside the band W.

If $$t = \frac{n}{2W}$$

When n is any positive or negative integer, then

$$f\left(\frac{n}{2W}\right) = \frac{1}{2\pi}\int_{-2\pi W}^{+2\pi W} F(W)\, e^{jwn/2n} \qquad \text{...(4)}$$

The values of the samples *f(n/2w)* determine the Fourier Coefficients in the series expansions of F*(w)*. The functions can be simply reconstructed from the samples by using a pulse of the type $\sin 2\pi Wt / 2\pi Wt$.

Let x_n be the nth sample, then the function *f(t)* is represented by

$$\sum_{n=-\infty}^{\infty} x_n = \frac{\sin \pi(2wt - n)}{(2wt - n)} \qquad \text{...(5)}$$

Any function limited to the bandwidth W and the time internal T can be specified by giving 2 TW numbers.

If we consider only signals whose average power is less than P, these will correspond to points within a sphere of radius.

$$r = \sqrt{2WTP} \qquad \text{...(6)}$$

If noise is added to the signal in transmission, it means that the point corresponding to the signal has been moved a certain distance in the space proportional to the rms value of noise. Thus noise produces a small region of uncertainty about each point in the space. A fixed distortion in the channel corresponds to a wrapping of the space, so that each point is moved, but in a definite fixed way.

The transmitter maps the message space into the signal space. The receiver maps the signal space back into the message space. It is possible to have more than one point mapped into the same point. This means that several different signals are demodulated or decoded into the same message.

Let us assume that the noise in the system is a white thermal noise band limited to the band W, and that it is added to the transmitted signal to produce the received signal.

Let P be the average transmitter power, and suppose the noise is white thermal noise of power N in the band W. By sufficiently complicated encoding system it is possible to transmit binary digit at a rate

$$c = W.\log_2 \frac{P+N}{N} \qquad ...(7)$$

with as small a frequency of errors as desired. It is impossible by any encoding method to send the bits at a higher rate and have an arbitrarily low frequency of errors.

Let a noise limited to the band W have power N and entropy power N_1. The capacity C is then bounded by

$$W.\log_2 \frac{P+N_1}{N_1} \leqq C \leqq W \log_2 \frac{P+N}{N} \qquad ...(8)$$

where P is the average signal power and W the bandwidth.

The capacity C measures the maximum rate at which a random series of binary digits can be transmitted when they are encoded in the best possible way.

If we have a channel of capacity C and a discrete source of entropy H, it is possible to encode the message via binary digits into signals and transmit at the rate C/H of the original message symbols per second.

If the source is producing a continuous function of time, it can be described as infinite rate of generating information. We cannot send continuous information exactly over a channel of finite capacity. A certain amount of discrepancy between the original and the recovered messages can always be tolerated. If a certain tolerance is allowed, then a definite finite rate in binary digits per second can be assigned to a continuous source. The rate may be described as the rate of generating information relative to the criterion of fidelity. If the message source has power Q, entropy power $\overline{Q}$, and bandwidth W_1, the rate R of generating information in bits per second is bounded by

$$W_1 \log_2 \frac{\overline{Q}}{N_1} \leqq R \leqq \log_2 \frac{Q}{N_1} \qquad ...(9)$$

where N_1 is the maximum tolerable mean square error in reproduction. If we have a channel with capacity C and a source whose rate of generating information R is less than or equal to C, it is possible to encode the source in such a way as to transmit over this channel with the fidelity measured by N_1. If $R > C$, this is impossible.

If the case where the message source is producing white thermal noise, $\overline{Q} = Q$. Hence the two bounds are equal and $R = W_1 . \log Q / N_1$. We can, therefore, transmit white noise of power Q and band W_1 over a channel of band W perturbed by a white noise of power N and recover the original message with mean square error N_1 if, and only if,

$$W_1 . \log_2 \frac{Q}{N_1} \leq \log \frac{P+N}{N} \quad ...(10)$$

Simple Digital System

There is a class of systems whose inputs and outputs are specified only at discrete time instants rather than for all time. Such type of systems are called discrete data systems. In discrete data system, the signals change only at discrete instants of time. Usually these instances of time are separated by some uniform interval. This type of discrete signal is required in digital system. Depending upon the requirements, the signals may be quantized in time and/or in amplitude. If the signals are quantized in time only, the system is called discrete time system or sampled data system. If it is quantized in amplitude only then it is called discrete signal system. If the signals are quantized both in time and amplitude, the system is called digital system. A simple digital system is shown in Fig. 1.2.

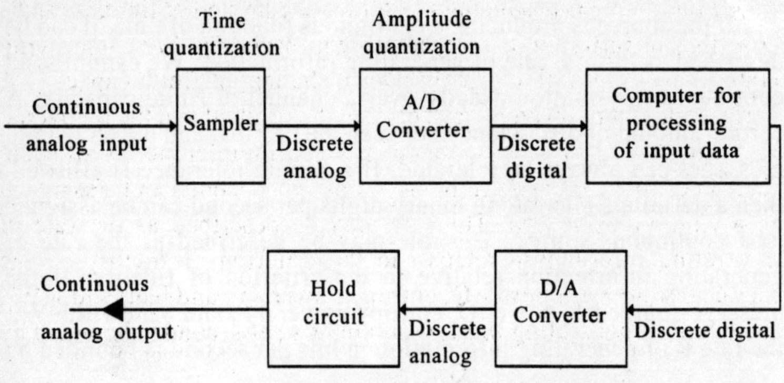

Fig. 1.2. Digital System.

Sampling of data is one of the fundamental operations in digital systems. Sampling process converts a continuous signal into a train of pulses. In a digital system only certain discrete values of amplitudes of the sample are allowed. Any sample which falls between the two allowed levels is converted into a sample of amplitude level nearest to the actual value of the signal. The process of approximation of signal by discrete levels is known as amplitude quantization. The sample is then converted into a code group by means of an encoder.

Digital Communication System

The problem of communication is to send the information from one place to another through noisy medium. It is desired that the information received is as close as possible to the information transmitted. Digital techniques have been widely used in the field of communication to reproduce the original signal seriously. One of the main advantages of digital signals is that it can be regenerated with switching amplifiers since the Zero-crossing of the digital signal carry the information and the linearity of the signal processing devices is of no importance. Also the use of digital techniques allows us to use special codes for the coding of messages.

The message from a source is converted by the transmitter into a signal adapted for transmission. A single channel can be shared by many messages. The technique of transmitting many messages over the same channel is known as multiplying. In this case, several sources of information are connected to the same transmitter. At the receiving end, the signals are converted back into respective messages. The transmitter block first converts the messages into digital signals and these digital signals are encoded before modulation. Encoding is a process by which the discrete data is converted into a code while modulation is a process by which some characteristics of the information carrier is modified in accordance with the instantaneous value of the input function. Modulation methods serve to improve the transmission reliability. At the receiving end, the received signal is first demodulated. It is then decoded and finally demultiplexed if more than one channel has been used. Fig. 1.3 shows a PCM communication system.

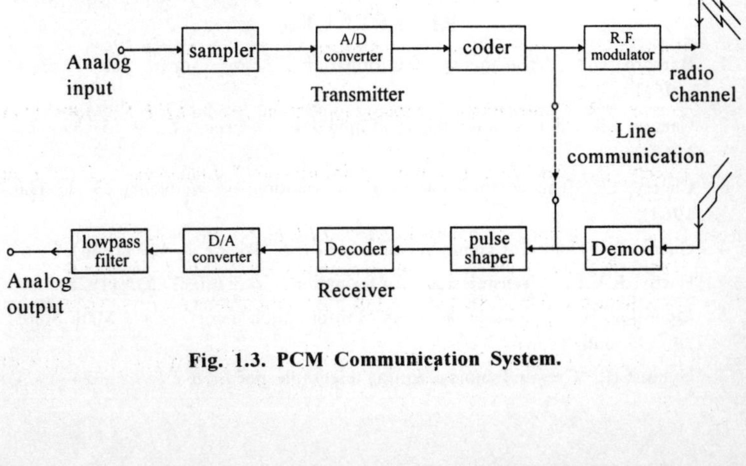

Fig. 1.3. PCM Communication System.

Conclusion

Information theory is the body of statistical mathematics which has developed out of efforts to understand and improve the art of communication.

Probably no single work in this century has more profoundly altered man's understanding of communication than Shannon's paper entitled, "A mathematical theory of communication", first published in 1948. He constructed simple mathematical models that describe the macroscopic functioning of each block of communication system. Also he studied how these models fit together. These resulted in theorems of great power, elegance, generality and beauty. They have shed much understanding on the elusive true nature of the communication process and have delineated its inherent limitations.

The ideas in Shannon's paper were soon picked up by communication engineers and mathematicians around the world. They were elaborated upon, extended and complemented with new related ideas. The subject thrived and grew to become a well-rounded and exciting chapter in the annals of science which is now known as information theory.

Most practical communication media are governed by linear time-invariant differential equations. Hence, the first applications of information theory have been to systems which are naturally best handled by the tools of Fourier or Laplace analysis.

REFERENCES

1. Barnard, G.A., "The theory of information", *J. Roy. Statist. Soc.* 13 B, 46 (1951).
2. Carson, J.R., "Notes on the theory of modulation", *Proc. I.E.E.E.*, 51,893 (Jun. 1963).
3. Cherry, C., "The communication of information," *Endeavour,* 23, 13 (Jan. 1964).
4. Gabor, D. "Theory of communication", *J.I.E.E.*, 93. Pt. 3, 429 (1946).
5. Hartly, R.V.L., "Transmission of information.", *B.S.T.J.*, 7, 535 (1928).
6. Mcmillan, B., "The basic theorems of information theory", Ann. Math Statist, 24, 196 (Jun. 1953).
7. Nyquist H., "Certain factors affecting telegraph speed," *B.S.T.J.*, 3, 324 (1924).

8. Rea, W.T., "The communication engineer's needs in information theory," Trans. *A.I.E.E.*, 75, Pt. 1, 805 (1956).

9. Shannon, C.E., "A mathematical theory of communication," *B.S.T.J.*, 27, 379 and 623 (Jul., Oct., 1948).

10. Shannon, C.E., "Communication in the presence of noise", *Proc. I.R.E.*, 37, 10 (1949).

11. Tuller, W.G., "Theoretical limits on the rate of transmission of information", *Proc. I.R.E.*, 37, 468 (1949).

12. Wolfowitz, J., "On channels without capacity," *Inf. and Control,* 6, 49, (Mar. 1963)

2

New Frontiers of Information Technology

Like a surging river, Information Technology (IT) has been reaching out for the latest knowhow from world leaders. Today IT is surging ahead to explore new frontiers of growth. This has led to the creation of global scale industries which are technically sound and commercially profitable.

IT is the combination of four important disciplines. They are: (1) Information Science, (2) Computer Technology, (3) Communication Technology, (4) Management.

People tend to label the software and hardware industry as the IT industry. A typical IT industry is one which treats information as a commodity and involves economics of information, viz., production, costing and marketing.

IT is the brain of hi-tech industry and telecom is the heart. IT, at a basic level, is the conversion of human intelligence and logic into software that propels the computer to crunch numbers. Telecom is the backbone for widespread informational growth. It provides the means to send the bytes of information soaring across the country or even to far-off countries via satellite uplinks. The reach and power of IT and telecom defy political and geographical obstacles. World Wide Web (WWW) spans across time and space to put cybersurfers in contact with each other.

Information is the fourth managerial asset (after people, equipment and capital). Wider use of IT would save money and time. Though scientific knowledge flows worldwide through formal and informal networks of publications, conferences, data-processing and computerised information communication systems, but the problem of determining ownership of scientific knowledge poses the question of its control, and the cost of its production.

Planned Information Technology Strategy

Adoption of well planned IT strategies are essential for organisations to be effective and competitive in today's dynamic business environment. IT strategy should include a well thought out and properly executed computerisation plan covering the entire functions of the organisation with proper integration among various systems.

There is no industrial sector unaffected by the revolution in IT. Successful project management requires implementation of projects according to specifications, within the scheduled time and at costs as originally estimated. Information is vital for the success of large, complex projects as their execution involves information flows relating to a variety of activities. There is enormous exchange of both technical and non-technical information generated by various work groups within the organisations and a number of outside agencies. This has to be coordinated effectively by monitoring the generation of information, data and documents by the responsible groups and making them available across the organisation for use by others functionally or for status monitoring and reporting.

IT objectives and applications in an organisation are :

1. Automation of normal and special functions such as design and engineering, material management, accounts, etc.
2. Coordination, monitoring and reporting of entire project activities. This requires capturing of data as and when generated for on-line availability across various users.
3. Building up comprehensive project data for future use.

Table 2.1. Twenty Top Indian Infotech Revenue Earners

S. No.	*Company*	*1993-94 (in Rs. crore)*	*1994-95 (in Rs. crore)*	*Percentage change*
1.	HCL	353.70 crore	605.50 crore	71.05
2.	Wipro Ltd.	380.83 "	572.29 "	50.20
3.	Pertech Computers Ltd.	204.35 "	369.48 "	80.81
4.	TCS	253.67 "	352.28 "	38.87
5.	ECIL	174.34 "	212.96 "	22.86
6.	Fujitsu ICIM Ltd.	160.30 "	211.49 "	31.93
7.	TISL	105.00 "	195.00 "	85.71
8.	DEIL	130.70 "	174.36 "	33.40
9.	NIIT Ltd.	95.35 "	162.07 "	69.97
10.	Tata Unisys Ltd.	120.40 "	140.77 "	16.92
11.	CMC Ltd.	115.00 "	140.24 "	21.95
12.	TVS Electronics Ltd.	70.75 "	114.91 "	62.42
13.	Aptech Computer Education	64.87 "	113.10 "	74.36
14.	Godrej & Boyce (EBE Div.)	91.00 "	96.59 "	6.14
15.	Zenith Computer Ltd.	60.50 "	92.00 "	52.07
16.	CMC Computer Ltd.	62.50 "	90.52 "	44.83
17.	PCS (Computer Div.)	65.00 "	85.00 "	30.77
18.	Modi Olivetti Ltd.	58.68 "	84.50 "	44.00
19.	Unicrop Computers	43.00 "	84.00 "	95.35
20.	Ultra Tek Device Ltd.	76.36 "	83.24 "	9.02

Table 2.2. Top Ten Indian IT Companies in 1996-97

S. No.	*Company*	*Turnover (in Rs. crore)*	*Percentage Growth over Previous Year*
1.	Wipro Infotech	Rs. 870 crore	11.38
2.	TCS	Rs. 721 "	40.15
3.	JTS Technology	Rs. 623 "	566.42*
4.	PCL	Rs. 589 "	23.69
5.	Tata Info Sys Ltd.	Rs. 533 "	62.91
6.	NIIT	Rs. 451 "	70.35
7.	HP India	Rs. 352 "	28.00
8.	Digital Equipp. India	Rs. 321 "	23.71
9.	APTECH Ltd.	Rs. 231 "	24.57
10.	CMC Ltd.	Rs. 228 "	26.27

IT application in an industry can be broadly divided into following categories :

1. Technical Applications : The hardware capabilities required for running technical applications is characterised by powerful CPU with floating point processing capability, large memory, high resolution graphic terminals with specialised printers, plotters, scanners and digitisers.

2. Commercial Applications : On line integrated commercial applications can be developed with appropriate linkage to the project management systems for transfer of necessary data across the systems.

3. Office Automation : Management of routine correspondence, communication, document exchange, etc., are important elements of project work. Office automation products like word processors, E-mail, integrated FAX/Telex facilities, document filing and retrieval systems are available. Large volume of documentation is generated during a project work in the form of reports, contracts, manuals, etc. Electronic publishing using Desktop publishing system can be used for printing the documents.

4. Communication : Integrated computer applications should have a strong communication foundation. These include both inter and intra office communication using Local Area Networks (LAN) and Wide Area Networks (WAN). Communication requirements to achieve integrated computer environment are as follows :

(a) Linking technical and commercial information systems.

(b) Integrating imaging systems with commercial, technical and office automation systems.

(c) Networking FAX/Telex facilities with computers.

(d) Establishing both LAN and WAN to connect the main, branch and site offices.

Vending Information

In 1953 Daniel Bell, a famous sociologist, coined the word "Information Society" and predicted that information would succeed all the raw materials, natural resources and energy as a commodity. The increasing complexity and competitions in the global market, the vast uncontrolled information explosion, just-in-time delivery systems, and socio-economic and cultural changes are already proving that the world is now getting turned to the information era. It has taken almost four decades for us to realise that the new wealth is neither money nor power but information and knowledge. India, is low gradually becoming a service providing nation to the countries which need reliable information at a cheaper cost.

In this attractive scenario, the industry which could exploit the computer and communication technologies along with the hard working manpower and the resources, to solve the problems due to the information explosion, would definitely become the prime mover of the entire world. The future lies in the hands of information producing or information vending industries. Information production is nothing but database making. These databases would be the goldmines for some countries especially the third world countries, which can get the information at a cheaper rate. Obtaining knowhow from foreign databases is 10 times costlier than obtaining it from India. India can provide on-line information at a cheaper rate due to the lower production cost.

Major activities involved in producing and marketing of information are: (1) Data/information collection, (2) Analysis, (3) Data processing, (4) Information storage, (5) Information dissemination, (6) Management. The analysis and interdisciplinary nature of these activities are given below:

1. Data/Information Collection : Information centre or library is the heart and soul of an IT industry. The people who are involved in this activity should have the following skills:

(a) Identifying the sources and services of data/information.

(b) Understanding the peculiar characteristics and the time value of information.

(c) Knowing different ways and channels of collecting the relevant data.

(d) Analysing the subject relevancy of the data/information collected.

(e) Categorising and classifying the information.

(f) Archiving and devising effective tools of retrieval.

Time value of the information is the life of a particular information. An information vendor should be able to provide the required information on time for the customer.

2. Data/Information Processing : Data/information collected is first analysed for relevancy by the subject analysts and processed by the computer professionals. This is the activity in which the computer technology is applied. As massive data processing is involved, an extraordinary computer centre with very high speed processors having greater memory is required. The output of this unit would be marketable information in the forms of databases and knowledge bases. These are packaged and disseminated through different media.

3. Information Marketing : The need for communication technology is inevitable for information marketing/dissemination. With the increasing complexity of the global market the urge to get the right information at the right time also increases. IT industry is required to have a global network so that information produced in one place can be marketed anywhere in the world. The network could also be used for data collection. There are many network providers, both national and international in India like VSNL, INET, DATA-LINE, INDONET, NICNET, etc.

The characteristics of information are so peculiar when treated as commodity, that the existing cook-book theories of management and production functions could not be applied to an IT industry. The need to change the managerial science is called for. The need of the hour is to control the information explosion and to provide new theories of management to cope up with the growing complexity in the global market.

The Indian IT industry is facing two problems:

1. Existing companies are creating databases for the same field, i.e., redundancy.
2. Foreign database makers are capturing unexploited areas of database making, e.g., Galileo's international computer reservation system is planning to capture the Indian market.

There are a growing number of database making companies available in the country. This is the right time for the Indian IT industry to start database making in unexploited areas.

Information Highway

The Information Highway is a nation wide data network that permits a two-way flow of information. The data travels in a split second from the database to the user's computer, electronically connected to the mainframe computer at an Information Centre. The prodigious storage capacity of computers permits storage of a monolith of national data and, more than that, their retrieveal at the user's convenient time.

The Information Highway will change the very business culture of the country. Business transactions, including banking, will be done on the Highway. Cellular telephones will allow seeing the person while talking; for money transactions, thumb impression can be taken and voice recorded to make them fool-proof. This reduces the need for frequent executive travel. The teleconference facility will minimise the need for air travel, too. The Highway will generate two kinds of employment : (1) purely technical and (2) business related. A lot of engineers and computer software personnel will be needed in the first category. In the second category, a lot of innovative business managers who can raise funds and create user friendly packages will be in demand. Prof. B.N. Jain of IIT, Delhi, is absolutely confident that India has the technological competence to build the Information Highway. We have the basic communication infrastructure. But we may have to import software packages and hardware. The ERNET is being shared by some 20,000 to 30,000 users. According to Prof. H.M. Gupta of IIT, Delhi, with globalisation, the volume of business is expanding so fast that FAX is no more fast enough. As business is being decentralised, there is greater need for inter-department

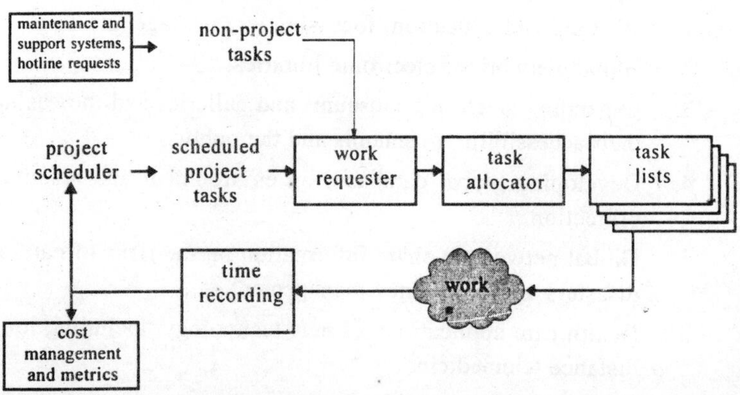

Fig. 2.1. A Simple View of Information Flows.

communication. Very often, the departments are located in different places. So the Information Highway is the only answer to communication bottlenecks and it will usher in the 21st century rightaway. On the software front, our industry and technical institutes can together face any challenge posed on this front. On the hardware front, our performance is dismal. Our investment, time-wise and money-wise, has been measly. Competent computer professionals who can adapt and innovate software packages are in short supply. Computer application needs much more brains, and is certainly much more paying. Hardware jobs are customer-related, design-related and product-related, and the segment is opening up.

Many computer companies are shifting their operations to Asian countries, because of the enormous cost of hiring brain-power in the West. Against a cost of $ 50,000 an ace computer personnel can be hired for $ 1400 a year in Asia. Global scales of economy would bridge the gulf in technology between the developed and the developing countries in a decade.

G-7 nations (U.S.A., Britain, Canada, France, Germany, Italy and Japan) have planned to set up a new electronically-linked information society which would encompass all nations. Countries in transition and the developing countries must be given a chance to fully participate in this process. All G-7 nations have approved of a package of eleven pilot projects for international cooperation in information technologies. Projects approved at the G-7 conference are:

1. Training and education, focussing on language teaching.
2. Global network of electronic libraries.
3. Expanding electronic museums and galleries and increasing their accessibility to schools and the public.
4. Developing global databases on environment and resource protection.
5. Global network to share information on the risks of natural disasters and emergency management.
6. Health care applications of new technology, including long distance telemedicine.
7. On-line exchanges between governments.

8. Making information more readily available to small businesses.
9. Maritime information exchange system to improve safety at sea and environmental protection.
10. An inventory of national and international projects and studies on the information society.
11. Global interoperability by linking the various high speed networks.

India's first information highway linking 14 cities with high speed satellite earth stations set up by the National Informatics Centre (NIC) was dedicated to the nation in September, 1994. The info-highway is superposed on the existing NIC Network (NIC-NET) which has 700 earth stations linking 500 centres. Broadcasting is expected to play a major part in linking all information networks in the country into a single information super highway (ISH). Introduction of the ISH would increase productivity by 20 to 40 per cent and create massive job opportunities. It will help in regional, state and local economic development, and electronic commerce.

The concept is being developed in countries like the United States, the United Kingdom, Canada and Japan and can be successfully used for networking data bank, telecommunication, education and health facilities. In India, the concept could help provide free exchange of information among educational institutions, hospitals, health care institutions and other sectors. Essentially, an Information Highway is a network of optical fibre, coaxial, twinwire, microwave link, with radio, television and satellite bringing together thousands of inter-connected and interoperable networks.

A large number of networks are already operating in India, and these could be linked to create ISH. Some of these include the educational and research network (ERNET) of the department of electronics and the remote area business message network (RABMN) of the department of telecommunications. To integrate these systems, the information network would have to be generated. Broadcasting is a powerful constituent of this because of the wide area covered by it with minimum investment, and the free service provided by it to the consumers. Broadcasting could also distribute video, audio and data off the air with limited interactivity through telephone. There were approximately 45 million TV households and 70 million radio households in country in 1994.

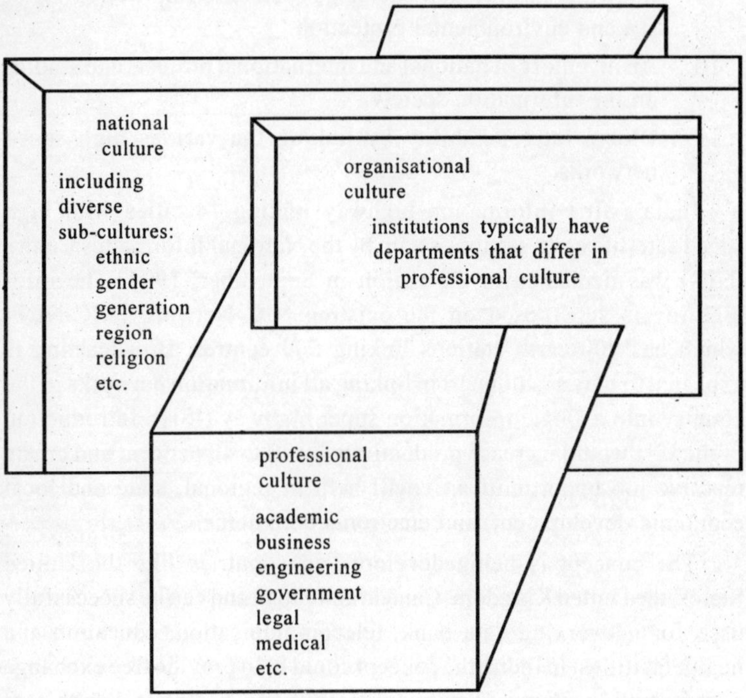

Fig. 2.2. Business Relationships Among People of Different Cultures.

Internet Access

Internet was introduced in 1969 as a pentagon research and development network. Today it has become an electronic global village. Now half of the Internet domains are outside the United States.

Internet is the fast growing network of computers around the world connecting millions of users through a simple telephone line. Today over 40 million personal computers (PCs) are hooked onto this network worldwide. Using the Internet, a person in Tokyo can look up to the train schedules in Europe, a high school student in San Francisco can persue course offerings at Cornell University in New York and people worldwide can exchange messages electronically in "Virtual Communities" devoted to thousands of distinct subjects. People are using the Internet to conduct long distance telephone calls. The Internet is growing quickly and the latest, least expensive technology

Table 2.3. Top Internet Users Countries

S. No.	*Country*	*Percentage Increase in July, 1995*
1.	New Zealand	22
2.	Norway	33
3.	Switzerland	35
4.	Sweden	40
5.	Canada	42
6.	United States	42
7.	Australia	49
8.	Finland	86

is being incorporated into it as rapidly as possible. Figures for Internet sites worldwide showed a jump to about 5 million in January 1995, from about 2 million in 1994. Among the Japanese, there is fear that if the language of computers remain English, it will be more difficult for them to compete in the information industries of the future.

India joined the global computer web on August 15, 1995 when the Videsh Sanchar Nigam Limited (VSNL) provided the gateway on commercial basis. Earlier VSNL was offering only E-mail services on Internet. This new arrangement would make it possible to access news, databases, graphics entertainment. It has been named the gateway internet access service (GIAS). Connections have been provided to Europe and U.S.A. via satellite and submarine cable through the VSNL's main node in Bombay. One only needs a phone, a personal computer and a modem to access the Internet.

Project ERNET of the Department of Electronics (DOE) has been providing this connectivity on non-commercial basis. At present, ERNET users can access Internet from eight cities – Delhi, Bombay, Madras, Calcutta, Pune, Bangalore, Hyderabad and Ahmedabad. In Delhi, for instance ERNET extends Internet access to 10 users simultaneously through a combination of leased telecom lines and VSAT links to the main gateway hub at Bangalore and Bombay. Other cities provide 40 more Internet access at the same time.

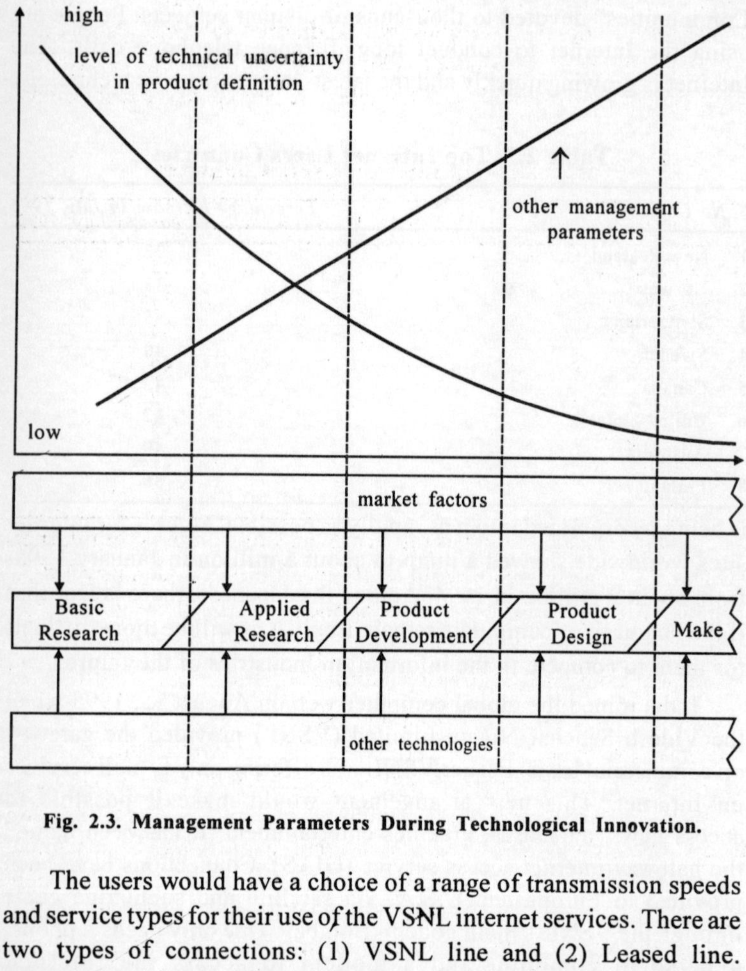

Fig. 2.3. Management Parameters During Technological Innovation.

The users would have a choice of a range of transmission speeds and service types for their use of the VSNL internet services. There are two types of connections: (1) VSNL line and (2) Leased line. Registeration fees of dial-in facility vary between Rs. 1000 and Rs. 10,000 per year for users other than students. Students have to pay Rs. 500/- per year. A student category subseriber with a terminal dial up account type is allowed a 2.4 kilo bites per second (kbps) access which allows for scanning of text and storing information in a floppy. The higher band-widths of 64 kbps to 128 kbps (the Tep/IP dial up account type) will get one to access graphics, sound and other audio/ video facilities. For leased access, tariff varies from Rs. 1.5 lakh per year for commercial organisations using a 2.4 kbps, leased line to

Rs. 25 lakhs per year at 128 kbps access speed. VSNL has provided connectivity from India to MCI, USA using multiple 64 kbps high speed links, which are to be upgraded to 2 mega bites per second (Mbps) later.

A cyber-prodigy virtually created a stampede on the Internet by co-authoring the Mosaic Web browser software. The software of Marc Andreessen, a computer genius, University of Illinois has opened the Internet, previously accessible mainly to the computer "nerds" to millions of ordinary mortals. Investors think that Andreessen is the next Bill Gates, founder of Microsoft. Netscape offers a free software programme that allows Internet users to travel fairly easily across Internet's World Wide Web. Microsoft is competing with it by introducing its own web browsing software as part of a new Windows computer operating program.

Netscape is working on an encryption process that will allow someone to use a credit card safely on the Internet. That could be revolutionary. Many people who use Netscape's browser on their desktop and do not know about stocks also bought it. The current craze in America is to own stocks. But an even bigger mania is the Internet.

Windows 95

Bill Gates is the leader of software giant Microsoft Corporation. He has launched the software giant's Windows 95 operating system. Now he stands at the pinnacle of the computer industry. He is the richest man in the United States with a stake in Microsoft valued at more than 13 billion.

Windows 95 is the most popular version of the software that runs more than 100 million world's personal computers. It is creating a stir in worldwide market. The $85 billion a year personal computer industry is recognised as a pillar of the American economy. As a gateway to the Internet, cyberspace and multimedia, the personal computer affects everything from how people communicate with each other to how children are educated. Windows 95 is a new operating system. An operating system controls the on screen look of a PC and the keyboard and mouse steps required to use it. More than 80 per cent of all PCs use Microsoft's operating software. Windows 95 is the most significant change. Microsoft has made in its operating program since 1990. That was the year the company introduced its first windows system which enabled a user to point and click on graphical icons instead of typing arcane commands. Some existing programs do not yet run smoothly on windows 95 and it requires more computer hard-disk space and random-access memory to use than the previous generation of windows. For Microsoft, the marketing campaign is essentially a $150 million insurance policy to make sure that nothing happens to prevent windows 95 from becoming by far the most successful product in the history of the business. Microsoft gets $50 in revenue for each copy sold. Selling 29 million copies in 1995 meant $1.45 billion in revenue to Microsoft.

Windows 95 users have the ability to run two or more operations simultaneously, such as sending faxes while checking spelling on a report and remaining connected to an on-line network. A reorganised desk-top makes it easier to see what files are available, and this can be customised for different family members. Opening programs and files is also simplified and getting rid of unwanted files is as easy as dragging an icon to a recycle bin. File names would not have to be limited to eight characters, as in the old system. So users can label their files as "letter to mom" instead of "letrmom". They also get improved protection against computer viruses and a single location to receive electronic mail and fax communication.

With the new software, new hardware and accessories can be installed without complicated reprogramming, because windows 95 senses the equipment being used. This feature is known as "plug and play". Microsoft says its 32- bit program is like having a free-way expanded from 16 to 32 lanes. Reviewers suggest the system works best with the newest computers with Pentium microchips, generous hard drives and eight to 16 megabytes of RAM.

Windows 98

Microsoft's Windows 98 is seen to be a hit with avoid Net surfers. This is because the operating system contains a host of features not available on its predecessor, Windows 95. Windows 98 users have the option of choosing the look and the feel of the desktop by selecting the Web-style desktop option, in which, the mouse pointers turn into the familiar "hand" whenever it passes over a folder or program icon and opens them with a single click. One can, for example, view live updates on the weather or stock quotes without actually spending to much time on the Net.

Folders now open in the form of a Web page interface with their own back and forward buttons. Microsoft claims that the operating system can be run even on a 486/66 MHz machine with about 200 MB of hard disk space also. The foundation of Windows 98 is the facile integration of a Web browser with the operating system.

Windows 98 supports major Net standard-Java and their own Active-X, in addition to bringing streaming data, including digital audio and video, to the desktop. Uses can make their online newspaper into the wallpaper. It supports new varieties of hardware devices like DVD drives and digital audio speakers, and standards such a Universal Serial Bus and IEEE 1394, thus making it easy to add serial devices.

Windows 98 is far simpler to use than Windows 95 version. Windows 98 is a very obvious move up from Windows 95.

Information Technology Industry

An infotech gateway was put into operation on 17th Jan, 1995 which allows live interaction between thousands of USA and Indian companies. This system is called the World Wide Web (WWW). The WWW system has been developed jointly by IBM computers, Sun Micro-systems, Bay Networks and Bolt Beraneck & Newman, and CP International. This will connect 5000 Indian companies with the US Trade Association. It will allow transfer of typed data, as well as colour picture transmission, and also enable live audio interaction over the network. The WWW system is an information retrieval system on a portion of the Internet. The web system will be most helpful to small and medium sized business companies who want to access data before they strike business deals with each other.

Silicon Graphic's new Alias/Wavefront subsidiary has launched its project Maya Software which is designed to help bridge the gap between the artist and the computer, using tools such as a pen-based system to replace mousebased graphic creation. Silicon Graphics also unveiled new software for its webfore authoring to create three dimensional graphics for WWW pages on the Internet.

Fig. 2.4. Multimedia Industry Growth in the USA.

Table 2.4. What People do on Home Computers (Survey in 1995)

S. No.	*Items*	*Men*	*Women*
1.	Games	64	53
2.	Personal Business	59	66
3.	Other work	45	37
4.	On-line service	43	31
5.	E-mail	25	27

Table 2.5. Women Embrace The Web (Survey in 1997)

S. No.	*Detail*	*Men*	*Women*
1.	On-line services	41%	47%
2.	To have a business home page	16%	23%

Presently the United States has 35 per cent of the world information and communications market, the European nations have 27 per cent and Japan has 16 per cent. The ballooning global information market was worth $1.13 trillion in 1994. The information society must promote and guarantee diversity.

A Rs. 500 crore information technology park has been set up at White field on the outskirts of Bangalore. The high-tech park has been established jointly by a consortium of companies from Singapore, the Tata Group and the Government of Karnataka.

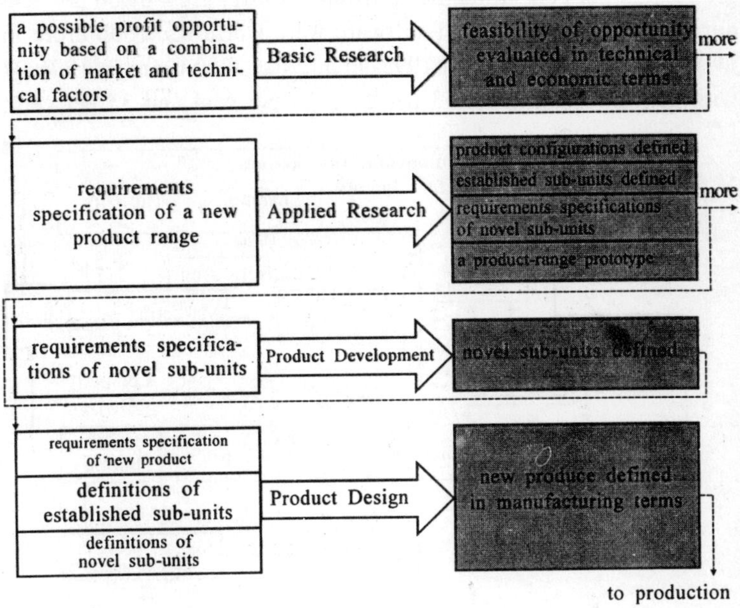

Fig. 2.5. Simplified View of the Technological Innovation Process.

The IT industry is on roll. During 1994-95, a total of 233990 PC units were sold in the country, while over 2 lakhs PCs were shipped out. Clearly, IT is rapidly making inroads into all facets of our economy and way of life. Be it banks, PSUs, the private or corporate sector or home, they are all getting wired into the information explosion In the last five years, this industry has recorded a Compounded Annual Growth Rate (CAGR) of 26 per cent which is roughly double the growth rates of developed countries.

The Indian IT industry which includes computer hardware, software and training, has crossed a turnover of Rs. 4364 crore during

1993-94 achieving an impressive growth rate of 34.42 per cent. It industry registered a 44 per cent growth during 1994-95 by posting a turnover of Rs. 6840.88 crore, according to an annual survey of the industry. HCL-HP had a turnover of Rs. 605.5 crore during 1994-95, Wipro Infotech had Rs. 572.26 crore, Tata Consultancy Services had Rs. 352.76 crore and PCL had Rs. 289.28 crore. The software industry grew by 55 per cent while the hardware industry grew by 56 per cent during 1994-95. Exports of software were worth Rs. 1560 crore in 1994-95, Rs. 2520 crore in 1995-96 and Rs. 3900 crore in 1996-97 with growth being about 53 per cent, 39 per cent and 35 per cent,

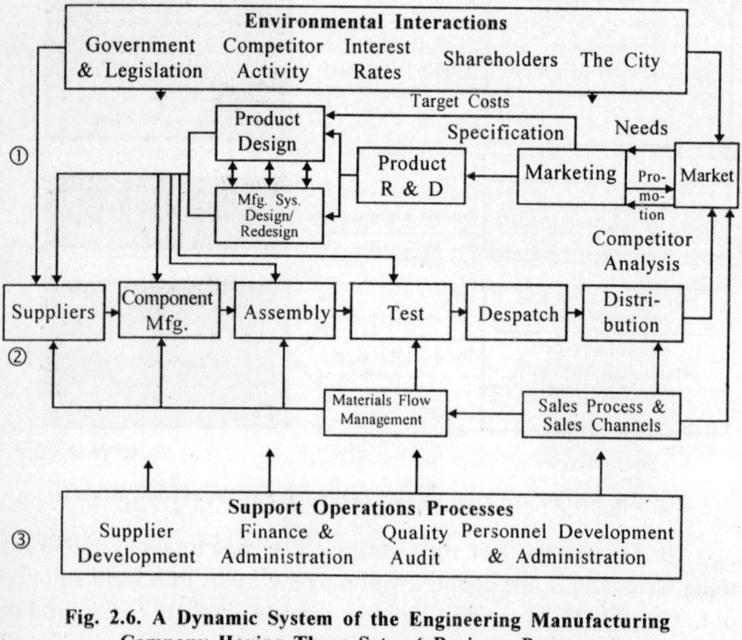

Fig. 2.6. A Dynamic System of the Engineering Manufacturing Company Having Three Sets of Business Processes.

respectively. Exports of hardware in these three years were Rs. 690 crore, Rs. 1000 crore and Rs. 1300 crore, respectively. The telecom sector has posted revenues Rs. 10206 crore in 1994-95, Rs. 12517 crore in 1995-96, Rs. 11767 crore in 1996-97 and Rs. 14035 crore in 1997-98. IT industry expected Rs. 10,000 crore from export and Rs. 5000 crore from domestic segment during the current year of 1998-99, even as hundreds of PCs get interconnected to the WWW.

The IT boom is all set to sweep across Indian Parliament. With the implementation of the computerisation project an MP, even while sitting at home, will gain access to data on all parliamentary proceedings, past and present, and parliamentary information in addition to a wide range of information relating to his specific constituency. Personal computers that will be provided to all MPs and other senior administrative staff at their residences will also enable them to avail of a wide range of office automation benefits such as E-mail, multilingual word processing, Fax facilities, voice mail, answering machine and multimedia facilities. The project is estimated to cost between Rs. 16 to Rs. 20 crore and will involve the setting up of a central computer machine at Parliament House, providing desktop computers to 50 computer-friendly MPs and laser and dot matrix printing facilities with corresponding software system.

Conclusion

The 21st century will be the century of speed as it will bear witness to space age and fast communication. Any waiting will be a great loss, not only of time but also of resources. The cyberspace of the 21st century will see the advent of fast personal computers, digital communication, televisions and high bands with cable and radio frequency networks.

The information highway is a catch phrase for an evolution that will unfold over the next decade or so, as the technologies of the computer, telephone and television coverage.

Many people expect to be able to tap a few buttons on a high-speed, high capacity information conduit in their homes to order and receive everything from Hollywood movies to books from Library of Congress. That is the vision of the information highway.

Information is the key for successful project management. The IT strategy should include a well thought out and properly executed computerisation plan covering the entire functions of the organisation with proper integration among various systems. Experience in the systems and project implementation fields will have to be properly merged to develop and implement an optimum, cost effective information system for efficient project management. Adoption of a well thought out IT strategy is essential for organisations to be effective and competitive in today's dynamic business environment.

An over-all IT strategy would enable formulation of computerisation plans and its implementation in a phased manner to meet the strategic objectives. Successful project management requires implementation of projects according to specifications within the scheduled time and at costs originally estimated. Information is vital for the success of large, complex projects as their execution involves information flows relating to a variety of activities. There is enormous exchange of both technical and non-technical information generated by various work groups within the organisations and a number of outside agencies. This has to be coordinated effectively by monitoring the generation of information, data and documents by the responsible groups and making them available across the organisation for use by others functionally or for status monitoring and reporting.

Technological innovations are sweeping the world, but their ownership remains in the hands of advanced countries. It is high time that the developing world form a collective science and industrial strategy.

VSNL has introduced "Gateway Internet Access Service" making Internet services available from anywhere in India on a commercial basis. VSNL has set up a network spanning in Bombay, Delhi, Calcutta and Madras through high speed data links, providing an avenue to access remote data bases, file transfer, news, bulletin board, remote log-in to host computers, electronic mail, etc. Subscribers can access the VSNL network by dialing in through a telephone or leased line. The services to users in other cities will be provided through I-Net packet switched network of Department of Telecommunication (DOT). VSNL is providing access to the full range of Internet services at the cheapest rates in the world.

The IT segment had a compounded annual growth rate of 26 per cent, placing the industry amongst the fastest growing segments in the Indian economy. Nearly 2.34 lakh personal computers were sold in India during the year 1994, registering a 45 per cent growth in value.

Window 95 has features like the plug and play technology which automatically connects the computer to compatible disk drives, sound cards and has built-in-softwares like Microsoft Exchange and the Microsoft Network.

3

Adding New Dimensions to Telecommunication

The technological explosion that has occurred during the past few decades has revolutionised the means of communication.

The current revolution in communications is likely to produce tectonic shifts in society, quite possibly accompanied by social upheavals the world over, at the end of which the globe would appear to be a smaller community than Europe or any other dominant civilisation in history has ever been.

Telecommunication is the life-line of a nation. In 1881, the first telephone exchange was installed in India. In America it was installed in 1878 and in U.K. in 1879. In the U.K., the post office gained control over the telephone through the Telegraph Act of 1868. The Indian Telegraph Act was enacted in 1885 almost on the same lines.

More than a hundred years of rapid reform in every single sphere of technology has transformed the way people live and work. With regard to telecom, computer technology has revolutionised communications in the last three decades. As computers and communication technologies converge, revolution will become a part of life. For example, services such as Radio-mail in the USA, offer mobile users access to E-mail and related connectivity to the global village using two-way paging technology. Telecom companies, computer manufacturers, software companies and entertainment companies abroad are out in the subscribers' premises today, testing technologies together that would enable the same cable to carry home voice, data and entertainment programmes. Teledisc will launch 84 satellites in the next decade to provide high speed connectivity to almost every point on earth.

In the 1950s the Americans started to build up the inter state highway system for rapid troop mobilisation. The government's vision enabled it to realise that it would give a tremendous boost to the American society and the economy. It would delink the economy from a handful of cities and bring the entire country together. The same vision was repeated with the ARPANET experiment. Started as a defence-funded experiment, it has evolved into the Internet, an operational network which offers low-cost communications to academicians, bureaucrats and corporate users. An estimated 50 million individuals communicate with one another on the Internet now and the number is expanding exponentially.

The soldier of the future will go to war with a computer on his belt, digital camera on his helmet and wireless transmitter on his rifle. The warrior will be able to identify the enemy electronically, photograph the battlefield for officers in command and aim at his opponents in battle without raising his head above the trench. This is the vision of "Cyberwar". The cyber warrior with his high-tech equipment may be ready to go into battle by 2010. The war of the future will then be above all a battle for information. Then destroying the enemy's information will become more important than destroying the enemy itself.

Indian Telecom Technology

Elsewhere in the world, telecom is regarded as the most important and fast growing industry. In India, telecom represents a grossly under-exploited industry. World wide, telecom companies earn returns ranging from 18 to 26 per cent almost without exception.

The Indian market of telecommunication equipment and services was about ten billion dollars during the period of 1985 to 1990 including private sector allotment. This compares to a world telecommunication market of 55 billion dollars and the U.S.A. market of about 25 billion dollars.

According to a study made by the Indian Institute of Foreign Trade (IIFT), direct international telephone service of the country has increased in terms of circuits, from 71 in 1973 to 1487 in 1987 and available to 48 countries in 1987.

The external telephone traffic of India has shown more than 70 fold growth between 1971 and 1987 from 1.8 million minutes to 128.9 million minutes. The international subscriber dialing service was available from over 450 cities and towns from the country to 164 overseas countries in 1987. Similarly, direct international telex service, in terms of number of circuits has increased from 64 in 1973 to 1166 in 1987, and in terms of traffic, the external telex traffic has risen from 2.15 million paid minutes in 1972 to 50.66 million paid minutes in 1987.

Table 3.1. Some Milestones in Indian Telecom

S. No.	*Year*	*Events or milestones*
1.	1875	First private telephone line (P.O. steam Nav. Co. and Fort).
2.	1881	Phones arrive with the installation of the first exchange. Licence to private parties to run telephone services in Madras/Calcutta/ Bombay/Rangoon.
3.	1913	First automatic exchange at Shimla with a capacity of 700 lines and 400 working connections.
4.	1943	Govt. exercises and option to purchase the assets of the phone companies.
5.	1948	Indian Telephone Industry set up at Bangalore.
6.	1956	Industry Policy Resolution reserves the right of manufacturing telecom equipment for the public sector.
7.	1960	First STD from Kanpur to Lucknow.
8.	1984	Manufacture of subscriber and equipment "Opened" to the private sector.
9.	1985	P & T was broken into DOP and DOT.
10.	1986	(a) Bombay and Delhi telephones converted into MTNL. (b) OCS was converted to VSNL. (c) INDONET was set up by CMC.
11.	1987	OILCOMNET was set up by Oil Coordination Committee.
12.	1989	ERNET network was made operational.
13.	1991	(a) First commercial electronic mail service was started from VSNL. (b) INET India's first packet switching network was set up.
14.	1992	Value added services operation was allowed to the private sector.
15.	1994	Telecom policy was tabled in the Lok Sabha.

The Indian Telecommunication sector has undergone a sea change in the last six years (1991-97). More than 90 lakh telephones have been commissioned bringing the total to 1 crore 41 lakhs connections. In the rural areas, telephone facility has been extended to almost 2.23 lakh villages. The rest 3.36 lakh villages will be provided with telephone facilities in the near future. The new policy envisages easy access to telecommunication facilities throughout the length and breadth of the country. It emphasises the qualitative performance of the network so as to ensure world class standards in all the functional areas. The number of telephone exchange has shot up from about 15,000 in April, 1991 to more than 22,000 in March 1997. Rural telephones have grown to almost 17 lakh connections. Telephone facilities are now available in 2.68 lakh villages. Now India is very well-connected with national subscriber dialing facility extended to 500 districts in the country. About 8000 stations have been provided with STD facility. A total of 254 satellite earth stations were in operation by the end of 1996. The Department of Telecommunication (DOT) is also coming up with good amounts of investment over the years. Its revised budget for 1996-97 was 5072.94 crore whereas it is 6231.29 crore for 1997-98. These have raised the telephone density to one phone per 100 persons.

The department of telecommunication has set a target of covering one lakh villages with public telephone facilities by March, 1996. These phones at tariffs subsidised by 50 per cent and having long distance (STD) connectivity, would be installed at post offices, gram

Table 3.2. Top Ten Telecommunication Equipment Manufacturers in 1993

S. No.	*Company*	*Country*	*Revenue in US $ Million*
1.	Alcatel	France	17351
2.	Siemens	Germany	11986
3.	AT & T	USA	11783
4.	Motorola	USA	10070
5.	NEC	Japan	8714
6.	Northern telecom	Canada	7861
7.	Ericsson	Sweden	7813
8.	Bosch	Germany	4718
9.	Fujitsu	Japan	4388
10.	Philips	Netherlands	3333

Table 3.3. Top Ten Telecommunication Equipment Manufacturers in 1994

S. No.	*Company*	*Country*	*Revenue in US $ Million*
1.	Alcatel	France	20400
2.	Motorola	USA	14400
3.	AT & T	USA	14300
4.	Siemens	Germany	12800
5.	Ericsson	Sweden	10700
6.	NEC	Japan	9500
7.	Nortel	Canada	8200
8.	Fujitsu	Japan	4800
9.	Bosch	Germany	3400
10.	Nokia	Finland	2530

panchayats, grocer shops or any other place easily accessible to the villagers. It is proposed to open a telephone exchange in a village having a demand for a minimum of 10 connections, irrespective of the anticipated revenue. By March, 1997, 2.68 lakh villages were provided telephone facility and 22,000 telephone exchanges were established i.e. 18000 for rural sector and 4000 for urban sector. All 500-odd district headquarters, 90 per cent of sub-divisional headquarters and 85 per cent of tehsil headquarters had already been linked with the facility by 1995. All manual telephone exchanges in the country had been replaced with modern automatic exchange and the telecom network was fully automatic.

The Centre for Development of Telematics (C-DOT) has taken yet another step towards indigenisation of telecommunication equipment with the development of the large digital switches. The switches for a 30,000 lines Main Automatic Exchange (Max-E) manufactured by the Indian Telephone Industries (ITI) has already been installed. The C-DOT switch is comparable to other digital exchanges provided by multinationals. The C-DOT had manufactured many rural automatic exchanges and also exported them in sizeable numbers to Vietnam and Bangladesh. As many as 3.155 million lines of C-DOT exchange of various configurations were now operational in the country constituting one-third of the country's total telephone capacity. Various C-DOT exchange manufacturers had manufactured 17,775 exchange by 1995. The centre had also released an enhanced software version for the rural automatic exchange (RAX) with 256 lines. One of the major achievements in the new software was the integration of 10 channel 600 MHz digital ultra-high frequency system with the 256 port RAX. C-DOT is working with a number of multinational telecom giants to develop state-of-the-art telecom equipment for exports.

Telecom Sector Reforms

To augment the Indian telecom sector with world class features, an array of value-added services have been introduced including radio-paging, cellular mobile telephone, electronic-mail, voice mail including Audio-Tex and 64 kbps satellite-based data service to propel the country into the era of advanced technology.

To meet the growing needs of the business sector in India INET, a packet switched public data network and a Remote Area Business Message Network have already started functioning. For this purpose, nearly 150 satellite earth stations have been commissioned, especially in the remote, hilly and inaccessible areas. To be launched shortly is "HVNET", a 64 kbps High speed data network. These space-age data services are designed to cater to the present and future requirements of the rapidly expanding network of business and industry. With the merging of Indian Telecom Network with the global plan, new vistas have opened stimulating technological advancement at every level.

Three-fourths of the Indian population lives in villages which constitute three-fourths of India's geographical area. Hence the development of our country is linked with the progress of rural areas. Although telecommunication has been recognised as the key infrastructure for this development, yet in 1993 only ten per cent of the telephones in the country were serving the 630 million living in rural areas and the balance ninety per cent were serving the 220 million living in urban areas. In recent years the Government has been convinced that rural development is only possible by providing rural telephone service. In the Eighth Five Year Plan (1992-97) DOT had taken a major initiative to provide a telephone in each of the 2.28 lakh gram panchayats by 1995 and a long distance public telephone (LDPT) within a 5 kilometre walk, in every village by the year 2000. On April, 1991 only 40,000 out of the total of 5.6 lakh villages had access to a telephone. The Ministry of Communication had therefore invited participation of private and multi-national companies in the development of rural telecom infrastructure. About 95 growth centres were identified of C-DOT RAXs to provide subscriber trunk dialing. The Confederation of Indian Industry (CII) had recommended the growth centre concept during the international conference on "Rural connectivity through Telecommunications-challenges and opportunities" held on December 17, 1992. It highlighted a timebound rural development project for setting up self-sustaining growth centres in rural areas. A cluster of villages and smaller towns were identified, suitably demarcated and developed into a potential growth centre by mobilising resources, acquiring skill, achieving competence, generating of employment opportunities and setting up specific types of industry.

This in turn opened up new avenues for investment, business opportunities and generation of income in rural areas. The development of the growth centre further accelerated by establishing efficient linkages among various development processes, activities and functions through telecommunications. The setting up of the telecom infrastructure has been integrated with the development of the growth centres through joint sector participation of Indian industry, non-government organisations and the gram panchayats.

The Department of Telecommunication has adopted the indigenous C-DOT technology for small and medium sized rural exchanges and also the "Mini-ILT" of Indian Telephone Industries for very small exchanges. These technologies have been specifically developed for ruggedness, reliability and easy maintainability in the rural environment of India and other developing countries.

Today the rural telecom market is growing fast in the developing world. In switching technology alone the market is expected to be around $14 billion for the period 1995-2000. There is, therefore, a great opportunity and challenge in globalising our indigenous technology. To tap this vast potential, the private sector should participate along with the government in pooling the resources and in

R & D for development of the products and services for the Indian and the rural markets of the developing world.

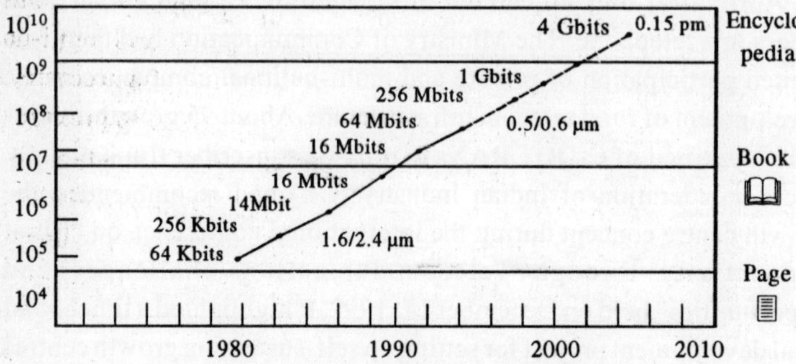

Fig. 3.1. Number of Bits Per Chip.

The evaluation curve for state of the art microelectronics, measured as number of bits per chip. The rate of development is 4 times every 3 years, or a factor of 1000 in 15 years. This exponential development is expected to continue at the same pace for at least another 10 years, giving us another factor of 100 in chip capacity, or 4 G-bits into one chip. This means that the paçe of development will continue to accelerate. This is what will allow new communications and information technologies to bring radical changes to society, e.g., PCs, hand-held video cameras and mobile telephones.

The Indian telecommunication sector is taking giant steps to ensure total connectivity of every village, town and city with the national telecom network. In this process special emphasis is being placed on the rural, remote, hilly and tribal areas. For this purpose, DOT has introduced a Rural Telecom package for subscribers in the rural areas. In addition to this, private initiative has been introduced in crucial areas such as basic services and value added services within the country. The drive to ensure total connectivity to rural India is aimed at providing quality services to people at large, particularly in the rural areas.

The village public telephones (VPTs) in rural areas are being provided on Multi Access Rural Radio (MARR) system in VHF and UHF bands. DOT had set a target of providing 1.20 lakh VPTs for the year 1996-97 and incorporating modern technologies like digital MARR and CT-2 systems.

Rapid advancement in rural telecommunication would go a long way to promote trade, exchange of information and make modern agricultural techniques easily available, resulting in better yield and increase in income of small farmers. In addition to this, strengthening up the telecom infrastructure in the rural areas will provide unhindered communication to inaccessible areas in times of natural calamities and other emergencies as well as speedy relief work in times of peril.

The Government had announced a series of attractive concessions for subscribers of telecom services in rural, hilly and tribal areas. The highlights of the rural package are :

1. Registration fee lowered by half to Rs. 1000/-.
2. Bi-monthly rental brought down to Rs. 100/- from Rs. 150/-.
3. The number of free calls per billing cycle increased to 250 calls from 150 calls.
4. Call charges for 200 additional calls (over and above the 250 free calls) lowered by 25 per cent.
5. Commission paid to panchayats for operating local PCOs increased to 50 per cent from 25 per cent at present.
6. STD, PCOs in rural areas to be paid commission of 25 per cent on gross turnover.
7. STD, PCOs in predominantly hilly/tribal areas to be paid commission at the rate of 20 per cent on a gross turnover of Rs. 50,000 per month and 15 per cent for that above Rs. 50,000.
8. In the rest of the country, STD, PCO franchisees to be paid commission at the rate of 16 per cent on turnover of up to Rs. 20,000, 15 per cent on a turnover of between Rs. 20,000 and Rs. 50,000 and 12 per cent for beyond Rs. 50,000.

The telecom commission had cleared a proposal to induct state-of-the-art integrated services dialling network (ISDN) in six major cities by 1995. This facilitated the introduction of a range of powerful telecom services that are significant for both the corporate sector and individual subscribers.

The ISDN services help a telephone subscriber in establishing at least two simultaneous and independent calls on the existing pair of telephone cables. ISDN calls can also be of any type–speech, data, image or video. This facility was initially offered in Delhi, Bombay, Madras, Calcutta, Bangalore and Ahmedabad. Jaipur, Ranchi and Hyderabad were identified for the second phase.

Orders were placed on some foreign manufacturers for the supply of 600 ISDN compatible terminal equipment like basic phone, video phone, video conferencing equipment, personal computers (PCs) decodic phones, Fax machines and modems. ISDN has emerged as a powerful tool for telecom services worldwide, with the main users being the corporate sector and PC buffs who are hooked on to the Internet and other similar information highways.

The type of services which ISDN offers to subscribers in India include video conferencing which has the potential to reduce the travel requirements of business executives. Besides, a range of "phone plus" facilities are also provided. These are:

1. Calling line identification.
2. Advice of charge.
3. Multiple subscriber number.
4. Call forwarding facilities.
5. Closed user group.

Table 3.4. Target for Telephone Lines during 1995-96

S. No.	*States of India*	*Number of Telephone Lines*
1.	Maharashtra	285000
2.	Tamil Nadu	270000
3.	Delhi	260000
4.	Kerala	200000
5.	Gujarat	145000
6.	Uttar Pradesh	145000
7.	Punjab	140000
8.	Karnataka	136000
9.	Andhra Pradesh	134000
10.	West Bengal	110000
11.	Rajasthan	110000
12.	Madhya Pradesh	85000
13.	Bihar	40000
14.	Haryana	40000
15.	Others	70000

Table 3.5. Cellular Telephone use in South-East Asia in 1995

S. No.	*Country*	*Percentage of People using it*
1.	Singapore	16
2.	Hong Kong	15
3.	Taiwan	8
4.	South Korea	6
5.	Malaysia	6
6.	Thailand	5
7.	Japan	3

Larsen & Toubro (L & T) has drawn up an ambitious expansion programme for its telecommunications division and proposes to enter the basic telephone services segment. At present, L&T telecom division concentrates on the manufacture of equipment and products like switching systems, EPABX, telephone instruments and Fax machines, and is a licensee for technology transfer by the Centre for Development of Telematics (C-DOT). This company is ready for providing basic telephone services in 20 industrial clusters and areas around it in the states of Tamil Nadu, Karnataka and Maharashtra. L&T has proposed a network, comprising fibre optic cables and wireless in local loop technologies. This company is in negotiation with several multinational service providers and equipment manufacturers from Korea, Australia, New Zealand and France for possible collaborations.

The Rs. 4000 crore Reliance group is negotiating with several multinational corporations to forge an alliance. Among the telecom majors being tapped are US West, AT & T, France Telecom and British Telecom. Initially the plan is to focus on Maharashtra and Gujarat, involving investments to the tune of Rs. 17,000 crore and Rs. 12,000 crore respectively, spread over a period of three to four years.

Australia will provide an assistance of $13.5 million (Rs. 31 crore) to the Indian telecom sector for setting up a network management centre (NMC) in Madras. Using advanced telecommunication technology developed in Australia, the NMC would improve the monitoring and control of telecom networks in

Karnataka, Andhra Pradesh, Tamil Nadu and Kerala. The NMC would manage and monitor all telecom traffic in the four states, including voice calls, faxes and computer data. Because of the large increase in the volume of traffic in India, congestion was occurring in some locations, while other parts of the system were not fully utilised. Under such situations, NMC would redirect traffic flow using all the capacity in various switch centres of the four states to maximise efficiency.

Table 3.6. Circlewise Allocation of Funds in 1995-96 for Telecommunication

S. No.	*State/Organisation*	*Amount in Rs. crore*
1.	Andhra Pradesh	424
2.	Bihar	214
3.	Gujarat	414
4.	Haryana	175
5.	Himachal Pradesh	138
6.	Karnataka	378
7.	Kerala	461
8.	Madhya Pradesh	429
9.	Maharashtra	496
10.	North-East	131
11.	Orissa	141
12.	Punjab	302
13.	Rajasthan	332
14.	Tamil Nadu	373
15.	Uttar Pradesh (West)	242
16.	Uttar Pradesh (East)	215
17.	West Bengal	153
18.	Calcutta Phones	132
19.	Madras Phones	234
20.	MTNL Bombay and Delhi	944

Depending solely on western technology imperils the interests of Indian industry. Instead of looking westwards our industry must look homeward for technological solutions. Presently what is needed for the growth of India is a strong indigenous R&D base which would supplement the knowledge inputs obtained from the collaborators for effective transfer and absorption of imported technology and generation of know-how capabilities. Unless we are able to dovetail our indigenous R&D efforts with the inputs received from the collaborators, we would never be able to produce state-of-the-art products through indigenous efforts. This calls for greater emphasis on research and development and a coordinated approach towards technological development in the country through closer interaction between various scientific research institutes, academic institutions and industry. We can create an environment and requisite facilities at our different centres for conducting continuous educational programmes in different disciplines so as to bring greater awareness amongst engineers about the new technologies, their impact on our lives and equip them with the latest knowledge to handle these technologies. Ideas are the fastest travelling commodity in today's world.

There is no illegality in the government's action of granting licences without framing rules for their regulation. Under section 4 of the Indian Telegraph Act 1957, the licences can be granted before framing of rules. Running of a telegraph system was the exclusive privilege of the government and in that sense its monopoly. This monopoly could be granted to private operators or to a corporate body by the government for a consideration making it in a sense some sort of. Telecom Regulatory Authority of India (TRAI) was set up on January 27, 1996. The functions and responsibilities of TRAI are:

1. To ensure technical compatibility and effective interconnection between different operators and service providers.
2. Revenue sharing arrangement between different service providers.
3. Spelling out and ensuring time frames for making available local and DOT long distance circuits between service providers.
4. Protection of consumer interests.
5. Protection of national security interests.
6. Strict enforcement of service quality standards.
7. To ensure compliance of licence conditions.

8. Fixation of tariffs for telecom service and ensuring price regulations.
9. Ensuring effective compliance of universal service obligations.
10. Resolution of disputes between service providers.
11. Rendering advice to the government in matters relating to the development of telecom technology and any other matter related to the telecom industry in general.
12. Levy fees at such rates and in respect of such services as may be determined by regulations.

Cellular Radio Telephony

Cellular mobile telephony is a revolutionary breakthrough in telecommunication that uses high frequency radio waves and high-tech portable mobile phones, small enough to fit in one's pocket. With a mobile phone one can communicate from and be accessible anywhere in the service area. Whether one is in a building, walking around, moving in a vehicle or even in a train. Cellular networks offer the users a freedom to move. This system consists of the following items:

1. Cellular telephone exchange
2. Radio base station
3. Subscriber stations : Mobile, fixed and semi-fixed station
4. Electronic exchange

The entire mobile service area is divided into geographic territories called "Cells". These cells are joined together in a honeycomb pattern within the service area. Every cell is equipped with one or more transmitters/receivers that send and receive messages. When a call is made on the portable cell phone, the message is relayed to the nearest station through the mobile switching centre (MSC) and sent onto the telephone network. The MSC interfaces with MTNL and it enables one to make and receive STD and ISD calls. When one is on the move from one cell to another the transmitters/receivers automatically reroute his call to the cell in which he is entering. All this occurs in a fraction of a second. The cellular system organises the automatic transfer from one cell station to the other once the signal becomes weaker than a particular critical level. Mobile phone service has an unlimited range, giving access to any place in the world.

The numbers of transmitters/receivers and their locations in a service area determine the clarity and sound quality of a mobile phone service. The service area of Delhi and its satellite towns have been divided into a large number of optimally located, compact cells equipped with nearly 700 powerful transmitters/receivers. While one is on the move this comprehensive network ensures that he is always in close vicinity of a powerful transmitter/receiver. And hence high signal strength is consistently maintained.

One essential part of radio network design is propagation prediction, which is used to estimate the coverage areas of the planned based stations. According to the terrain shape, antenna height, foliage, building density, etc. the field strength is obtained by adding correction terms to a distance-dependent basic median field strength. The coverage probability can be calculated, if the variance of the lognormally distributed field strength level is known.

Service quality consists of speech quality, coverage probability, reliability of signalling and probability of blocking. The last one is dependent on the number of channels at each base station. The first three are closely related to each other, and depend on propagation conditions between mobile and the base station. However, different kinds of interferences occur in cellular systems, the most severe being co-channel interference. Also adjacent channel and intermodulation interferences may effect the frequency assignment. Propagation attenuation has significant variations in different directions. Omnidirectional antennas improve coverage far away from the base station.

Global System for Mobile communication (G-SM) is a Pan-European standard and is the latest in cellular technology worldwide. The new GSM uses a digital computer language. The digital transmission eliminates background noise and other interferences. GMS's digital system allows a very large number of calls to occur simultaneously, enabling more people to use mobile phones. The frequency spacing standard of GMS stipulates that no two conversations ever take place on the same frequency. There is always a difference of 200 KHz between the two frequencies. Therefore, one will never find hearing others talking in the middle of his conversation.

Multiparty conference call is possible in mobile phone. With this facility one can simultaneously talk up to six person on his mobile phone, even if the other five do not have mobile phones. One can also use his handset for E-mail facility if he has a laptop with a PCMIA Card. In case one wants the fax facility, he needs to install a fax modem connected to a portable fax machine. The special alternate speech and fax facility switch will allow the user voice and data on the same line.

Cellular mobile telephone facility is presently available in Delhi, Madras, Calcutta and Bombay. In future it would be extended to all cities of India. At present, the number of cellular telephone subscribers in USA is over 2 million. The service revenues from cellular subscribers in USA is approximately $1500 million. By the year 2000, there should be at least 10 million subscribers across Europe.

Mobile phone has subscriber identity module (SIM) and personal identity number (PIN). To activate mobile phone one needs to insert the SIM Card in his hand set and punch in his PIN. Mobile phone is battery operated. It has a ringer, microphone, keyboard, built-in-memory and message display screen. Its computerised facilities allow data transfer, fax transmission, teleconferencing, etc.

The use of cellular phones in the country is set to boom with the launch of a PHS (personal handy phone system) model. PHS uses a high-frequency digital cellular system. Its major drawback is that users must be relatively stationary when using a PHS terminal, making the phones virtually impossible to use in cars. The monthly costs of using PHS in Japan is estimated at 5000 yen. Analysts say PHS has the potential to change Japanese life styles. The number of PHS subscribers will easily top one million in the initial year. Analysts say PHS will eventually become a niche market between more expensive cellular phones and pagers, without undermining long-term demand for existing communications. The launch of PHS will boost Japan's communications equipment market. The PHS system is a sophisticated wireless communication system which works as a digital cordless telephone at home and office as well as a mobile phone outdoors. This system can be used as an extension of basic telecom services by DOT and new private operators. The system was developed by the Japanese Association of Radio Industries and Business (ARIB) and it is working in Japan. It does not need a separate infrastructure and can be used with the existing basic telecom network.

Modi-Telstra made the country's first cellular phone call on July 11, 1995 at the Videsh Sanchar Nigam Ltd. Centre at Salt Lake. Modi Telstra would soon enable its subscribers to call and receive phone calls from the DOT network as well. Modi Telstra would be investing Rs. 80 crore in this project. The company's target is 20,000 subscribers during the first year of operations.

Tele-Conferencing and E-mail

Indian corporate houses are estimated to have spent Rs. 15 billion on their executives for seminars and conferences in 1994. The public sector units spend five billion annually, huge amounts by any standards. Video teleconferencing can help corporate houses hold "Virtual meetings" and cut down on the cost of travel and waste of man-hours. Today's teleconferencing technology is of three categories, namely : 1. Voice or data only, 2. Voice and video, 3. Video and data. Combining voice and video is technically advanced compared to an ordinary telephone call.

Video conferencing systems have been around for a decade or more, but have traditionally been expensive, difficult to use and offered limited benefits. As of now, most video conferencing is done through satellite. A teleconferencing solution must provide the benefits available in an in-person meeting. You want to be able to distribute a written agenda or a proposal for consideration or even pound on a virtual table to get attention. Most of the time video conferencing is done through VSATs (very small aperture terminals). New video conferencing and video phone systems are based on PC technology. Traditionally, such systems have suffered from two significant problems—image quality and speed.

Until a few years ago, prototype video phones and some low end video conferencing systems could either show images at either end as flickering, halting, black and white affairs or as even more halting colour images. Voices also tended not to synchronize with the images of the people who are speaking.

The image quality problems had a lot to do with the lack of high-definition small screens that could be fitted inside personal video phones. The screens used for video conferencing were often only marginally better. The biggest culprit was the speed of transmission. Most of the low-end systems produced in recent years, particularly those that operated over telephone lines, have only been able to show between 10 and 20 image frames per second. In order to achieve the full motion video, 30 frames per second are required. Sending 30 frames of complex video information down the telephone line every second is a difficult task.

The market of video conferencing system is now worth some $500 million a year and is doubling every year. Video conferencing has moved into the business communications main stream and is capable of offering a range of services extending well beyond face to face meetings between senior executives in separate locations. The enabling technology has been advances in compression techniques allowing full colour, full motion conferencing to take place over public ISDN telephone lines and the H.320 international standard for dial-up systems.

At present, Videsh Sanchar Nigam Ltd. (VSNL) provides video conferencing facilities at Bombay, Delhi, Calcutta and Madras. National Informations Centre (NIC) and Development Consultants Ltd. (DCL) are also interested in this field, therefore more video conferencing centres will come up in the near future. Tata Consultancy Services (TCS) has its own private video conferencing facility.

Electronic-mail is the electronic transmission of letters, messages and memos from one computer to another. The office automation software includes electronic desktop, electronic-mail, electronic filing, graphics and word processing and spelling verifier.

Electronic desk-top is similar to a standard office desk. The electronic desktop is situated where the user places his/her open documents to do work. In electronic desktop a mail is sent by selecting a document and moving it into the out tray.

The important functions of electronic-mail are:

1. People staying in different locations can communicate with each other through their terminals.
2. A typical simple electronic-mail system has a set of messages sent to each other user and stored in an area of the file system for incoming mail to the user.
3. Messages can be classified and filed accordingly.

In electronic filing a document is filed by sending it to the file server. The file system consists of drawers which contain folders. Each folder contains the documents.

As per a news, in 1993 North American business sent almost 6 billion electronic-mail messages. If each message has 50 words, it would be like sending 1000 manuscripts of the length of *War and Peace* (Tolstoy's novel) every day.

Electronic-mail is set to become a Rs. 500 crore market by the turn of the century in India alone and is expected to service nearby 400,000 users. Already, many corporations have begun their foray into this area. Large corporations who had planned their own communication networks for inter office electronic data interchange (EDI) have also scaled down their plans and are waiting for electronic-mail services to be in place for them. The cost of their own networks, with based lines or through dial-up is a lot more costlier than hooking onto a good electronic-mail service. A 24-hour service, with its host in Delhi, Sprint, the world's leader in electronic-mail will be first to offer a x.400 based service in the country. Worldwide, Sprint has more than a million customers. Sprint will be covering eight cities for a start : the four metros and Pune, Ahmedabad, Bangalore and Hyderabad through its dedicated network. A milestone in the field of communication has been achieved by putting the Indian station Maitri in Antarctica on electronic-mail network during the 14th Indian Scientific expedition. Now online data transfer to the various participating laboratories in the country has been possible.

Fibre Optic Communication

The fibre optic communication system uses hair-thin glass fibres for transmission. Laser beams are sent through these fibres which act as a waveguide and the beam is transmitted at a very low loss to long distances at exceptionally large bit rates.

It is totally free from radio frequency or electromagnetic interference besides being relatively immune to nuclear radiation and blasts. The normal communication systems are totally ineffective during radiation.

As compared to the co-axial and wave guide communication fibre optical communication is considerably cheaper, particularly over long distances, because it requires limited repeater stations. Fibre optic communication system is suitable for local area network, long distance trunk routes and installation in hazardous environment and power plants.

Fig. 3.2. Fibre Optics Communication Cables.

The Central Glass and Ceramic Research Institute (CGCRI') has developed optical fibre which is very suitable for all kinds of short haul communications. Now Universal Cables Limited (UCL) uses this know-how for fabricating multimode graded index optical fibre. Earlier the Hindustan Cables Limited and the

Madhya Pradesh State Electricity Development Corporation have entered into technological collaboration agreement with foreign firms manufacturing optical fibre cables in view of country's requirement of this fibre for national communication grid.

Optical fibres are currently carrying 75,000 or more telephone calls with the overall reliability. This is due to a new technique developed by British Telecom (BT). This company is claimed to be the first in the world to demonstrate coherent optical transmission over an operational network. The new fourth generation optical system can split the frequency spectrum in a fibre and send different groups of messages on separate wave lengths. Every colour of the spectrum has its own wave length and we can now send photons of light of specific colours. Each colour carries a different communication channel and they can all go down the same optical "Pipe". At the far end we can arrange for the receiver to filter and sort them out, without interference.

At the 1989 Hanover fair, Siemens had exhibited a new fibre optic cables made of plastic for the transmission of opto-electronic signals. Plastic fibre optic cables are less sensitive, lighter in weight, stronger, easier to install and cost less than conventional glass fibre optic cables. They are available in all desired lengths and as prefabricated cables with plug-on transmitter and receiver units.

As fibre costs are likely to fall over the next few years, the option of serial optical cables would be cheaper in rural areas. Fibres optic medium has been widely introduced all over the world as it has proved to be cost effective on accounts of superior characteristics such as wide band-width, low transmission loss, larger repeater spacing and light weight.

The Optical Fibre Cable (OFC) system offers larger capacities, flexibility in upgradation and covers vast geographical areas since the cable passes through the length and breadth of the country. The first long distance optical fibre communication system between Ahmedabad and Baroda was commissioned on 23rd January, 1989. The 1920 channel capacity system covering a distance of 123 km. between Ahmedabad and Baroda had

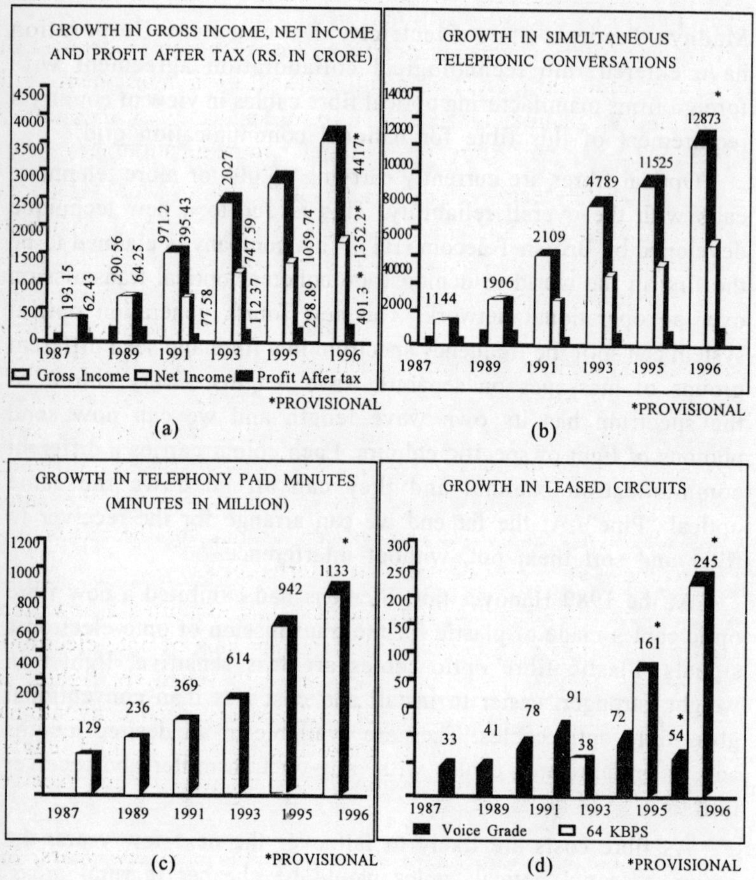

Fig. 3.3. The VSNL Achievements from 1986 to 1996.

been completed at a cost of Rs. 3 crores. There are four pairs of fibres in this optical fibre cable laid in this section and each pair is capable of carrying more than 7680 channels. About 16000 route kms optical fibre links have been commissioned in the DOT network by March, 1994. These systems mostly comprise 140 Mbps and 34 Mbps links with a few numbers of 565 Mbps links also. Both loose tube and slotted core configuration are in use. For the year 1994-95, it was planned to commission about 8000 route kms. About 40,000 route kms were planned to be commissioned during the Eighth Five Year Plan. The cables used in the network are jelly filled, metal free cables of six fibres, 12 fibres and 24 fibres capacity.

Another area where DOT planning to introduce optical fibre is in subscriber loop to provide better and reliable communication. Amongst the new technologies emerging in fibre optics the Synchronous Digital Hierarchy (SDH) technology provides a significant breakthrough. The main advantages of SDH technology are:

1. Network simplification.
2. Higher networks optimisation.
3. Improved network survivability.
4. Better network flexibility.

SDH has abundant overhead bits to carry large information for network management. The planning of the network is aimed at providing new services by introducing cost effective technology.

Role of Electronics

The world of electronics is surging forward at a tremendous pace, opening up new vistas in human life. The electronic industry in India made its humble beginning during the early sixties with the establishment of a few public sector units. This industry has made a remarkable progress during the last 15 years which one could not imagine. The turnover of the electronic industry has risen from Rs. 4100 million in 1976 to Rs. 34600 million in 1986.

In India, production of electronic goods is being carried out through the public and private sectors. The annual data received by the Data Bank and Information Division (DBID) of the Department of Electronics shows that the public sector units account for roughly 32 per cent of the total production and the remaining 68 per cent is contributed by the organized and small scale units in the private sector.

The total production worth of electronic products in the country during the year 1988 was about Rs. 63 billion. The growth rate in the area of electronics in India is much higher than the average world electronics growth rate. The production of electronic equipment had grown from Rs. 72,500 million in 1989-90 to Rs. 200,000 million in 1994-95, which represents an average growth of about 22 per cent.

Today, there is no field where electronics does not find its application either directly or indirectly. Electronics technology is used in a host of applications for improving the efficiency and productivity.

Table 3.7. Number of Direct Exchange Lines

S. No.	*Year*	*Direct Exchange Lines*
1.	March, 1948	82,985
2.	March, 1992	58 lakhs
3.	March, 1996	122 lakhs
4.	March, 1997	144 lakhs (Projected)

Table 3.8. State wise Number of Public Telephone Installed in Indian Villages (up to January, 1995)

S. No.	*State*	*No. of Telephone Installed*
1.	Madhya Pradesh	21221
2.	Uttar Pradesh	20485
3.	Andhra Pradesh	20105
4.	Maharashtra	16309
5.	Tamil Nadu	12289
6.	Gujarat	11176
7.	Bihar	10348
8.	Rajasthan	8261
9.	Punjab	8080
10.	Orissa	6952
11.	Haryana	6130
12.	Karnataka	5942
13.	Assam	5230
14.	West Bengal	4283
15.	Himachal Pradesh	2641
16.	North East	1704
17.	Kerala	1523
18.	Jammu & Kashmir	976

Note: North - East includes, Arunachal Pradesh, Manipur, Mizoram, Nagaland and Tripura.

Table 3.9. Electronics Exports from India

S. No.	*Items*	*1990-91 (in Rs. Crore)*	*1991-92 (in Rs. Crore)*
1.	Consumer Electronics	90.00	196.00
2.	Computer Software	250.00	508.00
3.	Components	220.00	300.00
4.	Telecom	135.00	71.00
5.	Computer Hardware	300.00	262.00

TABLE 3.10. Production of Indian Telephone Industries

S. No.	*Unit*	*1993-94 (Rs. Crore)*		*1994-95 (Rs. Crore)*	
		Target	*Actual*	*Target*	*Actual*
1.	Bangalore	467	352	491	227.42
2.	Electronic City Unit	182	173	140	98.44
3.	Naini	218	284	200	133.46
4.	Rae Bareli	180	130	164	87.35
5.	Mankapur	318	390	363	296.31
6.	Palakkad	146	160	175	115.22
7.	Srinagar	1	1	1	1.26
8.	I & M and Others	8	30	86	26.10

The role of electronics in the telecommunication sector has also been very pronounced during this decade going up from Rs. 1100 million to Rs. 5040 million and rising further to Rs. 7100 million in 1987. Currently, the range of communication equipments manufactured indigenously include telephone instruments, teleprinters, analog facsimile, switching equipment of strowger and cross-bar type, strowger telex exchanges, electronics PAXs and PABXs, transmission equipments such as open wire co-axial and microwave systems, troposcatter equipment in the two per cent 5 GHz band, FDM and PCM multiplexing equipment, satellite earth station equipment, two-way radio communication equipment in HF, VHF and UHF ranges, power line carrier communication equipment and data communication equipment, electronic switching systems (ESS). A number of private sector units have begun production of EPABX and electronic telephones. A beginning has also been made in the manufacture of data communication equipment with the introduction of modems and multiplexers. In the broadcasting sector too, equipment like video tape recorders, cameras, OB vans, digital video effects generators, AM and FM transmitters are being manufactured indigenously.

The manufacture of telephones, EPABX, data communication terminals, etc. have been allowed in the private sector. Other items can also be taken up by the private sector with Central/State Government participation to the tune of at least 51 per cent of the equity. The remaining 49 per cent in the private sector's share can include 40 per cent foreign equity.

The rationalization in the duty of a large number of equipment for telecommunication transmission, satellite communication, switching, data communication terminals, television transmission, studio and sound broad-casting, has been announced by the Government.

Conclusion

Telecommunication has been identified the world over as a basic infrastructure, essential for the socio-economic development of a country. Experience has revealed that there has been three per cent growth in GNP for every one per cent increase in the telecom infrastructure.

In India, today, telecom is being increasingly recognised as a priority sector. Digital exchanges have been introduced in major cities and long distance networks have also been digitalised through microwave and optical fibre systems.

In the strategy for long distance planning, DOT envisages the following:

1. Optical fibre shall be the main transmission technology serving the backbone routes linking all the SSAs.
2. Digital microwave systems shall supplement this fibre network wherein terrain or existing infrastructure dictates the use of microwave systems.

Optical fibres will thus form an integral part of the future broad-band network for communication and intelligent services which will transform the world into a global village, contributing to better living conditions.

As India's future unfolds, the demand for telecommunication and computer is growing steadily. Presently available wide range of technology will help connect the nation with a world class telecommunication network. It will fuel the growth of India's industry and economy. Also it will allow for the easy flow of communication among individuals, business and markets in India and abroad.

Approximately 20 lakh new telephone connections were issued by DOT during 1995-96. 17.69 lakh connections were installed during 1994-95. The Mahanagar Telephone Nigam Ltd. (MTNL) provided 2.6 lakh connections in Delhi and another one lakh connections in Bombay. Madras and Calcutta got 1.25 lakh and 90,000 new lines respectively. As many as 153090 new connections were given in Delhi during 1994-95. As against the Eighth Five Year Plan targeted of 75 lakh new lines, the DOT had been able to install 39.8 lakh lines in the first three years of the plan. The DOT had added a total of 57 lakh new telephones in the country's telecom network during 1992-95 as against a total of 57 lakh new connections during 1947-91. The number of telephones in the country had doubled in the past five years (1990-95).

Beginning with less than 86,000 telephones in 1947, the Indian telecom network reached a milestone of nearby one crore telephone connections by 1995. As on March 31, 1995, the country had over 19,200 telephone exchanges. The telephone density in the country, which was 0.5 per hundred persons at the end of the Seventh Five Year Plan, has now more than doubled.

Calcutta, Delhi, Bombay and Madras are among the 22 cities where radio paging services have started functioning. The services are being provided by one or more private operators. The other major cities covered under the service are Ahmedabad, Bangalore, Chandigarh, Coimbatore, Ernakulam, Hyderabad, Indore, Jaipur, Rajkot, Surat, Trivandrum, Vadodara and Vishakhapatnam. The MTNL has been operating this service in Delhi and Bombay. The Department of Telecom has licensed 14 Indian companies to franchise the radio paging services in 27 cities on a non-exclusive basis. All India Radio is also operating an FM paging service at a few centres.

4

Satellite Communication

Today, it is possible to establish instant contact the world over via global satellites. This has revolutionised our communication system. The first significant success in satellite communication came with the launching of Telestar by USA on July 23, 1963. Starting with the USA's Early Bird in 1965, satellites have made intercontinental television transmission an everyday feature for viewers throughout the world.

Artificial satellites revolve round the earth in circular or elliptical orbits. The period of rotation of a satellite depends on its altitude. The higher the altitude the greater is the period. For global communication the satellite have to move uniformly round a circular orbit with a period of $84.4 \frac{(R)^{3/2}}{r}$ minutes, where R is the orbit radius and r is the earth radius. At an altitude of 300 km. it takes about one and a half hours to make one complete revolution around the earth.

A special case arises when a satellite revolves in a circular orbit at an altitude of 35,680 km. where it takes 24 hours to make a complete revolution and this coincides exactly with the period of rotation of the earth about its axis. If the direction of travel of such a satellite is the same as that of the earth's rotation, i.e., from west to east and if its orbit lies in the earth's equatorial plane, the satellite moves synchronous with the earth and thus appear to be geostationary.

Principles of Satellite Communication

A Communication Satellite is essentially a microwave link

repeater. It receives the energy beamed up at it by an earth station and amplifies and returns it to earth at a frequency of about 2 GHz away. This prevents interference between the uplink and the downlink.

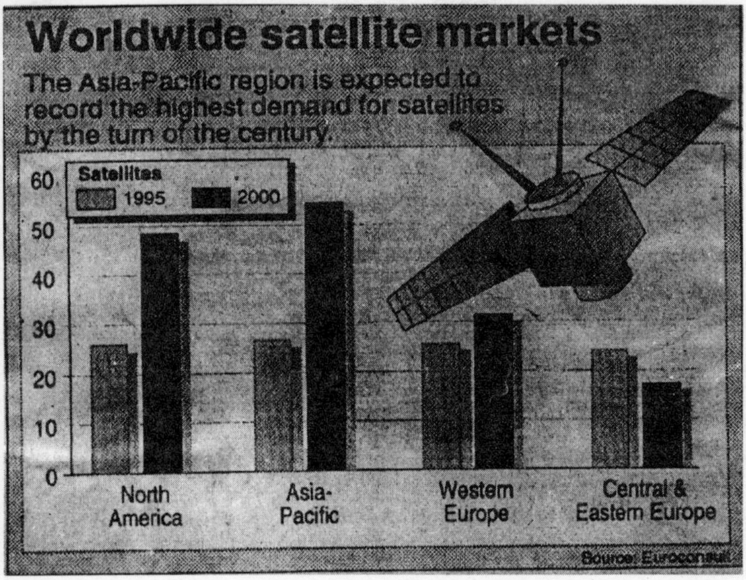

Fig. 4.1. Worldwide Demand for Satellites by the Turn of the Century.

A stationary satellite or a succession of satellites in low elliptical orbits can be used for global communications. Satellites in close elliptical orbits require relatively low transmitting powers and receiver sensitivities but must be tracked by the antennas of the ground stations. Stationary satellites present no tracking problems but are so far away that large antennas, high powers and high receiver sensitivities are essential.

A geostationary satellite acts as a line-of-sight device cum a sky tower to widen the visual horizon. It covers about one-third of earth's surface. If three such satellites are judiciously placed 120° apart around the equatorial belt, at least one of them will always be visible from any point on earth, except from the two poles. With three such global satellites in synchronous orbits around the equator, it is possible to cover a very large portion of the inhabited area of the world. In 1983, 100 operational geostationary satellites were in orbits all over the world. Eighty of them were for communications and broadcasting. Using synchronous satellites for speech purpose, there will be one way time delay of 240 to 270 milli seconds.

Satellite Communication in India

In India, the first satellite earth station was established by the overseas communication service of the Government of India at Arvi near Pune. The second satellite earth station was commissioned in Lachiwala, Dehradun in 1976.

A high power satellite ATS6 of NASA, USA was launched and loaned to India for beaming television and radio messages. With two earth stations, one set up atSpace Application Centre, Ahmedabad and the other in Delhi. India succeeded in August, 1975 in beaming programmes through this satellite. This ATS6 satellite was successful in sending TV programmes to 2400 remotely scattered villages in six different states : Rajasthan, Bihar, Orissa, Madhya Pradesh, Andhra Pradesh and Karnataka. It used a chickenmesh dish antenna and a front end converter coupled with an ordinary TV receiver to receive the pictures.

The Indian experimental satellite, APPLE (Arian Passenger Payload) was India's first 3 axis body stabilised geostationary satellite. It was launched by ARIANE launch vehicle of European Space Agency (ESA) from Kourou, French Guiana in June, 1981, to acquire competence in the utilisation of geostationary satellites for domestic communication on an experimental basis under the project called Satellite Telecommunication Experiments Project of the Space Application Centre of India.

Table 4.1. The Story of Indian Satellites

S. No.	*Satellite*	*Date*	*Launcher*	*Result*
1.	Aryabhatta	Mar. 19, 1975	USSR	Success
2.	Bhaskara-1	June 7, 1979	USSR	Success
3.	Rohini	Aug 10, 1979	SLV-3	Failure
4.	Rohini	July 18, 1980	SLV-3	Success
5.	Apple	June 19,1981	Ariane	Success
6.	Bhaskara-2	Nov 20, 1981	USSR	Success

S. No.	*Satellite*	*Date*	*Launcher*	*Result*
7.	Rohini	May 31, 1981	SLV-3	Failure
8.	Rohini	Apr. 17, 1983	SLV-3	Success
9.	Sross-1	Mar. 24, 1987	ASLV	Failure
10.	IRS-IA	Mar. 19, 1988	USSR	Success
11.	Sross-2	July 13, 1988	ASLV	Failure
12.	IRS-1B	Aug. 29, 1991	USSR	Success
13.	Sross-3	May 19, 1992	ASLV	Success
14.	INSAT-1A	Sept. 4, 1982	USA	Failure
15.	INSAT-1B	Aug. 30, 1982	USA	Success
16..	INSAT-1C	July 22, 1988	Ariane	Failure
17.	INSAT-1D	June 12, 1990	USA	Success
18.	INSAT-2A	July 10, 1992	Ariane	Success
19.	INSAT-2B	July, 1993	Ariane	Success
20.	IRS-1C	Dec. 28, 1995	Russia	Success
21.	INSAT-2C	Dec. 7, 1995	Ariane	Success

Table 4.2. Milestones of the 25 years of the Space Probe (From 1957 to 1982)

S. No.	*Date*	*Event*
1.	Oct. 4, 1957	Russia launches Sputnik-I, first artificial satellite.
2.	Jan. 31, 1958	USA launches its first satellite, Explorer-I.
3.	Sept. 13, 1959	Russia launches Luna-2, first probe to hit the moon.
4.	Apr. 1, 1960	USA launches first weather satellite.
5.	Apr. 12, 1961	Soviet cosmonaut Yuri Gagarin becomes first person in space.
6.	May 5, 1961	Alan B. Shepard becomes first American in space.
7.	Aug. 26, 1961	American Mariner-2 Spacecraft launched to fly within 22000 miles of Venus.
8.	July 26, 1963	USA launches Syncom-1, first geostationary, satellite.
9.	Mar. 18, 1965	Soviet cosmonaut Alexei Leonov conducts first space walk.
10.	Dec. 15, 1965	America's Gemini-6 austronauts rendezvous with Gemini-7 crew in orbit.
11.	Jan. 31, 1966	Soviet Luna-9 lands softly on moon.

S. No.	*Date*	*Event*
12.	Dec. 21, 1968	America's manned Apollo-8 conducts first manned flight round the moon.
13.	July 20, 1969	America's Apollo-11 makes first manned landing on the moon.
14.	Jan. 2, 1970	Two Soyuz-9 cosmonauts begin 18 days orbit voyage.
15.	Dec. 15, 1970	Soviet craft makes soft landing on Venus.
16.	Nov. 13, 1971	American craft orbits Mars.
17.	Dec. 3, 1973	America's Pioner-10 explores Jupiter.
18.	Feb. 8, 1974	American Skylab 3 crewmen spend 84 days in orbit.
19.	Jul. 17, 1975	Three Americans and two Russians rendezvous in orbit.
20.	Jul. 20, 1976	American Viking-I lands softly on Mars, returns high quality colour photographs and analysis soil.
21.	Mar. 5, 1979	American Voyager-I returns high resolution pictures of Jupiter and its moon.
22.	Oct. 11, 1980	Soviet cosmonauts set space duration record of 185 days in Salyut-6 space station.
23.	Nov. 12, 1980	Voyager-I returns first high resolution pictures of Saturn and its moon.
24.	Apr. 12, 1981	American space shuttle Columbia becomes first winged spaceship to orbit and returns to airport landing.

ISRO and DOT in a joint project under STEP conducted television and communication experiments, using the French-German Symphonism Satellite. India's outlying areas were put under effective communication links, utilising a fractional transponder leased from INTELSAT. The two main earth stations in New Delhi and Madras were linked with remote stations like Port Blair, Nicobar, Karavati, Leh and Aizwal.

Indian National Satellite Scheme was started in 1982. This INSAT system is a joint venture of various departments of the Government like ISRO, DOT, Indian Meteorological Department, All India Radio and Doordarshan. It represents a technical innovation for practical applications specific to India for cost-effective enhancement of national telecommunication, meteorological and mass communication capabilities. The INSAT scheme comprises basically space and ground segments. The ground segment primarily consists of earth station facilities like Network Operation Control Centre (NOCC) and Remote Area Terminals (RATS) for telephone links only. Eleven RATS are spread over the country. Five large earth stations are located at important places and 13 medium earth stations are located at other places in the country. There is one Master Control Facility (MCF) located in Karnataka and one Meteorological Data Utilisation Centre (MDUC) is located in Delhi. It has about 100 meteorological data collection and relay platforms. It has transportable terminals for meeting emergency needs in telephone and TV uplink feeds and also a scheme for rediffusion of Satellite television by terrestrial transmitters for national hookup within the country and emergency communication terminals mounted on transportable and air-liftable jeeps.

The MCF at Hassan form the major element of the ground system employed to support INSAT-1 Satellite operations after separation from the launch vehicle. The INSAT MCF consists of two independent satellite control earth stations each with a fully steerable 14 m diameter antenna. The main functions of MCF are as follows :

1. Satellite Commanding, ranging and testing.
2. Reception and processing of Satellite telemetry, ranging and test data.
3. Reception and processing of VHRR (Very High Resolution Radiometer) data for quick look evaluation.
4. Orbital Analysis, etc.

In addition, the INSAT MCF is the focal point for overall INSAT-1 system operations coordination in terms of links with the Network Operations Control Centre (NØCC) and with the Meteorological Data Utilization Centre (MDUC) at Delhi. Department of Telecommunication has started a new communication system to establish Remote Area Business Message Network through INSAT system. This network consists of Master Earth Station of large size (11 m. antenna) at Sikandrabad (U.P.) near Delhi and micro earth stations having antennas of 1.2 m × 1.8 m sizes at different user's locations. Stare configuration is used for easy command and control functions. Network control centre at Sikandrabad is connected to Delhi Switching Centre by optical fibre system.

These networks provide the following types of services:

1. Telex
2. Facsimile
3. Electronic Mail
4. Message Communication
5. Interactive data communication at speed up to 1.2 KBPS.

The capabilities of the INSAT scheme are enumerated as follows:

1. Utilization for thick routes, thin routes, remote area communication and TV programmes distribution on the 5935-6425 MH (earth to satellite) and 3710-4200 MH (satellite to earth) frequency.
2. Utilization for direct television broadcasting services to augment low cost community sets in rural areas, radio programme distribution, national television networking and disaster warning system though the frequencies of 5855-5935 MHz (earth to satellite) and 2555-2635 MHz (satellite to earth). It carries a very high resolution radio meter (VHRR) instrument with visible (0.55-0.75 microns), infrared (10.5 - 12.5 microns) channels with resolution of 2.75 km. and 11 km. respectively and with full earth coverage.

For the first time, the Atlantic Ocean Region (AOR) Satellites are being used by India to communicate USA. The VSNL has installed a roof-top antenna for the purpose at the Sanchar Bhavan, Bombay. Roof-top antenna are also installed at the other gateways at Madras and Delhi.

Intelsat Satellite System

The commercial use of communication satellites began with the successful launching of INTELSAT-I (Internation Telecommunication Satellite) in April, 1965. INTELSAT Organization Consists of about 102 member countries that operate a network of geostationary communication satellites positioned over the Atlantic Pacific and Indian Oceans for complete coverage of the earth.

Intelsat Organisation owns and operates telecommunication satellites which are used by many countries around the world for international communication. A number of countries are using these satellites for domestic communication. Intelsat global satellite system comprises two elements:

1. The space segment made of satellites owned by Intelsat organization.
2. The ground segment consisting of earth stations owned by telecommunication entities in the countries in which they are located.

A contract for the new generation of satellites was awarded to Ford Aerospace and Communications Corporation by the International Telecommunications Satellite Organizations (INTELSAT) in 1976. Today, there are over one dozen INTELSAT IV-IV-A, V and V-A satellites in the Atlantic, Indian and Pacific Ocean regions, offering capacities up to 12,500 two-way telephone circuits and two one-way TV channels per satellite. The INTELSAT VI satellites will be capable of providing up to 25,000 telephone circuits. Over 500 earth stations in nearly 150 countries use the INTELSAT satellites in the three ocean regions, to provide over 25,000 circuits and TV services for international and domestic use. The satellite was first launched in 1980. This satellite is a microwave repeater, receiving signals from earth stations, amplifying them at RF, and transmitting them to earth. This satellite uses 5.925 to 6.425 GHz frequency range for the uplink and 3.7 to 4.2 GHz range for the downlink. It also uses the 4.0 to 14.5 GHz range for a second uplink and the ranges of 10.95 to 11.20 GHz and 11.45 to 11.70 GHz for the corresponding downlink. The use of the 14/11 GHz range significantly increases the available system capacity.

An INTELSAT-V satellite has 11 low-noise 6 GHz receivers, consisting of a four stage silicon bipolar transistor amplifier and a low-noise mixer. Five of these receivers are operational at any given time, with the remainder on standby. The output of each operational receiver at 4 GHz, is fed to another four-stage bipolar transistor amplifier and then to travelling wave tube, whose output of 4.5 to 8.5 W is fed to one of the antennas for transmission to earth. Much the same arrangement is used at 14/11 GHz, except that this time there are four receivers. The front end in each case consists of a germanium tunnel diode amplifier, followed by a Schottky diode mixer and a five stage 11-GHz bipolar transistor amplifier feeding a TWT.

With its multiple receivers and antennas, the INTELSAT-V satellite employs a complex operational pattern of hemispherical zone and spot beams. Although a large proportion of the INTELSAT-V frequency spectrum uses frequency modulation and frequency division multiplexing, facilities are also provided for time division multiplexing and even digital speech interpolation at the earth station. Speech interpolation is a complex scheme for sensing silent periods between the speech bursts in a channel and filling them with speech bursts from other channels.

An earth station must be acceptable to INTELSAT before being allowed to work with a given satellite and must undergo exhaustive tests prior to commercial operation. Standard A stations have antenna diameters in the range of 27.5 to 30 m and are nowadays invariably parabolic reflectors with cassegrain feeds. They should be steerable. Standard B antennas have diameters of 11 m.

Standard C earth stations are designed to operate at the new 14/11 GHz frequency range and have antenna diameters between 14 and 19 metres. INTELSAT has also authorized the use of a number of non-standard earth stations for special purposes such as domestic leases.

The maximum power output of a standard-'A' earth station is up to 8 kW over the total band allocated to satellite communications. However, that would be only if the station transmitted over the complete spectrum of a satellite. In practice, each station is allocated a portion of the total bandwidth for its transmission, in proportion to its requirements and overall availability. The station High Power Amplifier (HPA) will have two multicavity Klystrons. These Klystrons are often driven by lower power TWTS and all the preceding amplifiers are solid state.

The station receivers are superheterodyne, with low noise parametric pre-amplifiers known as Low Noise Amplifiers (LNAS). The LNA is located close to the waveguide in the centre of the antenna and normally it is a multistage travelling wave amplifier. The parametric amplifier is thermo electrically cooled to about 230° K (–43° C) and its output is fed to a multistage FET amplifier. The pump for the parametric amplifier is a transistor oscillator with crystal frequency stabilization.

The foregoing amplifiers produce an overall gain of about 60 to 70 dh and are located close to the antenna receiving point. The signal is fed to the main amplifier via wave-guide. After still further amplification, the signal goes to a power divider and a series of filters. Whereas a station is capable of receiving signals anywhere wherein the 500 MHz passband of the downlink transmissions, it does not have to receive all the signals. Rather, it receives only the transmissions corresponding to the carriers which communicate with this particular stations.

Just as a satellite earth station is allocated carriers which it transmits, so a station allocates receive chains for the carriers which it must receive. Thus the output of the above mentioned power divider is fed to a series of bandpass filters, each of which is of a bandwidth sufficient to pass the wanted carrier. Each filter is followed by a mixer which downconverts the signal from the wanted carrier to an 1F of 70 MHz, where the signal is further amplified and then demodulated.

The output of the receiver chain is the baseband of that particular carrier, from which the wanted channels (if a so called multiuser group was transmitted, with different channels to different countries) are extracted. Sometimes the whole group is destined for this particular station, and often a supergroup or more. Either way the signals are suitably assembled into supergroups for sending via the terrestrial broadband link to the international terminal in the appropriate gateway.

Direct Satellite TV Reception

Direct reception of satellite TV programme has been made possible by using Direct Broadcast Satellite (DBS).

The programme generated in broadcast studios are transmitted to the satellite by earth stations. At the earth station the TV signals are superimposed on 6 GHz band carriers. These carriers, after power amplification to the order of a few Kilowatts, are beamed to the satellite by large parabolic dish antenna. These antennas focus the electromagnetic waves into a concentrated beam directed towards the distant satellite so that it can have the maximum signal strength for reception. The uplink has the potential to carry many channels as the bandwidth available at 6 GHz is generally 500 MHz.

Inside the satellite the active relay function is performed by the transponder. The transponder receives the uplink signals using small parabolic dish antenna, changes the frequency of the signals (generally to 4 GHz) for transmit-receive isolation, provides amplification (to the order of a few watt to tens of watt) and transmits them to the ground using the same or similar antennas. A transponder or the travelling wave tube amplifier (TWTA) in it may have a typical bandwidth of about 40 MHz and to utilize the 500 MHz bandwidth available, the satellite may employ multiple transponders or TWTAs. Some of the US domestic satellites carry 24 transponders for TV relay.

To accommodate more channels than is seemingly possible within 500 MHz, cross polarisation may be employed. In this case the adjacent channels overlap to a considerable extent but sufficient isolation is available between them because of the 90° difference in polarization of the microwave carriers of the adjacent channels.

The ground receivers are equipped with parabolic antennas pointing towards the satellite. There are essentially three types of ground receivers. The major TV earth stations form part of both the uplink and downlink. The smaller TVRO (TV receiver only) terminal is meant for reception only and may be used to redistribute the received programmes by means of cable network (CATV) or by means of conventional TV transmission by terrestrial transmitters (generally a limited rebroadcast station). In the third category are the simples community and home satellite receivers.

Now the Direct Broadcast Satellite (DBS) have the Effective Isotropic Radiated Power (EIRP) of the order of 60 so that the home receivers are less complex. Coupled with this power level, transmission in the 12 GHz band reduces the receiving antenna size to about 75 cm. diameter, making roof-top mounting easy. The cost of the home receiver can be further reduced by the use of low-priced GaAs FETS required for the front ends and coupled with Monolithic Microwave Integrated Circuit (MMIC) techniques.

INMARSAT Satellites

In July 1979, the International Maritime Satellite Organization (INMARSAT) was born. This system helps in establishing instant contact with ships at sea and offshore installations like oil rigs. The signatories to INMARSAT include Russia, the United States and

Inmarsat Dealers and Distributors

Company	Country	Contact	Telephone	Facsimile	Type of Outlet: Distributor	SCADA	FMS*
AFRICA							
Decca Contractors	South Africa	Clive Walker	+27 21 73 9400	+27 21 73 9410	●		
DVC	South Africa	Clive Grove	+27 11 886 5172	+27 11 886 1392		●	
Grinaker Telecom	South Africa	G. Engelbrecht	+27 12 655 0034	+27 12 655 0081	●		□
G-Track	South Africa	Pierre Burger	+27 21 758 460	+27 21 753 201			
Pertec	South Africa	Howard Smith	+27 11 805 1996	+27 11 805 2632	●		
ASIA							
ATS Pte Ltd	Singapore	Joshua Soong	+65 344 1533	+65 344 1332	●	●	
JRC	Japan		+81 3 584 8836	+81 3 584 8878			
KDD	Japan	Tatsuo Noma	+81 3 3347 6945	+81 3 3347 6306	●		
MCN	China	Wang Jialin	+86 1 421 3131	+86 1 421 3509	●		
Nera (SEA)	Singapore	Goh Yoke Lim	+65 281 3388	+65 383 9566	●		
VSNL	India	K P Tiwari	+91 22 262 4087	+91 22 262 3616	●		
AUSTRALASIA							
Electrotech Marine	Australia	Stephen Renkert	+61 2 905 6313	+61 2 905 6318	●		
Modac (CSIRO)	Australia	Ian Johns	+61 62 465 784	+61 62 465 800		●	
Sattrac	Australia	Ross Proud	+61 79 43 1377	+61 79 43 1272		●	
Tech Rentals	Australia	Charles Beavis	+61 3 879 2266	+61 3 879 4310	●		
EUROPE							
AST	UK	Gregory Darling	+44 1493 440 011	+44 1493 441 023	●	●	
BPI	UK	Richard Harris	+44 1425 479 064	+44 1425 478 485	●	●	
BT Inmarsat	UK	Sandra Hole	+44 171 492 4992	+44 171 606 4640	●		□
Bilton	Czech Rep.	Jaroslav Liska	+42 3 126 08 285	+42 2 401 5008			■

Company	Country	Contact	Telephone	Facsimile	Type of Outlet		
					Distributor	SCADA	FMS
Baumbach	Germany	M Baumbach	+49 911 48 26 00	+49 911 481 548	●		
CAS	UK	Christopher Sutton	+44 1708 437 666	+44 1708 437 667		●	
Catterwell & Assocs	UK	Bob Catterwell	+44 1306 743 223	+44 1306 881 951		●	
Comtrans	Netherlands	Antonio Grasso	+31 2159 49192	+31 2159 42208			□
CPN	Germany	Christian Nicolai	+49 67 23 70 26	+49 67 23 72 79			
CPRM	Portugal	Luis Rosa Santos	+351 1 720 7216	+351 1 795 5738		●	
CRM	France	Alain Biancheri	+33 42 32 99 09	+33 42 32 94 95	●		
Dantronik	Germany	Mathias Reinis	+49 461 811 00	+49 7545 89392			
Data Marine Systems	UK	Murray Cowie	+44 1224 725 133	+44 1224 724 962	●		
DeTeMobil	Germany	Hartmut Kreie	+49 251 977 3800	+49 251 977 3849	●		
East Anglian Elect.	UK	Tony Gillespie	+44 1224 725 552	+44 1224 722 874	●		
ELNA	Germany	A W Grube	+49 4101 301 00	+49 4101 301 214	●		■
Euro Traffic	Norway	F Ingebrigtsen	+47 67 58 1800	+47 67 58 1875			
Euro Truck Sat	Denmark	Frank Kupper	+45 74 67 5000	+45 74 67 0246			
Expoma	Austria	Evelyn Eder	+43 1 322 513	+43 1 328 242	●		
Fartskriver	Norway	Bjorn Carlsen	+47 22 64 58 60	+47 22 65 83 50			□
GEC Marconi	UK	Phil Gallagher	+44 181 732 0816	+44 181 953 5262			
Geolink	France	Phillippe Perrette	+331 40 56 34 33	+331 45 63 49 73	●		
Geostar	Finland	Kimmo Jappinen	+358 0 372 300	+358 0 377 214			■
GME	France	Martin Fierstone	+331 44 09 7575	+331 44 09 7631		●	
GT & T	Belgium	Mr. Gago-Garcia	+32 10 45 79 75	+32 10 45 79 79			
Hansabaltic	Finland	Matti Rapp	+358 0 754 4426	+358 0 754 4429		●	
Hermes Data Comms	UK	Stuart Castell	+44 174 323 5555	+44 174 327 1717		●	
ICS	Netherlands	Dick de Rover	+31 184 676 666	+31 184 676 333			■
ICS	Netherlands	Peter Janesen	+31 20 000 1570	+31 20 000 2017	●		

Company	Country	Contact	Telephone	Facsimile	Type of Outlet: Distributor	Type of Outlet: SCADA	Type of Outlet: FMS
Landata	Spain	F. Rionegro	+34 1 597 1916	+34 1 597 3146			□
Linkcom	Norway	Arild Garmannslund	+47 71 215 790	+47 71 215 717		●	
Livewire Digital	UK	Tristan Wood	+44 01372 744446	+44 01372 739421	●	●	
MCG	Portugal	Rosa Santos	+351 1 720 7216	+351 1 795 5738	●		
MTI	UK	James Green	+44 181 391 6043	+44 181 391 6026	●		
Maribel Coms	UK	Richard Lawless	+44 1494 431 062	+44 1494 434 205	●		
Martec	France	Elisabeth Loizeau	+33 1 46 23 79 09	+33 1 46 26 55 55	●		
Media Technology	Norway	Johannes Boe	+47 51 800 370	+47 51 800 853	●		
Metod Sari	France	Joel Gulgner	+33 6139 1292	+33 6139 1519			■
Morsviaszputnik	Russia	Leonid Pchelikov	+7 095 978 4417	+7 095 253 9910	●		
MVS USA Inc	Russia	Deborah Deffaa	+7 095 246 6873	+7 502 220 2220	●		
Nera	Germany	Hans Gunkel	+49 711 13285 10	+49 711 13285 99	●		
Nera	Norway	Ottar Bjaastad	+47 66 84 4700	+47 66 84 4621		●	
Nera	UK	Bob Chewter	+44 181 686 5701	+44 181 686 6811	●		
Nicolai Sat-coms	Germany	Christian Nicolai	+49 6123 5387	+49 6123 5387	●		
Nortel Dasa	Germany	Reiner Dietrich	+49 7545 88873	+49 7545 88509	●	●	
Nukem	Germany	E Rehfus	+49 6023 911 207	+49 6023 911 555			■
PCI	UK	George Mochrie	+44 1454 615 444	+44 1454 615 510	●		
PCM	France	Y Marceau	+33 93 755 801	+33 92 928 062			□
Prosoft Consult	Austria	Martin Novak	+431 545 33 10	+431 545 21 10	●		■
Radio Holland	Netherlands	Henk Hoonings	+31 20 667 8364	+31 20 667 8318	●		■
Remtec Systems	Finland	Charles Sederholm	+358 0502 40241	+358 0502 40242		●	
Roboteks Telecoms	Latvia	Sergey Sofyin	+371 714 4484	+371 728 0221			□
7E Communications	UK	Peter Beardow	+44 1344 872 737	+44 1344 872 276	●	●	
Satcom	Denmark	Mogens Birkelund	+45 97 56 8484	+45 97 56 8481		●	

Company	Country	Contact	Telephone	Facsimile	Type of Outlet: Distributor	SCADA	FMS
Servowatch	UK	Steve Smith	+44 1245 360 019	+44 1245 362 129		●	
Simac Systems	Netherlands	Bert Duursma	+31 40 582 922	+31 40 582 707	●	●	■
Skycom	Poland	C Neelsen	+48 39 125 038	+48 2 644 7673	●		
Sonal	Belgium	O De Clereq	+32 3448 0848	+32 3440 4019	●		
Starcom Systems	UK	A C McCarthy	+44 1493 655 429	+44 1493 655 428	●		
STN Atlas	Germany	Juergen Michel	+49 421 457 3535	+49 421 457 3935	●	●	
TD Com	France	Patrick Gibassier	+33 1 45 100 772	+33 1 43 86 06 60	●	●	■
Telemar	Italy	Marco Imperatori	+39 6 322 1800	+39 6 324 0148	●		
Telsis Elektronic	Turkey	Karem Resuloglu	+90 212 251 4728	+90 212 251 0787			□
Terrafix	UK	J B Rosson	+44 1782 577 015	+44 1782 835 667			■
Thrane & Thrane	Denmark	Per Thrane	+45 39 55 8800	+45 39 55 8888	●	●	■
3B Engineering	Netherlands	Jack Hoogewerft	+31 10 462 6377	+31 10 462 1825		●	
Tideland Signal	UK	John Gunning	+44 173 776 8211	+44 173 776 8192		●	
Transtema	Sweden	Iars Wallstrom	+46 31 680 450	+46 31 683 660	●		
Unisource	Netherlands	Katherine Bell	+31 23 568 6061	+31 23 568 6065	●		
Wenzl Hruby	Germany	Thomas Hoppe	+49 40 233480	+49 40 233489	●		
MIDDLE EAST							
Radio Holland (ME)	UAE	Rudi C Joustra	+971 6 543 002	+971 6 356 083	●		
NORTH AMERICA							
Comsat	USA	S Williamson	+1 301 428 2252	+1 301 601 5951	●		
CPCI	USA	C Van Wangner	+1 305 974 9601	+1 305 979 2943	●		
Globesat	USA	Gary Flaherty	+1 703 716 9000	+1 703 716 9003	●		
Glocom	USA	J D Pan	+1 301 309 1940	+1 301 309 1932	●		
IDB Mobile	USA	Jullie Madden	+1 301 214 8742	+1 301 214 8701	●		

Company	Country	Contact	Telephone	Facsimile	Type of Outlet		
					Distributor	SCADA	FMS*
ICG	USA	Nial Quinlan	+1 804 873 7753	+1 804 873 7760	●		
Landsea Systems	USA	Ken Ravenna	+1 804 468 0448	+1 804 468 0625	●		
Mackay Coms	USA	T J Finneran	+1 908 225 0909	+1 908 225 2848	●		
Magnavox	USA	M C Fernandez	+1 310 618 7046	+1 310 618 7001	●		
MTI	USA	John Legieza	+1 301 590 8500	+1 301 590 8558	●		
Navtek	Canada	P Kalogiannides	+1 416 491 4062	+1 416 491 0555			■
NEC America	USA	Mac Duncan	+1 703 834 4150	+1 703 481 6904	●		
Network Innovations	Canada	E Verheyleweger	+1 403 640 0550	+1 403 640 0342	●		
New East	Canada	Herb Davis	+1 709 364 5770	+1 709 748 4305	●	●	
O'Gara	USA	D Gallagher	+1 516 586 5100	+1 516 586 5531	●		
Quest Telecom	USA	Carl Sederquist	+1 301 431 5102	+1 301 497 2313	●		
Rockwell	USA	Scott Martin	+1 319 395 2067	+1 319 395 5918	●		
Scientific Atlanta	USA	Jack W Bright	+1 770 903 6395	+1 770 903 6388	●	●	
Seven Seas Comms	USA	Paul Adkins	+1 954 761 7671	+1 954 761 7668	●		
TD Comms (Canada)	Canada	Garry Beutler	+1 403 735 6063	+1 403 250 3779	●		
Voyager Systems	USA	J Tuoby	+1 212 864 6422	+1 212 864 6422	●		
SOUTH AMERICA							
Avibras	Brazil	L Guimaraes	+55 123 21 4465	+55 123 21 7014		●	□
Hobeco	Brazil	Gilson Feitosa	+55 21 2339 177	+55 21 2639 067		●	
Prosat	Brazil	Edson Galindo	+55 11 280 2870	+55 11 282 2983	●	●	
Scahin Cury	Brazil	A de Almeida Filho	+55 11 574 6667	+55 11 574 6667			■
Trucksat	Brazil	Carlos Xavier	+55 41 276 2007	+55 41 278 3463	●		

All firms listed here are members of the Inmarsat Partnership ** Fleet Management Systems*

China, besides India. This system helps in rerouting at short notice, diversion from congested ports, avoidance of ports which do not offer cargo and onward passenger reservation.

Over 20 INMARSAT earth stations are now in service, in a majority of the developed nations. A ship wishing to make a call, dials the operator at the appropriate earth station via its shipboard terminals, if the channels in its region are free then the operator would complete the call to its destination anywhere in the world. A call in the reverse direction is completed similarly. The shore station have antennas with diameters of the order of 13 m and the shipboard antennas are 1.2 m in diameter and generally contained in radomes.

The world's first production aeronautical satellite voice and data systems have been delivered by Britain's Racal Avonics to the Gulfstream aircraft company in the USA.

Racal has installed single channel SATFONE voice and data satellite communication systems into Gulfstream IV corporate business jet aircraft. Calls have already successfully been made through the INMARSAT geostationary satellite network, linking them to the public telephone network. Racal has received firm orders for 16 satellite communication systems around the world. Most of them are from Gulfstream Aerospace and other VIP/executive aircraft operators.

Regional and Domestic Satellites

A regional communication satellite system is a kind of mini INTELSAT designed to serve a region. The world's first regional satellite system was the Indonesian Palapa network which started functioning in 1970. Philippines was also allowed to use this satellite for their communication purpose. The Conference of European Post and Telegraph Administrations (CEPT) launched EUTELSAT satellite in 1980 through the European Space Agency (ESA). EUTELSAT provides and maintains the space segment for the European Communication Satellite (ECS) and individual countries provide their own earth stations as with INTERLSAT.

The ECS system came into service in 1983, operating in the 14/12 GHz band, with ground antennas very much like the INTELSAT standard-C antennas, but with lower ground and satellite transmit

Table

Land Earth Stations Contacts and Services

Country	*Operator*	*Telephone*	*Facsimile*	*LES*	*AOR-E*	*AOR-W*	*IOR*	*POR*
Australia	Telstra	+61 7490 9090	+61 7490 9094	Perth			A B C M	ABCM
				Virtual LES	B"M	B"M		
Brazil	Embratel	+55 21 216 7738	+55 21 233 9032	Tangua	AC			
Canada	Teleglobe	+1819687 3241	+1 819 687 8280	Cape D, Agullar (HK)			BM	BM
				Virtual LES			BM	BM
				Laurentides	B M	B M		
China	Beijing Marine	+86 10 421 3131	+86 10 421 3509	Beijing			AC	AC
Denmark	Telecom Denmark	+45 4252 9111	+45 4252 9341	Blaavand	C			
Egypt	National Telecom	+20 2 352 1220	+20 2 77 1306	Maadi	A			
France	France Telecom	+33 56 223 231	+33 56 83 1305	Pleumeur-Bodou	A"	A		
				Aussaguel	B" C M		B" C M	
				Virtual LES		BM		BM
Germany	T-Mobil	+49 228 436 6511	+49 228 93 66539	Raisting	A B C M		A B C M	
				Virtual LES		BM		BM
Greece	OTE	+30 1 611 8100	+30 1 806 3999	Thermopylae			AC	
Hong Kong	Hong Kong Telecom	+852 2888 2939	+852 2566 8900	Cape D' Aguilar			A" BM	A" BM
				Virtual LES	BM	BM		
India	Videsh Sanchar Nigam	+91 22 262 4020	+91 20 95 4321	Arvi			A B C M	
Indonesia	PT Indosat	+62 21 380 2614	+62 21 345 8155	Jatiluhur			BM	
Iran	Telecom Co of Iran	+98 21 86 1022	+98 21 85 8566	Boumehon			AC	
Italy	Telespazio	+39 6 407 93379	+39 6 407 93624	Fucino	AC			
Japan	KDD	+81 3 3347 5016	+81 3 3347 6306	Yamaguchi			A B C M	ABCM
				Virtual LES	BM	ABM		

Country	Operator	Telephone	Facsimile	LES	AOR-E	AOR-W	IOR	POR
Korea	KTA	+82 2 750 3745	+82 2 750 3749	Kumsan			AC	AC
Malaysia	Telecom Malaysia	+603 208 7972	+603 731 7899	Kuantan			BM	
Netherlands	Station 12	+31 255 545 111	+31 255 545 100	Burum	A"B" CM	AB" CM	AB" CM	
				Yamaguchi (Japan)				ABM
Norway	Telenor International	+47 22 77 7206	+ 47 22 77 7178	Eik	A" B" M	A B" M	A" B" C M	
Poland	Polish Telecom	+ 48 22 20 3887	+ 48 22 26 3665	Psary	A		A	
Portugal	CP Radio Marconi	+351 1 720 7226	+351 1 795 5738	Sintra	C			
Russia	Far East Shipping	+7 095 274 0046	Not available	Nakhodka				A
Russia	Morsviazsputnik	+7 095 978 7045	+7 095 253 9910	Virtual LES	BM	BM	BM	BM
				Perth (Australia)			BM	BM
				Cape D' Aguilar (HK)			BM	BM
Saudi Arabia	Ministry of PTT	+966 1 404 1515	+966 1 405 9008	Jeddah			A	
Singapore	Singapore Telecom	+65 331 0656	+65 334 6110	Sentosa			ABCM	ABCM
Turkey	PTT Genel Mudurlugu	+90 312 366 556	+90 312 310 9141	Ata	AC		AC	
UAE	Etisalat	+971 6 822566	+971 6 823 502	Towi Al Sawan			BM	
UK	British Telecom	+44 1278 727 342	+44 1278 772 222	Goonhilly	A" BCM	A" BCM		
Ukraine	Morcom	+7 048 268 3932	+7 048 268 3932	Odessa*	A*		A*	
USA	COSMAT Mobile Communications	+1 301 428 2400	+1 301 601 5953	Santa Paula				A"BCM
				Southbury	A" B" C M	A" B C M		
				Anatolia (Turkey)			A"	
				Eurasia (Malaysia)			B" M	
USA	IDB Mobile Communications	+1 301 214 8700	+1 301 214 8701	Staten Island	A			
				Niles Canyon		A		A
				Turkey			ABM	BM
				Virtual LES	BM	BM		

*Key: X = High speed data services available * = Commercial services temporarily suspended* powers. This system is used for intra European telephone, data and telex/telegraph services and also by the European Broadcasting Union for the distribution of its EUROVISION programmes.

The next regional satellite network is ARABSCAT system in the Middle East. There is conceptually not a great deal of difference between a regional satellite system used by a group of neighbouring countries and domestic system used by a large or dispersed country.

Telesat Canada was established in 1969 and in January 1973 inaugurated the Canadian domestic satellite system, using ANIK A1 satellite for the space segment. The United States of America launched Westar system in 1974 and later comstar, satcom, SBS, STC and Telstar networks. The comstar series is jointly owned by AT & T and GTE and operated on their behalf by COMSAT.

Many other countries now have domestic satellite systems using their own satellites, notably the Russia, China, Indonesia, India, the Scandinavian countries, Colombia and Australia. More than 20 countries, operate domestic services by means of leasing channels from INTELSAT, among them are Algeria, Australia, Brazil, Nigeria and Saudi Arabia.

Domestic satellite systems generally use the same frequency ranges as INTELSAT satellites, viz., 6/4 and 14/12 GHz, with similar parameters. In the earth segment, there are usually two sets of earth stations: One with 5 to 15 metres diameters antenna, owned and operated by the provider of the satellite system, and the other simpler stations with smaller antennas, owned and operated by customers. The resulting network provides point to point telephone, data and other services. Additionally, radio and TV broadcasting are available, by means of a signal originated at a major station and rebroadcast by the satellite to a large number of fairly small and simple, receive only stations located throughout a country. The rest of the system then works in the same way as community antenna TV with receivers connected by cable to the receiving stations. It is also possible for individual receivers to have their own satellite antennas and down-converters.

Conclusion

The feasibility of wide-band communication over large distance has been demonstrated by the telstar, relay, syncom and early bird satellites. A good quality service is ensured by a global operational satellite system.

The Government has prepared a comprehensive programme for setting up satellite earth stations to improve the communication system in the remote areas of the country.

INTELSAT satellites are used for global point to point communication. INMARSAT satellites are used for ships communication. Apart from INTELSAT there are a number of domestic satellite systems meant for coverage within a country or a region. Some of these are the TELESTAR of Canada, WESTAR, SAT COM and COMSTAR of USA, STATIONER of the USSR (now Russia), the ARABSAT for the Arab region, PALAPA of Indonesia and INSAT of India.

The DBS works in 12 GHz band. Direct reception of satellite TV programmes has become possible by these satellites.

5

Data and Voice Communication and Electronic Mail

The history of human endeavour is aglow with barriers that constantly challenge the human spirit to rise, shine and conquer. In the ever-changing world of complexity information technology goes on crossing many milestones of development.

Effective communication is a very important process in every aspect of life. Communication testifies the ability of an individual or a group to convey ideas and feelings to another individual or a group to evolve a response.

In any organisation an effective communication serves several purposes and benefits it in many ways. It acts as a basic foundation of the management. The formal organisational structure hinges on an effective communication system. It plays a pivotal role in planning, rational decision making, organisational control as well as building and maintaining of employees' morale.

A computer is connected with a telephone system by a signalling or data link which supports a protocol to carry command and status information between the two systems. The telephone system may be a PABX, an automatic call distributor, a key system or any other telephone switch. Computer systems often comprise a large number of personal computers linked by local area networks to a common file server. The telephone system itself may provide data links to personal computers, integrated voice and data terminals and so on.

Computers are a vital component in communication systems that employ satellite earth station and geostationary satellites designed specifically for communication purpose. The computer-directed system selects appropriate microwave circuits on which to transmit signal that completes a call. With the help of communication satellites signals are sent between any two points on earth having a straight line access. Undoubtedly such a communication system permits nearly instantaneous information exchange among people.

A computer network provides a powerful communication medium among widely separated people. With tele-conferencing, widely separated people can conduct a meeting by typing messages at their terminals. International contacts by human beings may be greatly enhanced by network based communication facilities.

Digital Communication

The outside physical world is mostly analog, with continuous variation in value. Analog to digital conversion is a method for a

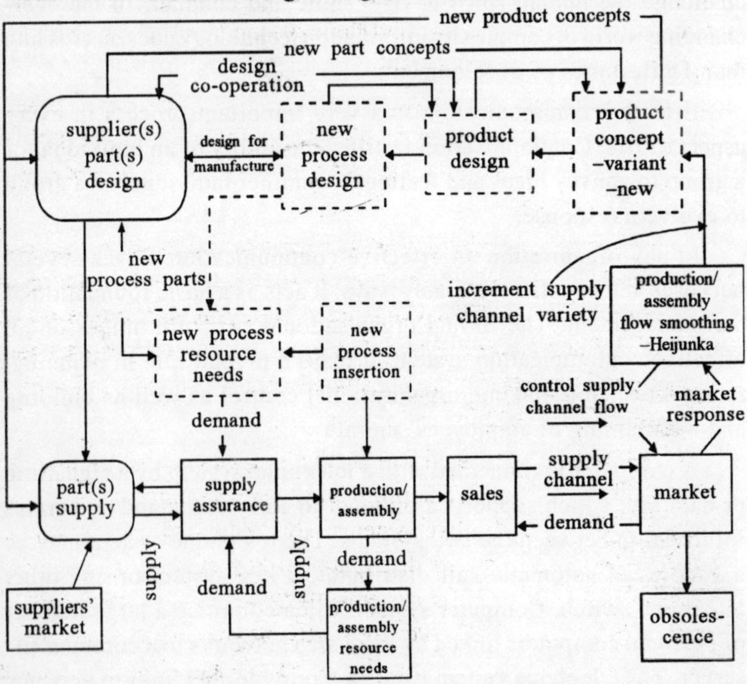

Fig. 5.1. Business Systems Engineering.

computer to sense the outside world and digital to analog conversion is the computer's method of talking with the outside world.

Digital techniques play a leading role in computers, control systems, signal processing, communication systems and measurement systems.

In discrete data system, the signal changes only at discrete instants of time. If the signals are quantized both in time as well as in amplitude, the system is known as digital system. Sampling of data are one of the fundamental operations in digital systems. Sampling process converts a continuous signal into a train of pulses. In digital systems a sampler may have a non-uniform periodic, cyclic-variable or random sampling rate. According to Sannon's theorem, no loss of information occurs if the signal is sampled at a rate which is at least twice as fast as the signal's highest frequency content. Since most of the practical signals are not band limited therefore the sampling frequency should be much higher compared to the twice of the highest signal frequency.

Digital techniques have been widely used in the field of communication for the improvement of signal to noise ratio. Digital communication can broadly be defined as a digital data processing operation at the transmitter and receiver end so as to faithfully reproduce the original signal. The digitized signals have many advantages over the analog signals with respect to data processing operations. One of the main advantages of digital signals is that it can be regenerated with switching amplifiers since the zero crossing of the digital signal carry the information and the linearity of the signal processing devices is not of any importance. Also the use of digital techniques allows us to use special codes for the coding of messages.

The technique of transmitting many messages over the same channel is known as multiplexing. In this case, if several sources of information are connected to the same transmitter, the transmitter converts the message into signals, encodes them and modulates them. After that signals are transmitted through different channels to the receiver end. At the receiving end, the sequence of events reverse to that of transmitter takes place. The received signal is first demodulated. It is then decoded and finally demultiplexed if more than one channel has been used.

Scenario of Communication Industry

According to the statement of Union Minister of Communications made on 10th July, 1993 the Department of Telecommunication had embarked upon an ambitious modernisation programme of increasing the telephone density from seven to ten per thousand by the end of the eighth plan. The minister claimed that by the end of eighth plan, 90 per cent of the telecom network would be electronic. The Telecom Department had provided as many as 8.87 lakh connections during 1992-93 against the target of 8.5 lakh, involving an outlay of Rs. 4500 crore. This included a rural component of 2.5 lakh lines involving Rs. 700 crore. During 1993-94 about 11 lakh new telephone connections were provided. This raised the level of direct exchange lines in the country to nearly 79 lakh, 2.32 lakh panchayat villages go connected with telephones by the end of 1995. Also 93 lakh lines were added to the network during the eighth plan period.

By the turn of the century India will be spending 25 million dollars to set up 15 million additional lines. As of today, our telecom network has more than 15000 exchanges, about seven million working telephones, 27000 route kilometres of coaxial cables, besides 37000 route kilometres of micro-wave system and about 6000 kilometres of optical fibre system.

Insatiable urge for innovation, appetite for handling of every single manual operation through artificial intelligence of computers and gradual elimination of human involvement, give rise to increasing automation.

Table 5.1. Communication Media within Fortune 100 Companies Used

S. No.	*Communication Media*	*1991 (in %)*	*1994 (in %)*	*1997 (Projected) (in %)*
1.	Printed memos, postings	66	57	42
2.	Electronic mail	6	20	41
3.	Face to face communication	20	22	21
4.	Video	11	12	18

Note: Survey of employee communications managers in Fortune 100 companies.

Highly versatile multichannel communication systems are now capable of handling diverse communication needs. Apart from being used as standard telephone, telex and teleprinters, they provide wireless media, like radio and satellite links. Information is created, edited, stored, processed and communicated from the users desk top. Similarly, information generated elsewhere is delivered to the users desk top at any time for the purpose of viewing, printing or filing.

Reliability of the communication infrastructure is vastly enhanced by the multichannel communication system. The Centre for Development of Telematics (C-DOT) has recently announced a much enhanced 256 port rural exchange which will not only help in increasing rural subscribers to be serviced from one exchange but also extend some of the essential telephony features to the village folks. EPABXs have contributed to better utilisation of the available telephone lines. The non–blocking function in an EPABX ensured that the lines remain free to make or receive a call.

Interconnection of private networks to public telephone networks is going to take shape. Such a strategy would reduce busy hour peak traffic in the DOT network, in addition to generating additional business. When all kinds of private networks would gain access to the national telecom network, the scope of allied activities would be much better.

Revolutionising the communication technology, optical fibres are now capable of performing simultaneous functions leading to availability of larger options to the end users. The wonder of optical fibre is, one single wire can at the same time transmit as well as receive telephone, television and fax signals, as well as computer data without their getting mixed up. Optimum utilisation of the band-width, sooner, may transform the Indian telecom to perform multiple functions.

Communication equipment manufacturers are gradually incorporating the latest technology to improve the product reliability and compatibility of the products to Indian environment. Facilities like automatic call back, call park, call forward, call pick-up, call camp on and conferences are provided by the EPABX manufacturers. Stored programme techniques are getting popular to minimise human intervention in telecommunication.

In 1867, Warner Von Siemens personally achieved a singular milestone by laying of India's first transcontinental communication link between Calcutta and London. On 29th June, 1993, Siemens has established another milestone with the inauguration of the EWSD

Digital Switching Exchange in Calcutta. Siemens is the first in bringing to India the most modern telecom technology which is already serving over 60 million lines around the world.

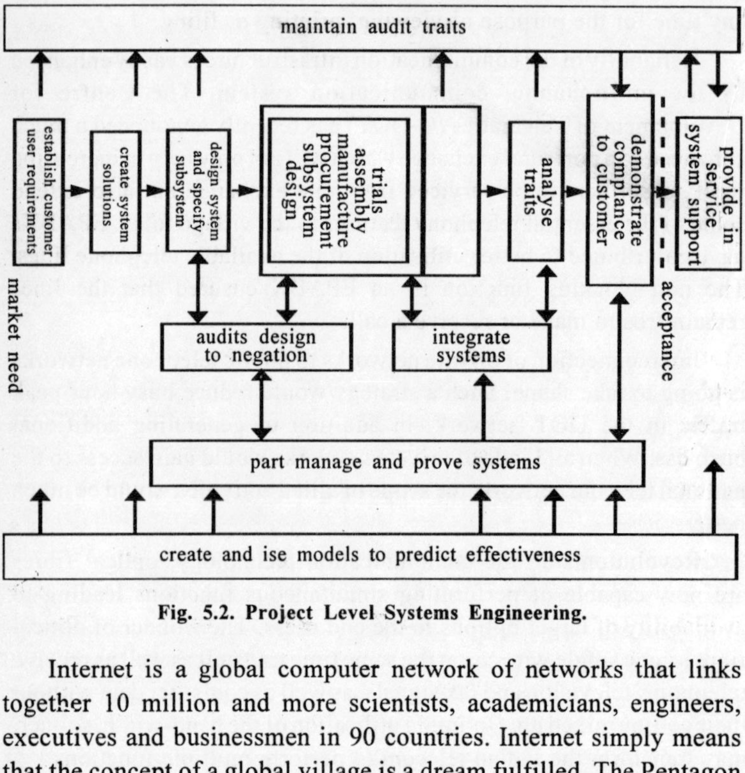

Fig. 5.2. Project Level Systems Engineering.

Internet is a global computer network of networks that links together 10 million and more scientists, academicians, engineers, executives and businessmen in 90 countries. Internet simply means that the concept of a global village is a dream fulfilled. The Pentagon Advanced Projects Research Agency created it in the 1960s.

Computer scientists and telecommunication experts believe that this could be the first step with which global computer networks will compete with or even replace traditional TV and radio networks that broadcast over the air or transmit by cable.

Computer Maintenance Corporation (CMC) owns one of the networks that are connected to Internet. This is called Indonet. The Department of Telecommunication (DOT) owns the second network called I-net. The third ER-net is called the education and research network and it is used by a few research organisations and educational institutes.

The Internet connection can either be a terminal or a network connection. In the terminal connection, the personal computer is hitched to a host computer with access to Internet. It can support only one session at a time. On the other hand, the network connection hooks one's computer directly onto the Internet chain and multiple sessions are possible. Internet is a combination of over 5000 networks that link millions of people.

The virtual phone is just a blank screen on a compact handset that offers access to voice communications, images and data. It is also a videophone. Future technologies will enable the virtual phone to be used over existing phone networks. It will also fully exploit the emerging asynchronous transfer mode (ATM) telecommunication technology, which is becoming the technology of choice for high speed networks carrying voice, video and huge volumes of computer data simultaneously. ATMs are still under development but are becoming available for area networks. Major long distance service providers such as U.S. based Sprint Corp. and American Telephone and Telegraph Co. have also recently announced alliances with Alcatel N.V. of France and Cisco Systems and Start Com respectively to develop ATM technology.

American Telephone & Telegraph Co. (AT & T) has made alliances with NEC Corp., Toshiba Corp. and Matsushita Electric Industrial Corp. to boost its position in the emerging market for personal communicators. AT&T's intent with its alliances is to create a standard set of hardware and software for this emerging personal communications market. Currently, there are a number of different incompatible technologies promoted for these devices. This device will cost from $2000 to $ 2900 plus the cost of a $800 cellular phone attachment.

Personal communicators are envisioned as a merger of today's cellular phones and notebook computers. They will allow users to communicate while on road, either by phone, by sending and receiving faxes or by sending and receiving printed messages. Most of these devices are also expected to contain electronic organisation tools, such as calendars, appointment schedules and phone lists.

Cellular Mobile Telephone (CMT) is like a cordless telephone with a range of a 100 km. Subscriber can make local calls, STD and

ISD calls. He can connect his laptop computer to it and access computer in his office through a modem or connect a FAX and send off documents anywhere in the world.

Cellular telephones work by dividing the city into imaginary hexagonal areas called "cells". Each cell contains a radio transmitter receiver system called a "Base Transceiver Station" (BTS). Each BTS is connected to a Base Station Controller (BSC) through a cable and microwave links. All the BSCs' in turn are connected to a central point called the Mobile Switching Centre (MSC). The MSC forms the central radial point of the entire system and connect it to the outside world, including the PSTN and ISDN. Whenever a call is made or received by mobile station, BSC allocates one of the available frequencies from the BTS to it, thus connecting the telephone to the system. Since this connection is made only when required, each available frequency or channel is maximum utilized.

Data Communication Devices

Data communication is defined as the process by which a computer communicates with other devices as well as other computers. Local

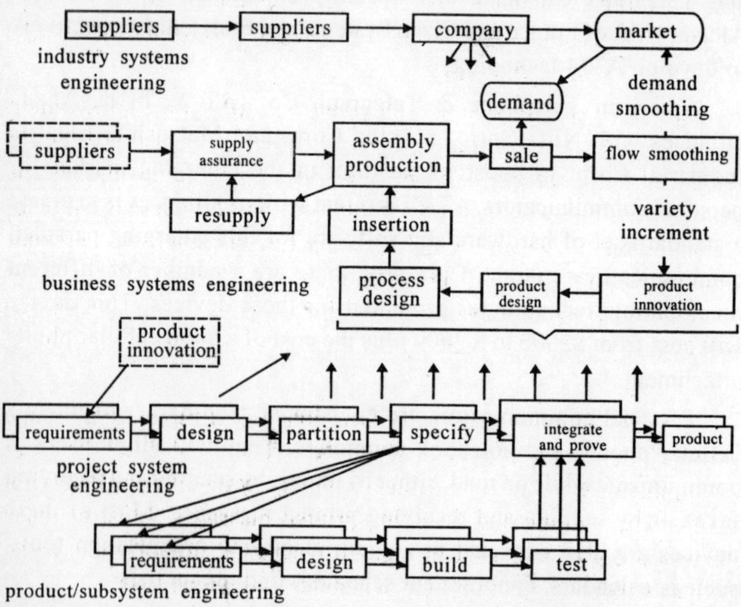

Fig. 5.3. Multi-Layered Systems Engineering.

area networks deal with the interconnection of computers within a precisely defined locale. Data communication includes development of modems, analog/digital converters and facsimile.

The modem or 'modulator demodulator' is the standard mechanism by which a computer can communicate via telephone lines. Modems operate by translating the binary data stream of the computer into a series of tones for transmission within the audio band of a telephone line. Modems are grouped according to communication, technique, speed and installation type.

The most common modems attached to computers are of asynchronous type. Asynchronous communications deal with data that comes in arbitrary spurts. Except for specialized communications with mainframe computers, all micro-computer modems are asynchronous. Synchronous modems used principally for communication with larger traditional computers at very high speeds, incorporate a continuous clocking pulse as part of the data stream. Asynchronous modems are self-clocking. Clock separation of data bits is based on internally provided timing signals which start with the detection of a "start bit". It reverses the normal idle state of the line and provides a standard starting point for bit separation.

Modems are serial devices, operating on a bit stream. The modem requires that the host system should provide a serial data. Most internal modems do themselves provide the necessary serial interface device. External modems required a connecting cable to the computer's serial port. Modem speeds are commonly expressed in bits per second (bps). Baud rate refers to the number of changes in the state of the data line in a second. Common modem operates at 2400 bps. Slow speed modems operate at 300 bps but the standard minimum speed generally accepted is 1200 bps. 2400 bps modems are rapidly replacing 1200 units and 9600 bps units are in their introductory stages now.

Presently modems are directly connected to the standard telephone wall jack. The majority of dial-up modems are "smart", with a resident microprocessor controller handling chores of dialing, answering, detecting busy signals and a host of other controls. Additional modem types include line driver modems. These devices amplify the normal serial port output to direct-drive a dedicated pair of wires for communication distances of a few thousand feet, usually within a single plant or complex. Amateur radio operators use a special tone based modem for radio wave digital communication. Optical modems use pulses of light over fibre optic light guide cables for short distance communication. Optical modems are impervious to electrical interference and eavespropping. A null modem is used to interconnect two computers.

With the rapid rise of facsimile transmission computer has been adapted as a form of facsimile machine. Facsimile requires a specialised modem and software. Budget facsimile subsystems for micro-computers rely on conversion of word processing files for text in and out. More elaborate systems use graphics scanners and laser printers for facsimile work.

Voice mail integrates voice input and output systems with computer control for message recording and retrieval. Several vendors have made available micro-computer based systems with varying abilities. Most common is the ability to leave user specific messages in private electronic mailboxes, accessible by tone phone command. Various outdial capabilities exist to make these systems into automated tele-marketing engines.

In virtual storage systems, paging is the process of transferring pages between real storage and external page storage. If a page is not transferred from auxiliary storage until it is actually needed, then paging is said to be done by demand. A fixed length block of instruction, data or both are transferred between real storage and external page storage of about 4 Kilo bytes. A programme will be divided into pages in order to minimize the total amount of main memory storage allocated to the programme at any one time. The pages will normally be stored on a fast direct access store and can be moved into main memory by operating system or hardware whenever the instructions of that subdivision need to be performed.

Word processing is the transformation of ideas and information into a readable form of communication through the management of procedures, equipment and personnel.

Fax machines today are becoming faster, cheaper and more sophisticated with some new models even boasting colour transmission. Today there are about 15 to 20 million fax machines worldwide, they are generally group 3 machines capable of sending A4 sheet across the world in seconds for the price of a phone call.

The new group 4 machines can handle (Integrated Services Digital Networks (ISDN) speeds of sending A4 page in 3 to 4 seconds. Enhanced Fax can broadcast virtually simultaneously to as many as 10,000 fax machines all over the world. Jet fax produced by Fujitsu connects to laser printers directly and enable the incoming faxes to print directly or send anything on the screen as fax.

Office Automation

The information technology available today achieve three business strategy objectives:

1. It improves internal office efficiency, enhances external effectiveness and helps develop new markets.
2. It helps to adapt to market changes quickly and adjust to market conditions, customer demands, employee expectations and take advantage of latest available technology.
3. It is the engine which initiates change, brings in pro-active corporate culture, increases company risk taking capability and individual responsibility, raises information technology awareness, helps redesign the shape of the organisation.

The business automation will be able to dramatically improve the productivity of an office worker by reducing the time to receive and send information, reduce transport and travel and improve organisational performance due to greater participation by the company personnel. It will reduce the time spent on meetings and leave each one with more time to do the job rather than talk about it.

Fully integrated office automation solutions are coming up. Software for business in some specific area of the world is available. For example, software for doing business with Europe or USA is available. The trend today is towards open systems so that one can connect to all the systems anywhere in the world. This will make possible a true international data exchange, enterprise to enterprise.

The main components of office automation are :

1. Telephone connected with high density datacom, fibre optics and satellite networks.
2. A modem to convert voice and analog signals to digital and vice versa.

3. High speed and high quality laser printers.
4. Copier which can produce copies in different colours.
5. Monitors or flat screens to keep in touch with what is going on, where, how quickly and for any alterations thereon.
6. Computer for coordination.

Office Equipment Manufacturers

Methodex is a household name in the field of office equipment, systems and business supplies. Methodex combines its technical expertise with top marketing strength and underscores the whole strategy with foreign collaboration (Minolta Camera Company of Japan).

The range of products which they manufacture includes plain paper copier, fax machines, micrographic equipment (cameras, processors, reader printers), laser printers and full colour laser copier.

Methodex is a service company with a full back-up of a strong research and development department. Information is an important resource and the company highlights this in their names Information Resources (INFRES).

Chinar Communications is a service-oriented company, serving the needs of business communications and office automation requirements. It represents top brands in the country, prominent among them are Escorts Key Telephone systems and Mini EPABX systems and Canon Facsimile machine.

Ultimate Tele System (P) Ltd. has equipped itself to meet the business communication challenge. It has cutting edge technologies and operates with a product mix which can meet the challenge of the next generation of communication products.

Salora International Ltd. is a fast growing company. Their Japanese collaborators, Matsushita Electric Industrial Co. is a global leader manufacturing famous National and Panasonic products including Panasonic facsimile machine and personal fax. Their TAMFAX combines the functions of an answering machine, dictaphone, telephone, copier and fax.

India Telecomp Ltd. has brought the latest fax machine with high speed transmission, speed dialling, delay transmission, advanced polling, half tone reproduction and fully automatic operation. It has one touch dialling to ten destinations, speed dialling to hundred stations. It has automatic document feeder and has answering machine interface.

The New Canon Marketing Pvt. Ltd. has launched an advanced plain paper Fax B-70. L&T has introduced multifeature fax machines Fax-260 and Fax-340. L&T has entered into manufacture of Digital Microwave Radio (2 GHz to 8 GHz) to meet the requirements of DOT, Railways, ONGC, Defence and others. L&T is the first company to manufacture computer peripherals in India. Godrej and Boyce Mfg. Co. Ltd. has tied-up with Matsushita of Japan. M/s Matsushita is a popular name in office automation, printing solutions CAD/CAM and system products.

Business India has analysed the information and communications requirements of Indian business. They have designed a number of information products which help in decision making process. It has started from Telephone Directories with Business Pages also known as yellow pages for various cities in India. It is now producing special information products such as Exporters Series, The Business Pages Series and Made in India series. The first product in the Made in India series is the Computers and Office Automation Directory. This includes complete information on the subject needed by the businessmen.

Commsys Inc is a team of young professionals in the field of communication. The company is very strong in the area of marketing and personalized services.

Network is a pioneer company which introduced the electronic type writer in the country. They are introducing now new products and the latest Fax 6000 facsimile machine.

Computer Zone (CZ) was established in November 1991 with the objective of making licenced software available at reasonable cost.

Electronic Mail

Electronic mail is the electronic transmission of letters, messages and memos from one computer to another. The office automation software includes electronic desktop, electronic mail, electronic filing, graphics and word processing and spelling verifier.

Electronic desktop is similar to a standard office desk. The electronic desktop is situated when the user places his/her open documents to do work. In electronic desktop a mail is sent by selecting a document and moving it into the out tray.

The important functions of electronic mail area:

1. People situated at different location can communicate with each other through their terminals.
2. A typical simple electronic mail system has a set of messages sent to each user and stored in an area of the file system for incoming mail to this user.
3. Messages can be classified and filed accordingly.

In electronic filing a document is filed by sending it to the file server. The file system consists of drawers which contain folders. Each folder contains the document.

Globalization of Communication

India, the second largest populated country, needs to improve her communications and become part of the global scenario if the country wants to progress economically. The communication scenario is fast changing worldwide and telecommunication companies are becoming giant players. Telecom investment alone will be worth $100 billion globally in the next three years.

We are now talking about voice mail, electronic mail, data communications, paging and cellular telephony, all coming together and making it almost difficult to attain the objectives. Private sector is interested to chip in but the money market is tight and bank finance is scarce, indicating that development of these services in the immediate future look dicey.

The problem in most developing countries is the lack of global perception and the fear of being swept over by multinational corporations.

Unless developing countries see the opportunities, take advantage of those being offered and join hands to improve the country's communication, they will continue to remain economically backward and progress will be adhoc, or at best haphazard instead of leapfrogging the barriers of telecom technologies.

INFOTEK'93 focused on every aspect of information technology with emphasis on emerging areas of cellular telephony, radio paging and value-added services. For the first time live demonstrations of ISDN, Minitel, Videotex and other new services were shown straight from France by the French PTT, France Telecom. Participants were HCL, Hewlett-Packard India, L&T, Gurusons, Automation International, New Canon Marketing, Mekastar Telecom, Singapore Telecom.

Vikram Land Earth Station (VLES) at Arvi near Pune provides shore-to-ship and ship-to-shore telephone, fax, telex and high speed data services to and from Inmarsat's terminals. A terrestrial digital microwave link extends communication channels to and from VLES to the international gateway digital telephone and telex exchanges of VSNL Bombay. VLES then interfaces with the Inmarsat network and the land-based network.

Today the global telecommunication industry is the centre of massive political, economic and technological changes. Technological advances have removed barriers of distances, time and cost. This industry needs a striking balance between competition and cooperation. The competition must be centred around network and network intelligence while cooperation must bring commercial application of satellites. The geostationary satellites provide global coverage with transmission of voice, data and video.

Conclusion

Today the computer is playing a pivotal role in information processing which is considered a part of information technology. It includes sending and receiving messages, via modems, telex, fascimile machines, word processing, desktop publishing and sometimes simply dialling distant telephone numbers. A computer can be used as a diary or a telephone book tool.

The telephone connections are increasingly becoming the gateway to sophisticated communication services. Video, audio and data transmissions are being integrated into a single fibre-optic system.

Mobile communication systems are institutionalised as portable phones, facsimile machines, pagers and beepers. Computers are making 24-hour accessibility routine.

Digital sketch pads, optical scanners and voice recognition systems are becoming popular. Their uses are increasing day by day.

Modern technology and communications do bind people and ideas beyond national boundaries. Now technology and information are the key to a free world, free expressing, free enterprise and new alliances.

The revolution that IT is expected to bring about in organizations can be viewed by the human aspects involved in the IT systems. It is now commonly acknowledged that it is the not the hardware or the software that often frustrates successful implementation of systems. It is the people to adapt to the systems and technology. The development of human resources is inextricably linked with the implementation of information system.

6

Man Versus Computer

The greatest creation of God is human being and the greatest invention of the 20th century by a man is computer.

Computers have taken the world by storm. After proving their efficacy in business, engineering, transport, communication and banks, now they have entered the domain of fashion, adding new dimensions to it. Better time management, designing of communication channels, accurate patterns and drafting, reduction of sampling costs and colour production are only a few areas in which computer has displayed its effectiveness as a production tool.

Basically, computer is a machine which computes or calculates. Today computer can process, store and retrieve miscellaneous information automatically which may be of audio, visual or linguistic type. A computer does not possess any intelligence of its own. It has got no thinking, arguing or decision making power of its own. The power to work intelligently is conferred on a computer through proper programming methods by persons handling it. Characteristics of a computer are: speed, accuracy, reliability, storage capacity (memory), integrity, power of making logics, superiority of manufacturing, etc.

Human brain is made up of many billion neurons which are the basic information gathering centres. Thousands of fibres extended out of the neurons are called dendrites. These dendrites establish link with different neurons. Total length of these dendrites in a human brain is approximately one lakh kilometre. There is a small gap between two dendrites known as sympose. Through these gaps the nerve cell collects the signal and transfers it to concerned human parts. Electrical and chemical impulses generated by nerve cells start the process of thinking and psychology. The human brain resembles with a digital computer.

Digital Computer

A special purpose computer will automatically execute the desired sequence of operation under the control of a fixed control unit executing a fixed program. The general purpose computer, however, can be programed by the user to execute any task. This flexibility in the general purpose computer is achieved by an instruction register in the control unit which stores the present instruction to be carried out by the computer.

A computer consists of four main blocks, namely: Memory unit, the Central Processing Unit (CPU), control unit and Input/output devices.

The memory unit which generally consists of random access type of memory is used to store both the sequence of instructions needed by the control unit to carry out a given task and the data needed by the Central Processing Unit to make the computations.

The CPU consists of a set of registers and logic circuits to carry out the basic logic and arithmetic operations required to perform the given task.

The control unit governs the operation of the overall system. The control unit does two main functions. First, it controls the order in which the instructions are carried out and second, it controls the operation of the CPU and other parts of the system during the execution of a particular instruction.

The input/output devices serve as interface between the system and the outside world. Sometime input/output information flows through CPU while at other times the information transfer takes place directly between the input/output devices and the memory unit.

Emperor of the Mind

Behind forehead lies the greatest powerhouse in the universe. Human brain is three pounds of wetware inside which swim all the thoughts and emotions along with dreams, drives, fears and fantasies. Human brain can be compared with the modern computer. According to some scientists, future computers will be able to do all that human brain can do. Indeed, artificial intelligence (AI) may even be able to replicate itself, according to some scientists. AI may, thus, be the next step in mankind's evolution.

During the last decade, many models of our intelligent biological system have been formulated. Each was designed to function the way our brain and nervous system functions. The intelligent biological model is called the artificial neural system model. This model uses a representation of a single human neuron and the interactions between neurons as a basis. In classical AI, experts are used to supply their own tested methods and knowledge to give the computer the basis for appropriate answers for a specific domain. A system constructed by the contribution of each expert is called an expert system. A neural system learns directly by interacting with the domain. It does not need any expert knowledge about the domain. Given enough time and experience, the neural system will learn everything about the domain.

Prof. Roger Penrose, world's foremost mathematical physicist's of UK vehemently disagrees. According to him, natural intelligence is superior to the so-called artificial one. Modern computers are inferior to human brains in some elusive but profoundly essential ways. He agreed that a sufficiently powerful computer equipped with sophisticated programs could emulate many of the computational or algorithmic functions of the human mind. In fact, computers are already better than most humans at computation. But that does not mean computers have a real mind. He says understanding, self-awareness or creative insight are the aspects of human intelligence and impossible to program. He discovered the concept of helicity or spin of electrons based on twistor theory of space-time. Could a computer have connected the fall of an apple with gravitation? And supposing it fell into a bathtub, could it have connected the rising level of the water to the *Eureka* reaction? Never, says Prof. Penrose. A computer can only compute with the rules that you program it with. It can neither understand nor think or be intuitive. The infamous Hall, the murderous computer of 2000, A space Odyssey, is purely an imaginary creature. Born in the mind of Arthur C. Clark, brought to the screen by the creativity of Stanley Kubric. Understanding is itself a mysterious thing. Present research by Libbers and his colleagues is very important. They do indicate that there is something very strange going on in relation to our conscious perceptions. They also indicate that there is something strange about the relationship of our consciousness and the passage of time in the ordinary sense. The very fact that time has a passage, that it passes at all, is a feature of consciousness.

In the late 1980s and early 1990s, Nobel Prize winning geneticists and biochemists like Gerald Edelman and Francis Crick and leading physicists like Stephen Hawking have published books investigating not only intelligence but also consciousness, because the tools and technologies for such scientific endeavours are now available for the first time in the history of humanity.

Scientists are beginning to seriously investigate questions such as "What is consciousness? How does the mind emerge from the brain? Can we construct a computer which not only has intelligence but also consciousness?"

The physical matter underlying the mind is not at all special. It is made up of carbon, hydrogen, oxygen, nitrogen, sulphur, phosphorus and a few trace materials. The organisation of the brain is special. These ordinary chemical elements form extraordinarily complex structures in the form of cells of living tissues of human brain. These cells are called neurons. They have the property to receive and transmit information between each other, thus forming an interactive neural network. The brain is a mass of such interacting neurons. These neurons also interact with nerves in the rest of the body. The neural network develops due to the inputs from the senses, resulting in a physical and/or psychological reaction like memory, learning, anger, joy, etc. The development of this network depends on what the neurons actually do. There are about one million billion connections in the brain. If we consider how these connections may be combined, the number would be hyperastronomical. Now scientists are trying to understand the interactions and messages which are responsible for anger or ambition. Research has now reached the point where joy, sorrow, selective perception at the level of neurons is being understood, albeit in a very tentative and elementary way.

There is a tremendously exciting and serious new field which has recently been given the name of "molecular computing". Neural network computers, using DNA (Deoxyribonucleic Acid) instead of integrated circuits, have been developed which can solve certain problems much faster than conventional computers, because they use massive parallel processing, like the human mind does, and not step by step sequential processing like conventional computers. Computers use only binary digits which are 0 and 1. DNA consists of A, C, G, T letters, therefore its capacity is enormously greater than that of a binary machine. Brain Josephson developed a circuit which had tremendous potential for making computers mind-bogglingly faster. Imagine a chip lodged in your head which grows nerve cells so that the rest of the brain can communicate with it. If the muscles of the mind are not exercised, if traditional functions of the brain such as memory, logic and even so called "Original" thinking is replaced by technology, will the brain wither?

Tale of Brain Expansion

Modern humans evolved when areas of the cerebellum, the part of the brain just above the brain stem that controls the movement, and frontal parts of the higher cortex, both expanded. At the time, rudimentary connections between them also expanded, forming a unique circuit. This expanded circuit may have resulted from a mutation in one or more genes that help in shaping the developing brain. The part of the brain that gives humans motor dexterity enlarged to give them mental dexterity. Dr. Peter Strick found direct nerve cell connections between a part of the cerebellum that is known to have evolved relatively recently and a part of the higher cortex that is involved in memory. Motor regions lie outside this circuit supporting the notion that the cerebellum does more than coordinate movements. It may play a role in cognition but it would involve imagining movements to improve actual motor performance or thinking about speaking words aloud or taking actions that require muscle movements.

The cerebellum is a fist-sized structure that lies just above the brain stem at the back of the head. It has two lobes—the left side connects to the right cortex and vice versa. The cortex is a thin layer of folded tissue that forms a cap over each of the brain's two hemispheres.

Most higher brain functions are carried out in separate regions of the cortex, with extensive feedback loops into middle and lower brain regions. Among these higher regions is a strip near the front of the brain called the motor cortex where movements are planned and mapped. Further into the forebrain, motor functions trail off and cognitive functions involving planning and thinking about the future begin. According to Dr. Leiner when you dissect a human brain, you can see with the naked eye an enormous cable of 40 million nerve fibres decending from the cortex to the cerebellum. There are more nerve cells in the cerebellum than the rest of the brain and spinal cord combined. It is a huge computational network.

Now with powerful tools like Positron-Emission Tomography (PET) and Magnetic Resonance Imaging (MRI), neuro-scientists have begun to actually map changes that occur as thoughts arise and emotions flicker across nerve networks.

Each population of sensory cells, from the eye, ear, nose and skin, sends its information to its home area on the outer surface of the brain, known as the cerebral cortex. An image may be reconstructed from all cells that are firing in a particular rhythm at a particular instant. Like traffic lights interneurons are rhythmic and well coordinated and could control the flow of cognition. When interneurons are damaged, the result is epilepsy which is a storm of uncoordinated electrical activity in the brain.

Different brain regions may have evolved their own temporal binding codes, said Dr. Rodolfo Llinas, a professor of neuro science at New York University. The cerebellum is a structure that coordinates movements, relaying a barrage of signals from higher brain regions where decisions are made to the muscles.

The brain stem contains a nucleus of cells that burst at a rate of 10 Hz. These cells, inferior olivary neurons, send long fibres upto the cerebellum, where they make dense connections, thus amplifying their signals. Information flowing into the cerebellum is regulated by these bursting cells making sure that the movements occur only10 times a second. The oscillation literally binds brain commands with muscle movements.

Researchers have come to realize that emotional brain circuits are just as tangible as circuits for seeing, hearing and touching. Emotions are largely the brain's interpretation of our visceral reaction to the world at large. Pioneering experiments on emotions have produced the following interesting concepts:

1. Emotional memories involving fear are permanently ingrained into the brain. They can be suppressed but never erased.
2. The body, as represented in the brain, is the frame of reference which humans experience as mind. Our thoughts and actions, which are our sense of subjectivity, use the body as a yard-stick.
3. Emotion is an integral part of the ability to reason. While too much emotion can impair reasoning, a lack of emotion can be equally harmful.
4. Guts and intuition are indispensable tools for rational decision making, without them humans would have great difficulty in thinking about the future.

Dr. Joseph Le Doux, neurobiology professor, New York University, says that a basic emotion like fear and the circuits that support its expression are highly conserved through evolution. Understanding fear mechanism in human is important because many psychiatric disorders, including anxiety, phobias, post-traumatic stress syndrome and panic attacks involve malfunctions in the brain's ability to control fear. Much of the research is centred round the amygdala, a tiny structure deep in the brain that is crucial for the formation of memories about significant emotional experiences. While animal experiments have helped scientists trace exact pathways for fear, the question of how emotions such as sadness, anger or shame are wired in the human brain is more difficult to answer. Advanced imaging techniques that can look inside the brain of the subject while they experience emotional feelings are bringing forth a neurobiological explanation of emotion. When specific parts of the brain are damaged patients may lose the ability to feel emotions, sometimes with disastrous consequences.

The human brain has evolved specialised circuits, called feature detectors which can be used to decode aspects of both speech and music. The temporal lobes at both sides of the head contain cells that recognize and process pitch which is the unitary pattern of frequencies that one hears when a musical instrument or the vocal cords are vibrated.

Researchers are beginning to model these special music circuits in computer neural networks and to map them in living brains. When sound waves enter the human ear they stimulate neurous called hair cells that lie on a flat plane. Depending where it is located, each hair cell responds to a characteristic frequency. Those at one end respond to high frequencies, those at the other end to low frequencies. The signals are then passed up through the brain stem, where information from both ears is integrated to help in locating the origin of the sound. From these they enter the primary auditory cortex, which contains cells that specialize in particular frequencies.

Scientists have found a fundamental brain flaw that may be a major factor in the development of some forms of dyslexia, a learning disability that affects millions of school children and adults. The research finding suggests that dyslexia is at root neither a visual nor ordinary hearing problem but a flaw in a specific brain circuit that handles rapidly flowing auditory information.

The study found that the left brain hemisphere of dyslexic children usually contain few cells of the kind that specialize in comprehending rapid sounds and that this comprehension problem is a major factor in their later difficulty in learning to read.

New research on reading difficulties points to a deficiency of cells in a region of the left brain that handles fast processing of sounds. The region, the medial geniculate nucleus of the thalamus, processes impulses on the way to the auditory cortex, which interprets speech. Scientists have already identified a similar problem with visual processing in cells in the lateral geniculate nucleus. The auditory problem affects areas that are active when the brain absorbs fast changing sound like tone triplets, syllables and words.

Power within Thoughts

Thought is a product of the mechanistic properties of the brain since anything mechanical can be reproduced. Therefore, thought which is a function of conditioning is locked in and can be reproduced in an automatic device, i.e. in a machine. Scientific enquiry aims at reproducing and controlling the minds as a function of its mechanistic properties, while the spiritual enquiry is to comprehend and be free of it.

Our imaging faculty can be defined as a process by which we create mental pictures in our mind's eye. In fact the process by which we envision and formulate goals within, long before they are actually achieved, is the play of our controlled imagination.

Our entire thought processes and feelings are in fact a series of photographic images which flow through the mind. As we read these ideas, images are formed in minds. Thoughts form mental pictures on our inner screens. We produce and direct the pictures that run through our minds. These pictures govern our attitudes and performances. The ability to choose, control and discipline one's imagination positively is one's greatest creative power. For professionals to achieve outstanding success in the upper echelons in any field of human endeavour, it is imperative to first tap the incredible dormant creative energy forces within the subconscious.

Nothing in this world is more magnetic, more powerful than an intensified, focused thought. A single clarified thought from one's mind contains within it unsurpassed power when linked to a specific purpose. Thought is the fountain-head from which all the higher powers of mind flow. We all are the direct result of a thought. We relate to everything on our planet through thoughts. All knowledge and thought achieve dynamic impact when acted upon. This is where thoughts get converted into things.

The greatest power of thought vibration also go undetected by our eyes. Dreams come true when we channel creative cosmic energy from a higher source, by becoming attuned to guidance from the universal mind. There are many who do the possible, but right within us is also built the desire-fulfilling drive, to turn such dreams into reality. Only that will remain impossible to man which in his mind he believes to be so. By becoming open-minded and receptive enough, many wonderful adventures will unfold and be worked through you. Most wonderful within man is the harmonious working of the conscious and subconscious mind. The subconscious mind is like the soil where seeds of all kinds grow freely when cultivated. The conscious mind is exactly like a camera lens, and the subconscious is like the negative where all photographed images get impressed. All positives are only as clear as the image on the negative.

The conscious mind is the rational, logical, surface level of mind whose primary function is the thinking and reasoning faculty. It takes cognizance of the world by the five outer limited senses. The conscious mind is mechanical, negative and non-creative. The subconscious is located just behind the solar-plexus, and is sometimes also referred to as the abdominal brain. It is the irrational level of the mind. This phase of mind, governs independently twenty-four hours a day all our vital inner processes like the beating of our hearts, breathing, digestion and assimilation. Its working is not limited by time or space dimensions. The subconscious takes cognizance of its environment by means of the independent of the physical senses. It perceives by intuition and its higher faculties of telepathy, clairvoyance, clairaudience and the sixth sense. It talks to us through hunches, inspirational flashes or insights to follow a certain course of action.

To become creatively effective we need to mentally choose, accept and radiate a vivid image of our clarified desire. Creativity is the most basic manifestation of a man or woman fulfilling their being in the world. The optimum condition for creative ideas is the mood of quiet intuitive concentration, when you are inward by turned.

The arena of mind holds within it fathomless possibilities. Tapping even a fraction of these is what professionals today need give serious thought to. Staying with the known is always comfortable, yet actualizing the move towards the unknown is where useful breakthroughs await discovery.

The Johari Window was discovered by behavioural scientists Joe Luft and Harry Ingham. It offers a tool for increasing self-awareness and, inter-alia, effectiveness. It depicts four windows of our self. These are obtained by an interplay of two main dimensions. They are aspects of a persons behaviour and style that are known to him (self) and aspects of his behaviour known to those with whom he interacts (others). An interplay of two dimensions reveal four areas of knowledge about the self. The open window relates to those ideas, thoughts and feelings that we are aware of and share with others freely. These include biographical details and other aspects. The closed area corresponds to secrets. Blind spots are aspects others notice but we are blissfully oblivious to. The fourth area is the dark area inaccessible both to the person and to others, relating to the subconscious. The open window is opened wider by reducing the closed area as well as the blind spots. The closed windows open with sharing your thoughts and feelings. Blind spots can be reduced by being open to feedback, by seeking feedback. One would have to develop a receptive attitude as well as create or permit a relationship to exist whereby others feel safe and comfortable to give one the feedback. Inherent in the Johari Window concept is the premise that openness is good. The more open a person is, the better is his psychological health. On the other hand, everything has a context. The degree of desired openness has to be viewed against the backdrop of the openness that exists in a culture. Too large a variance, even on the positive side, would lead to maladjustment for the individual, causing stress unless one is exceptionally strong.

Computer Neural Networks

In 1982 several researchers, including John Hopfield at the California Institute of Technology, suggested a way to adapt an existing technique, called connectionism, to design something more like a brain. This approach rejected the conventional concept of a computer as a complex central processor running a specific program. Instead, the machine they built had many very simple processors, connected much as the neurons are in the biological brain, and no program at all. Then they started to teach it. The results were startling. These "neural networks" showed a very uncomputer like ability to learn.

A basic neural network consists of three connected layers of anything from a few to a few hundred "neurons". These neurons are simply junctions between pathway that can carry electrical signals. Every neuron in the first layer which is the input layer, has a single pathway leading into it and then many pathways leading out, one connected to every middle layer neuron. Signals from the first layer of neurons thus become the inputs for the neurons of the middle layer, which are in turn individually connected to every neuron in the final layer. The neurons of the final layer which is the output layer, have single pathways leading out of them. The neurons and links could be the real prices of silicon circuitry. Today's neural networks are "virtual machines", made by simulating the behaviour of these components of a traditional computer.

When data are put into a neural network as a set of signals to the input neurons, each one sends a corresponding signal to every neuron in the middle layer. The middle layer neurons add up all their inputs and pass the sum along as another signal to the neurons of the final layer, which in turn add up the network's ability to learn. Each of the pathways into and out of the middle neurons can be adjusted so that the signal travelling along it is amplified or reduced. To the outside world the neural network is simply a "black box" with a set of inputs and a set of outputs. Inside it the influence of one on the other is the result of a weighted combination of all the many different connections between them.

The primary problem is that, by comparison with the brain, neural networks are small. Because most networks today are simulated on traditional computers, they are limited by the speed of such machines to a few thousand neurons. A cockroach's brain, by comparison, contains about 100,000 neurons; the human brain about 100 billion. As a result, neural networks take a long time to train. They can remember only few things. Whereas we might have to teach a child the alphabet a hundred times, a neural network can require thousands of training sessions. Building neural networks in hardware, on a silicon chip, would make them much faster than today's virtual versions, and therefore potentially bigger. Neural networks make more sense every year as the computer power on which they ride continues its exponential growth. Someday they may even realise their full potential.

Altos India Ltd. is planning to make touch sensitive computer screens. The touch screen functional computers are aimed towards the hotel and tourism industry. This is expected to revolutionise the service sector, as it would give customers the opportunity to see options on travel, booking, food on screen. All they have to do is to touch the preferred choice on screen for instant acceptance. Customers in hotels can also order a meal knowing a particular dish's recipe.

Markov's most famous feat of modelling was to predict statistically the sequence of words as they appeared in Pushkin's verse novel, *Eugene Onegin*. Until recently, all this work could only be done on large and fast mainframe machines. Over the next five years, speech recognition is going to become standard on every computer. These voice recognition machines can be used by people who have never used a keyboard or a mouse. The computer combination of text, video, sound, graphics, animation, etc. will become so user friendly that anyone can use it in future. Evocations of the future like these invariable contain a lot of hype. No body is sure that what kind of machines will eventually be available in the coming years. The changes surrounding us are not mere trends but the workings of large and revolutionary forces. Growing up around these in a new, information-age economy, whose fundamental sources of wealth are knowledge and communication rather than natural resources and physical labour.

According to Michael H. Spindier, CEO, Apple Computer, "An Upanishadic credo cries out for a movement from darkness to light". But the credo of New Order will be a movement from light to light. Ideas, thoughts and expressions have no physical boundaries, therefore, in this knowledge age, work will go to the people. Today ideas and thoughts are transmitted by digital networks. When ideas move so fast, it means that those companies that are able to get information assimilated throughout their organisation for discussion and action will have a strategic advantage over others and will be able to customise their products for individual customer needs. This disintegration of mass in the economy has not been accomplished yet. But we are moving towards what we call mass customisation. Companies like General Motors and General Foods in the United States will have to think and act like specific Motors and specific Foods.

Computers dictate the modern work ethos, but we are also suffering their tyranny in the form of impaired vision and bad health. Eye strain, headache, backache and pain in the hands, wrists, arms and shoulders are the symptoms of the Repetitive Strain Injuries (RSI). If ignored, a person can be weakened within five years and even be crippled permanently.

Dawn of the Cyberman

According to Prof. Peter Cochrane, leading futurologist of Britain, a physical connection could be created between the carbon based memory of the human brain and the silicon memory of the computer chip. Nerve strands could be passed through an implanted chip, allowing a process called "listening in", which could enable us to follow and alter the electronic trail in the brain's 50 billion nerve cells. The scenario for tomorrow is that researchers will have the expertise to replace every part of the human body except the soul.

In future, scientists want to insert electronic chips in our heads so that we can plug directly into information super highway. In a generation, people with a peppercorn sized chip in the back of the neck will be able to talk to computer.

The idea, being developed by academic and military scientists in Britain and America, on a device is to read the mind and transmit instructions in computer code. Teams on both sides of the Atlantic are working on commercial and military uses. Airforce pilots, for instance, would be able to fly aircraft and fire missiles by "electronic telepathy", using the chip to send instructions to the planes computer. There would in principle, be no need for manual controls. Other applications include trying to restore feeling and movement in paralysed limbs, and sight in blind people. A recreational use would be "virtual tourism", with signals sent to the brain to evoke a mental landscape of sights and smells.

According to Michael Deering, Sun Micro Systems, California, "One can duplicate any human emotion or create any human experience with this technology". He believes people will eventually communicate on Internet without computer keyboards or telephones. The theoretical work on which "Chip grafting" is based, has been carried out by a group led by Grg Kovacs, professor of electrical engineering, Stanford University, California. British academics are part of his team. Early results show that rats with artificial legs can feel through their prosthetic limbs when these are joined by a chip to the nervous system. Deering is studying the potential for implants in the neck. The chip is placed at the point which is the centre for nerves at the base of the skull. Nerve stands are passed through the chip, allowing a process called "listening in". This would create a gateway between the mental and material worlds. Since nobody wants a plug in the neck or wires trailing from the skull, the chip would be attached to a tiny infrared transmitter to send out signals from the head.

Age and Ability

Change is an inevitable part of life, occurring internally and externally with the passage of time. And, as the body changes, so does the mind, evolving with the age and use. It has always been thought that the mind is at its peak up to the time of adulthood and then the process inevitable decline begins. Mental functions such as memory invariably decrease in efficiency as neurons die and produce irreversible organic changes.

Research has shown that the mind is constantly adapting to its functional environment, finding short cuts to the final goal, compensating at each stage for any deficiency caused by age. Helping out is the biology of the brain itself, as neurons use a "buddy" system of working together, one replacing another which cannot cope. Recent data from experiments on rats has suggested that the vast number of glial cells or astrocytes, which have so far been thought to act just as supporting structures for nerve cells, do play a more significant role in mental functioning. These are believed to actually communicate through gap junctions, relaying messages not only between themselves, but also intercepting and implementing those from the neurons as well. Neuro-psychologists at the University of California, Berkeley have shown that active minds cause new dendrites to sprout which connect with other neurons and establish lines of communication. The new courses first appear in visual association areas of the brain, gradually expanding the entire cerebral cortex and continuing as long as stimulus is provided. An interesting finding is that the caps or telomeres at the ends of strands of DNA fray over time at the rate of about 35 amino acids a year.

With the stimulation of everyday living and education, the brain cells that exist multiply, widen their scope and expand the network of connections and thus capabilities. New routes over which messages can travel are formed by complexes of dendrites, each getting increasingly sophisticated and providing a range of choices for the pattern of any particular activity.

At each stage of this refining process, the mind is filtering out what it cannot use, rejecting one pathway for a more economical, efficient or just plain enjoyable alternative. New strategies are learnt at every stage, knowledge becoming specialized and techniques and manner of using it even more so. In experiential expertise, information is used in a particular way to suit a particular purpose, and is one mental resource that, in stead of declining, is improved with time and application.

The neuro-transmitter norepinephrine is involved with the mental ability to focus attention and screen out unwanted influences. Age could cause this system to be thrown off gear, thus affecting the mind. Some day, there may be a way of compensating for a decline in norepinephrine production or for mental sluggishness.

Conclusion

In the late 1940s and early 1950s, Alan Turing, a brilliant mathematician, began to develop conceptually a machine which was as intelligent as human brain. Even today his model is the essential base of all computers.

There has been an exponentially explosive growth in the speed, memory and power of computers in the past four decades. The cost of computers has dropped dramatically, therefore, they are to be found everywhere, doing virtually everything. The software has become so good that today virtual reality is possible. Todays computers can beat every chess player in the world.

A brain is a wonderful thing to fake. It is made of lots of switches (neurons) linked together by a lot of wires (synapses), just like a machine, really. Computer scientists have created whole industries round the pursuit of artificial intelligence and smart machines. But until the early 1980s, the comparison always seemed a bit forced. Brains do not work through the rigid logic of computers. There is no program, no lock step march of instructions from question to answer. Instead, brains just seem to know and when they do not know, the process of working something out is a mysterious combination of logic and intuition.

Brain is one of the most complex organs of the human body. It has as many as 100 billion neurons with some having 100,000 or more connections with neighbouring neurons. The number of potential pathways is beyond the realm of even supercomputers.

As many as five types of memory have been identified. Semantic memory, implicit memory, remote memory, working memory and episodic memory. The trick to keep the memory related functions optimal is to continuously force the brain to work.

According to a Yale University professor and noted computer expert, science will never be able to create a computer that truly duplicates the human brain until researchers find a way to program a computer with emotions. Mr. David Gelernter, associate professor, says that if the goal is to truly duplicate the human mind, then it must mimic our ability to wonder, to dream, to draw analogies, to think intuitively, to come up with insight. Rational, logical, analytical thinking is just one end of a spectrum ranging from high focus to low focus thought. The high focus end is where problem solving usually begins, while inspiration, creativity, insight, and intuition, all are found at the low focus end of the spectrum.

In my lifetime, it would not be possible for a computer to compete with the human brain. Probably the coming generation will see whether the man made computer at that time will be able to compete with the God-given brain of a man. Because, nobody knows what is hidden in the womb of future.

7

Computers: Past, Present and Future

The history of humankind bears testimony to man's insatiable thrust for knowledge, to his unrelenting endeavour "to strive, to seek, to find and not to yield".

Alfred Tennyson

Since the beginning of recorded time, a significant amount of human activities has been used to organize and process information so that it could be more easily understood and learning could take place more effectively. History verifies that those people who improved methods for handling information and communicating it to others, have had a disproportionately large impact on the rest of the world's population.

The modern electronic digital computer is essentially a machine for organizing and processing information.

Computer industry has made spectacular progress in a short time. In the beginning, computer systems were highly localised, usually within a single large room. The concept of the "Computer Centre" as a room with a large computer to which users bring their work for processing is rapidly becoming obsolete. The old model of a single computer serving all of the organisation's computational needs has already been replaced by one in which a large number of separate but interconnected computers do the job. These systems are called computer networks.

Presently available very powerful computers in the world market are known as supercomputers. These computers made a major impact in the field of science and technology.

Almost everyone in the world is directly or indirectly influenced by computers. Today it is extremely important that everyone should know about computers because they are playing an increasingly important role in our life. Each person should find out about potential personal benefits derived from knowing how to use a computer. Writing computer programs and learning about computer applications are pedagogically sound means to become knowledgeable about societal impact of computers.

As the speed of electronic components is slowly approaching the theoretical limit, very expensive technology is required for achieving very high speed of computation using sequential processing. Parallel processing computers can achieve the same speed of computation using less expensive technology and therefore offers a cost-effective method for achieving the high computational speeds required in a variety of scientific and engineering applications such as aerodynamics, structural analysis, weather forecasting, remote sensing, artificial intelligence, missile tracking physics, computational chemistry, etc. Efficient utilization of a parallel processing system requires a close interaction between the machine architecture and the algorithm. Inspite of rapid developments in the field of parallel hardware architecture, parallel processing systems have been slow to catch on because of the slow pace of development in the design of parallel algorithms and applications and in the design of user friendly parallel programming environments.

Presently the computer engineers and scientists are actively involved in man's exciting adventure to extend the frontiers of his intellect and his never-ending persuit of excellence. They distill the knowledge of the yesteryears and harness it to contemporary hi-tech expertise to make possible tomorrow's progress today.

Computer's Past

The simplest and the most ancient computing device is the abacus which was invented by the Arabs many centuries ago. The hand or motor driven computers were technical improvements of the ancient abacus. Real progress in the development of fast computing machines began during World War II.

In 1944, a machine called the Mark I was completed under the direction of Howard H. Aiken. He continued improving the technique and started working on the Mark II model but that too was an electromechanical machine. He designed and directed the construction of two later computers called Mark III and Mark IV. The Mark computers revolutionised scientific and statistical research.

While Aiken was developing his computer, three engineers : John V. Atanasoff, John W. Mauchly and J. Prespao Eckert, were working on calculating machines destined to be even more powerful than the Mark I.

The Mark I was an electromechanical machine. It handled numbers in decimal form and did its arithmetic in 23 digits of accuracy. The time required to perform an addition operation was 0.3 second. Multiplication and division were done by using a multiplication table built into the machine's circuitry. Numbers were stored in strings of relay switches, on punched paper tape and on a series of hand-manipulated switches set up for each computation. The sequence of instructions was punched in numerical form into a ribbon of paper tape, which was moved automatically by the machine, instruction by instruction. George Stibitz of Bell Telephone Laboratories also developed a computer in 1946 which was similar to Mark I. Stibitz's computer was the first to have storage facilities, although it could store only twenty seven digit numbers.

The Atanasoft and Berry Computer (ABC) was completed in 1942. This machine incorporated the vacuum tube as the basic counting device rather than the relay used in Aiken and Stibitz. It was capable of solving large systems of algebraic equations.

Mauchly and Eckert completed a machine in 1946 named Electronic Numerical Integrator and Calculator (ENIAC). It was consisting of 47 panels of electronic parts and wires, each panel being 2 feet wide, 9 feet high and one foot thick. Among its components were 19000 vacuum tubes, 70000 resistors and 10000 capacitors. It had 500,000 soldered joints. It used 150,000 watts of electrical power each day when operating. It could perform 5000 additions of ten-digit numbers each second. It had a memory of 20 storage locations. It did everything Aiken's Mark I had done but much faster, about 1700 times faster. It also incorporated the memory feature of Stibitz's machine. The machine weighed 30 tonnes and occupied 15000 square feet of floor space.

Von Neumann's innovation in computer science was the concept of storing the program (the set of instructions for the machine) in the memory of the machine along with the information (numbers) on which those instructions would operate. The design of such a computer, called the Electronic Discrete Variable Automatic Computer (EDVAC) was began in 1946. A team headed by Maurice V. Wilkes developed a machine called Electronic Delay Storage Automatic Calculator (EDSAC) patterned after the EDVAC.

The EDSAC performed its first automatic calculation in 1949. Thus the EDSAC was the world's first stored program computer. It was a much smaller machine than the ENIAC. It contained only 3000 vacuum tubes compared to the ENIAC's 9000. It required only 15 Kilowatts of power to operate. It operated with about one-seventh the speed of the ENIAC, being capable of executing about 700 additions per second. The important advantage inherent to the EDSAC was its ability to store instructions in its working memory.

The first commercial computer UNIVAC I (Universal Automatic Computer) was delivered by Remington Rand to the U.S. Bureau of the Census in 1951. This machine was able to perform just under 4000 additions of five-digit numbers in one second. Its instruction set made it possible to process both numeric and alphabetic information. Remington Rand Corporation was the first in the world to market computers. The IBM Corporation started manufacturing the commercial computer in 1951. It is estimated that 16200 IBM commercial computers had been installed in the USA alone from 1951 to 1962. By 1975, this figure was well over 80,000.

The ABC, ENIAC, EDSAC and UNIVAC I were the first electronic computers and they used vacuum tubes as the basic counting device. During 1950s many of these vacuum tube computers were built and marketed. This group of computers is now referred to as first generation computers. Their computation speed was in the range of 1000 to 5000 additions per second, a tremendous increase in computational speed over precomputer days. With the advent of transistor, the computer designers started using transistors as the basic counting device instead of vacuum tubes. Thus, from 1958 to 1964 a large number of such computers were built and marketed. Computers utilising transistors came to be known as second generation computers. This generation computers had calculating speeds ranging from 2000 additions per second for the small machines to 500,000 additions per second for large machines like IBM 7090. Memory capacities were large enough in some of the machine to provide 65000 storage locations in the main memory (the working memory of the computer) and several million storage locations in the auxiliary memory (the secondary memory from which information could be retrieved at a slower rate). After 1964 the integrated circuits were used in the manufacture of computers. The IC's make it possible to construct faster computers with larger memories than ever. Also the cost of a given computer of certain capability is less than it was before. Computers utilising IC's as the basic counting device are referred to as the third generation computers and have been marketed from about 1964. The third generation computer perform as many as 10 million additions per second and many have the main memories of more than 100 million locations. Presently available computers are called fourth generation computers. They use very large scale integrated (VLSI) chips. Present trend is to connect all the computers installed in different places in a network. The fifth generation computers will do the processing in parallel.

Computer's Present

Intel Corporation, USA has produced the fastest and the biggest microprocessor chip which contains over 2.5 million transistor. This chip is called 1860 XP. This chip combines supercomputer performance and microprocessor technology to accelerate the development of the high-end computing systems. This is the only microprocessor with inherent support for multiprocessing, parallel processing and visualisation, all on a single chip.

Pertech Computers Limited has launched a six processor mini-computer. This computer is based on Intel 80486 microprocessor. This can support more than 200 active users simultaneously.

NEC Corporation, Japan, has introduced a new supercomputer SX-3 44R in the market which is the world's fastest computer. This computer has a sequential computation speed of 25.6 Giga flops or 25.6 billion calculations a second. This computer exceeds the peak speed of 24 Giga flops of the top model of Cray Research Inc., USA.

Convex has produced the first supercomputer C 3800 implemented in GaAs technology. C 3800 is the direct coupled FET logic (DCFL) supercomputer. It is claimed to match the speed of ECL but with about a quarter of ECL's power requirements. This computer operates at a speed of 2 Giga flops for vector operations. It is low power, low cost and small in size.

The university of London Computer Centre has become the first establishment worldwide to replace a Cray supercomputer with one from Convex. The system installed is a C 3840 worth £4.5 million, with four processors and one Giga byte of main memory.

The Convex system will assist the evolution to interactive super-computing which speeds up the research cycle by allowing users to observe and monitor results as they work.

The Convex supercomputer offers good networking facilities and provides a high degree of compatibility into the existing Cray environment.

Toshiba Company of Japan has developed 16 Mega byte EPROM (erasable programmable read only memory). According to Toshiba, the new device has the largest memory capacity ever achieved in EPROM with an access time of 150 nanosecond. It is expected to be used mainly in design and development of word processors, laser printers, telecommunication and medical equipment where a large amount of data is required.

SGS-Thomson Microelectronics has developed the fastest 4 Mega byte EPROM. It has an access time of only 80 nanosecond. The new device is intended for use in laser printers and many other embedded applications where both high speed and high EPROM capacity are required. Other applications include PABX equipment, fax machines, robot systems, simulators and industrial control systems.

The V90 rapid access storage system from TANDEM, is based on WSI (Wafer Scale Integration) technology. The capacity of the basic memory element of the V90 is 40 Mega byte, each memory model being formed from two six-inch wafers configured to give 20 Mega byte of memory per wafer. With its fast access time, typically 200 microsecond, the V90 can provide significant performance improvements in applications that demand frequent access to key data.

Motorola has introduced a Fibre Distributed Data Interface (FDDI) chip set, implementing the physical layer and the media access control sublayer of the OSI seven layer model. The new chip set has four components: (i) FDDI Clock Generator (FCG) (ii) Elasticity buffer and Link Manager (ELM) (iii) Media Access Controller (MAC) (iv) FDDI system interface (FSI). Additional support, including station-management software and an application development system is also available.

The new ceramic superconductors would make it less expensive to make superfast electronic switches called Josephson junctions. Economic Josephson Junctions would make the computers many times faster and smaller in size.

A supercooled computer that will work at an incredible speed is the goal of the new research activity in Japan. Japan has already developed high temperature superconductors which are oxide materials that lose electric resistance at liquid nitrogen temperature. Mr. Takeshi Kobayashi of Osaka University says the logic step is to combine semiconductor and superconductor technologies to create micro-electronic logic devices for high speed computers of the future.

Computer's Future

Future supercomputer will rely increasingly on parallel designs because the operational speeds of vector computers are inherently limited to 50–100 Giga Flops (billion floating-point operations per second), even allowing for technological advances over the next decade. In contrast, massively parallel supercomputers will offer teraflop (1000 Giga Flops) performance.

In Japan, there has been widespread installation of supercomputers in the last five years in the universities, research institutes and industry. As per the statement of Japanese Government, the massively parallel computing is the country's most important priority for the 1990s. U.S. Senator George said in his introduction to the National High Performance Computer Technology Act of 1989, "The nations which most completely assimilates high performance computing into its economy will very likely emerge as the dominant intellectual, economic and technological force in the next century".

The computer has come into vogue as a very important device in bringing new benefits to the society. Computer-based forecasting is one of the most significant tools in planning the future. In fact much of the future is controlled by today's decisions. The world future society forecasts that mind reading computers may be in use by the end of this century. This telepathic computer could electronically pick up human thoughts.

In future, computers will have computation speed 10 to 50 times faster than today's computers. Increased computation speed will cause people to attempt the solution of even greater and more complex problems.

The combination of faster computation speeds and large computer storage capacity, all for less cost, will enable people to attempt computer applications hitherto felt impossible. Computers will communicate with one another and will share stored information. The availability of inexpensive computer terminals will have more impact on society than any other future change in technology.

Computers are a vital component in communication systems. In future, instead of telephone line circuits, the computer directed system will select appropriate microwave circuits on which to transmit the signal that will complete a call. Communication satellites would not have the restrictions associated with the need to find an available telephone line. Signals could be sent between any two points on earth having a straight line access to communication satellites. Undoubtedly such a communication system would permit nearly instantaneous information exchange among people.

Computers are already being used to control the environmental conditions inside large buildings and huge enclosed spaces such as Houston's astrodome.

In future computerised shopping will be very common. As per a report, by the year 2005 Singaporean shoppers might not need to try on new clothes before buying them. Instead, when a customer chooses the cloth and cuts of a suit, he will see on a large wall screen, a computer generated image of himself wearing the finished product. Then if he decides to buy, the price will be automatically deducted from his bank account. There is a plan to turn Singapore into a world leader in information and communications technology. Such screens could soon become as common in the city State as the telephone.

Conclusion

A few years ago, computers were the domain of MIS or EDP departments but now all the successful executives are found with a PC on their desk. Local Area Network (LAN) have made it possible to share information and files among various users, facilities like Electronic mail allows to communicate with other PC users thereby practically obviating the paper work in the office. The PC revolution is the net result of amazing information technology which offers a tremendous amount of speed and accuracy. PCs have offered a viable solution to deal with the problems of clerical manpower and expensive office space. Today in the USA and many other western countries, computers maintain diary, make telephone calls, send and receive telex and fax, keep track of appointments, take dictation and type out a memo ready for signature. These and other developments have made a PC an integral part of an executive's life.

In the last 40 years, there has been a 10,000 fold increase in the computing speed but the insatiable demand of scientists for computing power in some areas continues to challenge the designers of parallel processing systems.

Distributed memory multiprocessors consisting of a number of processors each with local memory communicating with each other by sending messages are examples of parallel computers which exploit coarse grain parallelism. Intel IPSC, NCube, C-DAC's PARAM are examples of distributed memory multiprocessors.

We know the major areas of computer applications and are aware of some of the implications to society of the widespread use of the computers. All indications are that the future holds even more spectacular surprises in the way computers will be applied to everyday life.

8

Role of Computers in the Coming Years

The driving force in modern economy is the continuing process of technological innovation. Sweeping changes through technology are thus dramatically affecting the quality of life. A computer is an information processing device capable of interpreting and executing programmed commands for inputs, outputs and logic operations. Computers have been largely used for data processing. Data are generated through transactions. Therefore processing of the transactions themselves promises much greater returns. A by-product of transaction processing system is information.

The goal of a Computer Integrated Manufacturing Systems (CIMS) would be optimization of the total business rather than optimizing individual components. CIMS has to link automated manufacturing functions such as numerical control, process planning, material requirements planning and CAD/CAM and then further integrate Management Information Systems (MIS) to data process functions such as financial, accounting, inventory control and payroll.

Computer Society of India

The Computer Society of India (CSI) was founded in the early sixties when the first computers were installed in India. It is a body of computer professionals dedicated to spreading the productive use of computers by encouraging interaction among these professionals, upgrading and updating their knowledge and skills, spreading computer literacy and cooperating with the government in choosing the right policies. The CSI has branches all over the country. These branches organise various activities to achieve the professed goals of the CSI. These include organising courses on computer languages such as Basic, Fortran, and Cobol, etc. as well as on systems analysis, design and PC software. The CSI has evolved the national standard test for competence in programming competence which has been recognised as proof of proficiency.

Information on Tap

Initially, computers were introduced in business data processing as batch processing machine. The inherent requirement of handling data in batches leads to delayed reports, irrelevant business decisions and all-round confusion at the user level. A user can avoid such situations in batch processing environment only by adhering to very strict self-discipline in the areas of data preparation, i.e., design and preparation of input sheets from source documents, immediate response to check lists generated by the validation runs, preparation of supportive data, etc.

Even the batch processing machines cannot fully meet the requirements of today's business world. At management level today's manager demands up-to-date status on sales, pending orders, stock positions, money on hand, etc. because decision taken on the basis of yesterday's or last week's information may not be relevant tomorrow. The most promising alternative is managing up-to-date information with on-line computer systems. In an on-line computer system, the user himself can enter the data almost as soon as it is generated. On-line validation facilities lead to marked reduction in data errors, and whatever errors are detected can be immediately updated by the user. Airline and Railway reservations are typical examples. Only with on-line systems any particular booking centre can refer to a central database, which is being continuously updated by the information flowing from all centres and accordingly commit a seat.

On-line information technology thus offers diverse benefits in business applications. The implementation process is extremely complex initially but ultimately the benefits will outweigh the costs and expertise required for the same.

Computer Aided Design

Computer Aided Design (CAD) is being extensively used in the advanced countries to speed up the design development cycle for increased manpower efficiency, improved product quality and reduced costs.

Eniac Computer

John Presper Eckert was the inventor of "Eniac", an acronym for "Electronic Numerical Integrator and Computer". It weighed 30 tons, had 18000 Vacuum tubes, occupied a whole room and had flashing pink lights and miles of cable. Its first real job was to confirm the design calculations for the atomic bomb in 1945. Todays desktop computers, though a thousand times faster and a tiny fraction of the size, use the same principles as Eckert's machine.

This sophisticated technology is now within the reach of the Indian designers. Integrated package consisting of a computer, a digitiser, a high resolution plotter along with suitable software are customised to meet a customer's specific requirements. The range starts with PC/XT and PC/AT based systems at the lower end and goes up to very powerful 32 byte supermini computer based ones.

These packages aim particularly at the engineering industry for design, drafting and technical analysis, architects for plans and drawings, and graphics designer for visuals and illustrations. The computer stores the drawings, retrieves and manipulates them according to the requirements of the designer.

The images can be seen and changed on the screen to arrive at the desired result. For professional CAD/CAM/CAE requirements, a high resolution graphic terminals are available. The digitisers allow the design to be fed to the computer with ease. After the design has been finalised, the plotter can make an accurate rendering of the design. A wide variety of internationally proven CAD/CAM/CAE software for all kinds of design applications are available.

Computer Networks

As computers have become smaller, cheaper and numerous, people have become more and more interested in connecting them together to form networks and distributed systems. Computers have made spectacular progress in a short time. The merging of computers and communication has had a profound influence on the way computer systems are organized. The old model, a single computer serving all of the organization's computational needs is rapidly being replaced by one in which a large number of separate but interconnected computers do the job. These systems are called computer networks.

Fig. 8.2. Future Intelligent and Speaking Computer.

Networks are being developed both to connect existing machines and to take advantages of the low cost, high performance micro-processors the semiconductor industry is turning out. Most networks have a collection of hosts communicating via a subnet. The subnet may utilise multipoint-to-point lines between its interface message processors (IMP), or a single common broadcast channel.

Different Types of Computer Networks

(a) Satellite Links for Indonet: Telecommunication department has approved the use of satellite communication, VHF radio and dial up access for its national computer network, Indonet. According to

Mr. Gupta, Chairman and Managing Director of CMC Ltd., Indonet's coverage would increase very soon from 8 to 35 cities of India : TDM/ TDMA would lead to optional use of satellite space. He further says this technique, together with the use of the three metre roof-top earth station, would lead to an effective cost and highly reliable backbone network.

Data transmission would take place at 64,000 bytes per second, a thirty-fold increase over what was currently available.

CMC is using "digital packet radio" technology. Radio-cum-data equipment are being used in this technology. By this system many users can simultaneously utilise a single VHF radio frequency for two-way data communications. Use of dial-up facilities in metropolitan cities like Mumbai, Delhi, Chennai, Bangalore, Calcutta would allow in-frequent users to also utilise Indonet services as charges would be levied only on the basis of each call.

Nowadays many organisations of both public and private sectors are utilising Indonet, for example, Oil & Natural Gas Commission, Shipping Corporation of India, the Steel Authority of India, Coal India Limited and many more. The State Bank of India is also using Indonet for its foreign exchange operations.

(b) Telecommunication Network of ONGC: The Oil & Natural Gas Commission had decided to have its own communication network for WRBC. The operational areas of Western Region Business Centre (WRBC) of the ONGC stretches over a 300 km. long belt from Mehsana in the north to Hazira in the South. To cover the whole operational areas of Western Region, it was needing a highly efficient, versatile and integrated communication network. This network is connected through digital radios having the digital time division multiple access (TDMA) system.

The connections are established through nodes or base stations connected to one or two computer controlled telephone exchanges. The TDMA system is point-to-multipoint communication system with computer control telemetry-cum-telesupervisory facilities. This system is connected through microwave links.

(c) Packet Switched Public Data Network "Vikram". Recently a public data network operating in packet-switching mode was started in India. This network will fill the need for a highly reliable data network making the most efficient use of long distance media. It will support data communication switching amongst terminals and computers of different speed and protocols. All data switching facilities as per international standards (CCITT) will be provided through this network.

The user's information may be provided in packets (16-1024 characters) or characters/8 bit codes which can be converted by packet switch into packets. These packets are switched between subscribers who are connected to each other in a "Call". These packets are exchanged between the connected subscribers with little error which is less than 1 in 10^9 and with a small delay of less than 0.5 second. They can access the packet switch in different ways. They can be connected by dedicated cable pairs. They can dial a telephone number allotted to a packet switch and communicate with use of PSTN-dat/dial up modems. They can use their telex machines to get connected to the network and work with others in the network. This will be achieved by dialling a telex number allotted to the packet switch at each of the locations.

Proper communication is possible among them even though they work at different speeds and codes. Depending on the type of access, the subscriber has to adopt a certain procedure (Protocol) for communication in the network. These procedures will be CCITT standard procedures (*x*.25, *x*.28).

The Subscribers who are using *x*.25 procedure can support various simultaneous calls to other subscribers on a single link to the switch. This will facilitate computers, etc., to support multiple calls from different terminals spread over the network in a time sharing mode. To protect the lines to the packet switch against failures all subscribers will be provided with the option of accessing the switch through the telephone network using the normal and PSTN (dial-up) modems. The protocol adopted in such a case is *x*.32 which is very similar to *x*.25.

The initial network covers 20 locations. Bombay, Delhi, Madras and Calcutta are major switching modes. Ahmedabad, Pune, Bangalore and Hyderabad are minor switching modes. There are 12 remote access facilities.

Micro Computers

Microprocessor is the biggest break-through in electronics after the transistor. The microprocessor had come as a result of a powerful thrust in digital electronics towards miniaturization. Today the microprocessor is an integral part of our everyday life. Microprocessor controlled instruments and instrumentation systems are becoming a rule rather than an exception. They are also gaining even more ground in management, information and process control systems, telecommunications, electronics, medicine, public services and toys. The microprocessors form the heart of all microcomputer which invade the society in all walks of life.

The integration of the microprocessors into instruments capable of measuring many and diverse electric and non-electric quantities has impressively enhanced their accuracy, reliability and speed, extended their capabilities, simplified their controls and offered a tool for tackling problems that were entirely unmanageable before. The microprocessors are thus poised to play a pivotal role in the development of electronics in the decade to come.

Mr. Anant Agarwal, an Indian born computer wizard, had developed a computer SPARC (Scalable Processor Architecture) based on RISC (Reduced Instruction Set Computer) architecture which is rated to have a capacity of ten MIPS (Million Instruction Per Second) as compared to the capacity of one or two MIPS credited to the conventional chips which are used in personal computers. These chips can be employed in a wide range of computers from personal computers to super-computers. RISC technology can be acquired from M/s. Sun Micro Systems, USA. Presently M/s Sun Micro Systems is developing a chip of 40 MIPS capacity at a cost of about one-tenth of the market price.

According to SCL Chairman and Managing Director, Mr. Virendra Mohan, micro-chip will be developed for personal computers soon. This micro-chip will reduce the cost of personal computers significantly.

Computer Software

Export of software touched $ 600 million by 1996 and is likely to expand even further if the government continues to support the Indian Software Industry.

According to the Confederation of Engineering Industry (CEI), India's software industry represents one of its lead areas and would be able to sufficiently increase production of software exports to meet the world demand. The USA is the largest consumer of Indian software. Almost 90 per cent of India's total software enters in the USA market.

Demand for standard software products and packages is also expected to rise and grow in the coming years.

Use of Computers in ONGC

The following is a list of the various business and support groups in ONGC and major functions in each group requiring computer support at corporate, regional and project levels:

1. ***Exploration***

   Planning, monitoring, resource management, interpretation laboratory analysis and reservoir monitoring.

2. ***Drilling***

   Planning, monitoring, resources management, formulation of drilling norms, optimisation of drilling practices, etc.

3. ***Operation***

   Planning, monitoring, resource management, installation management, etc.

4. ***Technical Service***

   Planning, monitoring, workshop management, equipment maintenance, material management, engineering and design, surveys, construction management, logistics and transport manpower.

5. ***Materials Management***

   Planning, procurement, goods clearance, storage issues and receipts, inventory control, vender analysis and market research.

6. ***Finance***

   Profit planning and revenue budgeting, capital budgeting and control, profitability and security, costing and control systems, tax management, Accounting and Audit.

7. ***Personnel***

   Manpower build up (recruitment, posting and transfer), manpower forecasting, executive bio-data, grievance handling, ACRS, executive development, personnel statistics, house allotments, seniority lists, leave records, etc.

Rural Computers

The World Bank had lobbied the government of India for pilot project on village level computerisation. The project was lobbied on behalf of the World Bank by one of its communication experts, Mr. Bernard Woods and Mr. Srinivasan representative of Appollo Computers, a USA firm.

The funds for this pilot project proposed in India, came from a World Bank administered UND programme. In establishing local area computer networks, the attempt would be to integrate into the system the computers being installed at block and village level by the government agencies. The maintenance and support of the hardware and software would be entrusted to a combination of bodies consisting of the Computer Maintenance Corporation of India, the private sector, trained non-government organisations and village level workers.

The decision about the kind of software to be imported and adapted for the pilot program would be taken after reviewing international experience in the area as well as the National Mission and other on-going village-based programmes in India. It is being suggested that the software developed in India may later find a ready market elsewhere.

The networks developed under the pilot program would serve a variety of sectors and would also provide information to the villagers on non-agricultural employment, environmental preservation and women's development. Experience gained from the pilot program is expected to provide a basis for large scale application on new information technology for rural development programmes in the future.

How to buy a Computer?

The modus operandi of purchasing a computer is not fundamentally different from that of any other high technology product. The first step is to establish the need for computer. Be sure of what you want and then home in on it. This is done by faithfully translating your needs to specifications that will have to be given to the computer vendors. Computers come in all sizes, power, capabilities and configurations. Your ability to communicate your requirement to the vendor will decide whether you will get the right machine or not.

The specifications should clearly outline hardware and software requirements, installation and maintenance support, training and warranty. If you ask the vendor to develop one or more applications for you, be sure to clearly state the terms of the development activity, the time frame envisaged, the boundaries of the vendor's task, the help that would be given to him during the development stage and other related matters. A real price advantage could be gained by going in for a tender-based purchase. Alternatively, you could negotiate with some selected suppliers.

Evaluation of the offers is the most difficult task. The best way is to go through the offer item by item, comparing it with the specifications and allotting points. The offer which gets the maximum points, will be your choice. Factors which should be examined in the evaluation of the offer include the quality of the hardware, through put of the machine which can be tested by running benchmark programs, field upgradability of the machine, the warranty period, the type of training offered, the maintenance support promised and its cost and the quality of the software offered.

The vendor should be committed to the industry, should be financially sound and able, and even keen, to give prompt and quality after-sale service in maintenance and software support. It is always better to entrust the maintenance of your hardware to the vendor because he knows the machine best.

Buying the computer from the right person is important. The purchase of the computer is an important activity. Make sure that you are not investing your precious money on junk.

Computer Scenario of ONGC

The following is the visualization of the computer scenario of ONGC:

Powerful computers are being used for scientific applications at various regions and corporate offices. These powerful computers provide sophisticated database technology, graphics, plotting, etc. at all the regions. Important projects are having microcomputers. Drilling sites also have terminals or small micros. A micro-computer becomes as standard part of rig equipment and operatives. Multiple computer systems for commercial data processing are being provided at all regions.

Data network will be operational at all the levels, i.e., drill site to project, project to region and region to corporate office. Office automation will be a part of office working environment enhancing the productivity of office staff.

Sccurity of data base will become an important consideration. Paper may get replaced by electronic mail. Tele-conferencing will be a reality. Senior and functional executives will have terminals allowing them to interact with each other as well as with intelligent machines connected through data network.

Conclusion

The computer is very much a part of the present day life. In the coming years, the computer will be indispensible. Everything will be on computer. Computerised manufacturing automation can be applied in a wide range of industries. This implies moving away from the mechanical model to an information based organic model. Design engineering and manufacturing technology in highly developed countries have been completely revolutionized through computer aided design, manufacturing, technique of management, etc.

A computer, no matter how sophisticated, is useless without intricate and expensive application software which programs it for specific tasks.

To conclude with the remark that in the coming years, behind every successful executive, there will be a computer.

9

The Great Internet

"Arnold Schwarzenneger has a long one, Michael J. Fox has a short one, Madonna does not have one, The Pope does not use his any more. What is it'?

Answer is last name"

—Internet Humour; Source: *The Times of India*

The most happening thing in the world of ITis Internet. It is going to touch everyone's life like nothing has before and change the face of global economy. It is like the coming of petroleum and the steam engine before it. It is the next biggest thing and it will bring in an era that will destroy national boundaries.

Until the advent of the Worldwide Web in 1994, the Internet was little more than a playground for computer freaks. Now a simple click-and-point access, it has opened to everyone and become a rapid-growing business tool.

UPS, the international courier company, reckons to be saving about $2,00,000 a day by using the Internet. In just six months the number of UPS's American customers using the Internet has grown from 25 per cent to 59 per cent and more growth is coming. In the next six months, 75 per cent of American business, or at least the companies that do business with UPS in the USA, will be using the Internet.

There were 50 million Internet users worldwide in July 1997, with an installed base of over 100 million computers. Estimates suggest that Internet users are growing at the rate of 12 per cent per month with the service becoming a vital business resource and international commerce through it will be $6.6 billion by 1998. In India, there are

1.5 million computers and only 30,000 Internet users. According to the government's estimate there will be 5.29 million computers in the country by 2000 and Internet users will grow to 750,000 and to 1.6 million by 2002. By contrast, there are already 3.5 million Internet users and 850 ISPs (Internet Service Provider) in Japan, 500,000 in Malaysia and 400,000 in Mexico.

Table 9.1. Internet Host Computers in the World

S. No.	*Year*	*Internet Host Computers*
1.	1987	Very few
2.	1988	Few
3.	1989	0.3 million
4.	1990	0.57 million
5.	1991	0.70 million
6.	1992	1.12 million
7.	1993	2.82 million
8.	1994	5.14 million
9.	1995	9.71 million
10.	1996	16.10 million

Internet users in India can look forward to better accessibility and a wide range of services like E-mail, File Transfer Protocol (FTP), Chat-sessions and Web-site/page design. The Department of Telecommunications (DOT) is planning to slash the prices of Internet services to Rs. 10,000 or 12,000 per annum for 500 hours from Rs. 15,500 at present.

IBM e-business solutions can help the company people work together more effectively wherever they are, at home, at office, or on road, giving them access to the up-to-date information they need on their jobs, just when they need it. Connecting Internet or Extranet to the Internet makes the information it contains accessible from anywhere in the world using ubiquitous browsing software.

Knowledge as Capital

The explosion of information has rendered complex its control and dissemination. The task of information generation has been facilitated by computers, especially, online access to data bases, fax and other document delivery and reproduction facilities. Publishers have also been aided likewise through desktop publishing, online receipt of a manuscript directly from an author's terminal, photo-offset printing and computer assisted typesetting.

Rapid advances in science and technology are possible now because users get information faster. Nearly one million articles on science alone are published every year. The developed countries have long ago realised that information is power and have invested substantially on research in this area. Within the last three decades they have developed a host of innovative equipment for storage, processing and dissemination of information. As information became a marketable product the commercial houses and big computer companies also produced computers, information-related products and machines in competition with each other. Thus world has become the market for the new equipment and products like computers, optical discs, CD-ROMS, VDTS, modular charging desks, modems, microform readers, word processors, disk drives, printers, facsimile transmitters, etc.

As information got stored in mainframe, mini and microcomputers the cooperation and sharing of resources are now connected through networking. The concept of networking has been upgraded. By now the different computers of the world have been connected through communication networks.

Information has no value until it becomes integrated knowledge and therefore useful. Information, processed by human brain into knowledge and integrated and intuited into wisdom, has quite suddenly become the world's most important resource. It will be playing the prima donna role in world history that physical labour, stone, bronze, land, minerals, metals and energy once played. Information expands as it is used. It is less hungry for other resources. The higher the teck, the less energy and raw materials are needed. It can, and increasingly does, replace land, labour and capital. It is readily transportable and it leaks tool. It is shared, not exchanged.

Indeed, the growing importance of information in creating wealth has turned out to be a very good news for countries less endowed with geological riches and arable land. Japan, for example, was forced by the lack of physical resources to bet on the only sure resource it had, the minds of its own people. By contrast, in the countries whose people have been kept in ignorance, it hardly seems to matter which riches lie in the space they occupy. Most of their citizens become the peasants of the information society.

So in a rapidly changing information environment there is going to be much less excuse for depriving whole populations of the benefits of development that could benefit the many, not only the few. The enormous advances in information science and technology have now made the human species, for the first time, the lead actor in its own evolution.

Managers have access to more information than they could ever have dreamed of years ago. They can all up Web pages on the Internet, they can tap into databases and they can call on corporate expertise by using internal networks. The problem is that it is all too easy to confuse data with knowledge and information technology with information. As ever-increasing volumes of data become available, the difficulty of shifting, sharing and exploring it has become more acute.

It is all part of the failure of modern management to face up the changes which are taking place in business, commerce and government. Today, we depend on information more than ever before, highlighted by advances in technology, and the growth of global companies, yet most managers fail to ask whether they have the necessary and sufficient information to do their jobs.

IMPACT programme has been developed for Boards of Directors to enable them to understand the issues and set the direction and policy for their companies. This involves thinking through how they manage their existing assets and concentrating on the similarities between information and physical assets. The problem is that because information assets are intangible and not quoted in the balance sheet, people pay too little attention.

It is no use talking about corporate knowledge if you do not know what corporate information you have to represent and/or you mismanage it. Information management is, therefore, an essential discipline to corporate knowledge.

Guide to Internet

The Internet has two types of computers involved, the clients and the servers. The clients are the users, who access the information stored on the computers known as the servers, which are the information storage banks.

The collection of these information servers is known as the World Wide Web, and the servers themselves are known as Web servers. The tremendous amount of information on the web servers can be accessed by the clients by using a simple user—friendly interface known as web browser. A web browser allows users to accept text, graphics, audio- and video-based information from these web servers. Each web server is identified by a unique address, which in called URL (Uniform Resource Locater) or simply a web address, which looks something like this http://www., some server. com. Here "http" stands for Hyper Text Transfer Protocol. Protocol is a rigidly defined set of rules and formats that computers use to communicate with one another. "www" stands for worldwide web and someservercom. is the name of the web server being accessed. To access the Internet the user must have a telephone line connection.

Important information required about equipment and Internet policy are:

1. *Desktop Computer* : Considering the current demands of audio, video and graphical date present on web server, the computer must be a Pentium 100 MHZ with 16 Mb or more of RAM (preferably 32 Mb) a 1 Gb hard disk, (in case the user wishes to download the audio, video and textual stuff on the Internet), it must be equipped with a CD ROM, a high quality resolution SVGA colour monitor and a good quality sound card with speakers.

2. *Modem:* It is required to connect the computer to the telephone line. Preferred speed of the modem depends on what the line conditions and ISP (Internet Service Provider) can support. It can range from 1200 bps to 33600 bps. But the right choice for the Indian conditions is at least a 33600 bps modem.

3. *Browser Software:* Any web browser which is easily available will do. The preferred choices are Netscape Navigator or MS Internet Explorer. A lot of modem companies offer this as a complimentary add on to their Internet Ready Modems.

4. *Internet Policy:* The Indian government has announced its new Internet policy to permit an unlimited number of private service providers. The announcement ended the monopoly on Internet services by Videsh Sanchar Nigam Ltd. (VSNL), but the government said VSNL would continue to provide Internet services in major cities. The government would spend Rs. 1,200 crore ($300 million) on setting up an information infrastructure backbone and encourage banks and financial institutions to motivate new entrepreneurs to enter the field.

It said it would allow foreign firms to take stakes of up to 49 per cent in private Indian ISPs (Internet Service Providers). It promised to waive the licence fee for private ISPs for five years and to grant them an initial licence for a period of 10 years. The government also said that it would allow ISPs to use surplus communications capacity owned by the railways network, the Power Grid Corporation of India, and State Electricity Boards. But voice monopoly for covering long distance and international calls will continue to remain with the department of telecommunication (DOT)/Mahanagar Telephone Nigam Ltd. (MTNL) and VSNL. All licensees of DOT, including basic telephone service providers, pager and cellular phone operators can also apply to become ISPs.

The department of telecommunications (DOT) plans to set up a National Internet Backbone (NIB) built on Optic Fibre Cable (OFC), microwaves and other media to carry Internet traffic across the country and to VSNL gateways. An investment of Rs. 170 crore has been earmarked for upgradation of the long distance network.

In pursuit of its policy to promote Internet services at the grass-root levels, the Government of India has commenced Internet services at village levels to encourage exposure of the rural populace of this powerful electronic medium of communications.

Demonstration links have been initiated in 15 identified villages all over the country, termed as "Tele-Villages", as a bold step forward to provide hands on experience for the rural population. Popular Internet applications are E-mail, World Wide Web and File Transfer with extensive use in business communications, agriculture, education, research and entertainment. Major applications such as Electronic Commerce and Virtual Private Networks are also gaining popularity on the Internet.

Launched on August 15, 1995 in India, commercial Internet service is now available from 20 nodes like Ahmedabad, Aurangabad, Bangalore, Calcutta, Chandigarh, Chennai, Dehradun, Ernakulam, Guwahati, Gwalior, Hyderabad, Jaipur, Kanpur, Lucknow, Mumbai, New Delhi, Panjim, Patna, Pune and Thiruvananthapuram.

5. *Charges:* VSNL offers two types of Internet access, one is a shell account that allows a user to connect one's own computer through the VSNLs like a terminal and get information only as text. The other is the TCP (Transmission Control Protocol)/IP (Internet Protocol) account.

Currently for an individual, VSNL charges a onetime fee at the beginning for 500 hours of usage of their service and the user will have to pay again either on using up 500 hours or on completion of one year, whichever is earlier. VSNL charges Rs. 5,000 for a shell account and for an individual TCP/IP account, it charges Rs. 15,500.

6. *Getting Internet Connection:* The next step is to approach the nearest ISP for an Internet account which facilitates connection to the Internet. As long as the ISP is local, the telephone call is also local.

All what now the user has to do is to fill the required form and get his Internet connection.

Harnessing Web Technologies

Introduction of Web technologies has redefined communication in a major way. Web technologies used in Internet and Internets have revolutionised the world by enabling connection of millions of computers across several support platforms and around the globe.

There are several technologies that made the Web a success. First, the links between computers became faster and wider because of improved telecommunication network like fibre optic and satellite link. Secondly, invention of standards such as HTTP, HTML and TCP/IP that enabled text, pictures, audio and video clip to be transmitted.

Table 9.2. World Wide Web Sites Visited by users in a Month in 1997

S. No.	*Internet Online Service*	*Percentage*
1.	aol. Com	46
2.	yahoo. Com	38
3.	netscape Com	31
4.	microsoft Com	22
5.	gescities. Com	21
6.	excite. Com	20

Hyperlinks enabled users to jump from one document or page to another by simply clicking on a word, a phrase or a visual irrespective of which computer in the world the document was physically stored in. Thirdly, the ability to support across all platforms, thus the information is presented in the same way to every computer.

Organisations and business world over have been reaping the benefits of Web technologies. The World Wide Web presents exciting opportunities that few would have dreamed possible. The advantages that of putting up a site on the World Wide Web are several. The most striking benefit is its international presence. The Web is the shortest and the cheapest way to reach across to an international audience that totals 60 million and an NRI audience of 3.5 million.

The Web site can be used to disseminate information about the activities and achievements of organisations. One can use it to sell his business and services globally. Among Indian companies, ICICI Bank increased their NRI deposits from 4.5 per cent to 10 per cent in one year. 80 per cent of its NRI customers are coming through the Internet. Kotak Securities raised a few crores of rupees from NRIs for the public issues that have promoted, using the Internet.

The Internet has myriad possibilities. It transcends geographical boundaries and is open 24 hours. One is able to get in touch with one customer directly and explain to him about one's products and services. It also gives one a good understanding of the consumer psyche through the feedback that one receives from them.

There are several service providers who help create, host and manage Web sites. These companies provide a host of services ranging from developing a web strategy, domain registration, server set up, site construction, content creating, site management, search engine registration and site updating.

The cost of putting up a site on the web is not very high. Compared to traditional medium like print and electronic, the money that one needs to spend is chicken feed. In India, the costs of putting up a simple site of just two or three pages would come to around Rs. 15,000 to Rs. 20,000 per annum. This would include cost of registration. Each update costs approximately Rs. 500. A medium size site of around 10 to 15 pages would come for around Rs. 50,000 to Rs. 75,000 per annum.

Table 9.3. Internet Access in the USA in May 1998, which use the Different Media for Getting News

S. No.	*Different Media*	*Average Hours Per Week PC Users*
1.	Broadcast TV	5.7 hours
2.	Cable TV	5.0 hours
3.	Radio	4.5 hours
4.	Newspaper	3.6 hours
5.	Internet/on-line news	3.5 hours
6.	Magazines	2.4 hours

Updates are a very important feature for the web site. A onetime publishing of information is not enough. The information should be kept up-to-date and fresh. This will keep one's site alive. It is also important the one advertises his web site like business card, letter-heads, brochures, newsletter, popular web sites and traditional advertising medium like newspapers, magazines and television.

As the Internet revolutionises the world, internets are transforming corporate organisations in India and the world. Internets involve use of web technology within the internal network of an organisation. They cater only to the internal users of an organisation and enable the use of same type of servers and browsers used for the World Wide Web.

There are several advantages. First of all, since Web technology is based on open standards, it is available for nearly all operating systems and hardware platforms and can integrate with existing system. One of its most important advantages is the ease of use. Hyperlinking, that essential Internet tool enables users to easily navigate and find information by simply clicking a word or graphic. Internets are also relatively inexpensive both in initial purchase and in training and development.

Among the more popular uses of Internets include communication between departments and project teams. This saves the cost of producing, printing and shipping corporate information. It is also useful for application requiring two-way interactions. It can be used for sales and marketing information such as on line training materials and sale presentation, programme calendar, pricing chart, etc. It enables employees within the organisation to share up-to-date information on customer problems, respond to customer queries and complaints.

In India, Internets are being considered by several corporates to connect their offices all over the country. Indian ERNET has more than 50,000 subscribers. This network enables educational and research institutions to communicate with each other and link with institutions across the globe via the Internet.

Finland has the highest per capita use of the Internet and mobile phones in the world. It is estimated that more than 60 per cent of the country's five million people are linked to the Internet.

The AT&T Pocket-Net service provides access on a specially equipped cellular telephone to e-mail and an online personal organiser, as well as news, financial reports, weather forecasts, sports scores, airline schedules and national directories.

The Pocket-Net service also comes with a password, protected private Web site from which subscribers view and manage their personal information, such as a calendar and address book from a Pocket-Net compatible cellular phone or a personal computer. The phones are manufactured by Mitsubishi Electric Corpn. and Samsung Electronics Co. Ltd., and sell for $229. Subscriptions cost $29.99 a month plus the subscriber rate for basic cellular phone service.

Intel introduces "quick Web" technology on the computers called servers that Internet services use to store and replay data. The combination of Intel hardware and special software compresses all the graphic images that are piped through the server, boosting access speed. It is like putting the Columbia river through a garden hose.

For years, a major complaint about the Internet has been the long down—load tines required for graphics and data—hogging files over a typical 28.8 kilobit per second modem. The increase in speed varies, depending on the content of the Web page. Text will not get much boost, but some graphics could be more than twice was fast, even seven times as fast.

The quick Web system boosts the speed of existing computer networks without having to invest in new infrastructure such as high-speed cables, fibre optic lines or satellites.

Lycos Inc was awarded a patent on a technology widely used to search and index information, from the World Wide Web. The technology, which uses automated software robots, or "spiders", to wander the Internet and collect information from Web sites, plays a part in many of the most popular Web search services.

The number of visitors on the Web increased tenfold between 9 p.m. to 10 p.m. on July 4, 1997, the might of the Pathfinder landing on Mars. This was the single most popular event on the Web so far because the act of landing on Mars struck a visceral chord in millions of Americans and also the images were so spectacular, millions of non-scientists consulted the Web for information. NASA reported that about 45 million people visited its Web site and mirror sites between July 4 and July 11, 1997.

The critical mass of interest in a proactive approach to gathering news was seen as a turning-point that could affect the way news is reported, consumed and interpreted for many years to come.

Table 9.4. Events Remembered not only for their Historical Significance but the way People Received their News

S. No.	*Event*	*Year*	*People Received Their News*
1.	American Civil War	1861	Through Newspaper. The New York Herald readership grew from 77,000 in 1860 to 107,520 by April 13, 1861.
2.	Japanese Attack on Pearl Harbour	1941	By radio. On December 8, 1941 sixty million people turned into President Franklin D Roosevelt's address to Congress, a day after the bombing of Pearl Harbour.
3.	Kennedy Assassination	1963	By T.V. broadcast. On November 22 from 4 p.m. until 11 p.m. more than 50 per cent of the 51.6 million homes with T.V. sets turned into the news of the assassination.
4.	Attack on Baghdad, Gulf War	1991	By live T.V. coverage. On January 17, CNN's ratings hit a record high for its continuous coverage of the bombing of Baghdad.
5.	Exploration of Mars	1997	Through Internet. NASA reported that about 45 million people visited its Web site and mirror sites between July 4 (the day Pathfinder landed on Mars) and July 11.

Television network news in its heyday fostered a sense of security and shaped national attitudes towards major events by providing a collective viewpoint. By contrast, the Web caters to a creed of individualism that allows people to get the information they want when they want it.

Shifting through mass material at their own time and pace is precisely what so many enjoyed about the Web. Because electronic publishing is relatively cheap and more details are available online than anywhere else.

Marketing via Internet

"Electronic commerce opens up a host of possibilities for some altogether new business," says Daniel C. Lynch and Lestie Lundquist, authors of *Digital Money*, a new book on Internet-based commerce. Now, Internet-based enterprises include the buying and selling of hard goods, services centred around the Internet, and information-related businesses.

In hard goods industries, brokers could purchase any type of goods via a Internet for companies, individuals, or even parties wishing to remain anonymous. In services, many new job descriptions may be created. A person could become a Web architect, designing and consulting on home-page construction, or an Internet salesperson, specially in online resources. Even an interactive actor, performing in computer games, can offer multiple outcomes.

Table 9.5. Books sold by the first Internet bookshop Amazon Com

S. No.	*Year*	*Cost of Sold Book*
1.	1996	$16 million
2.	1997	$148 million

Traditional fields such as advertising, entertainment, and mailing —list brokerages can find new ways to prosper on the Internet. Advertising people can become "sales counsellors", able to provide on demand information about specific products. Entertainment people will be able to use the Internet to download "digital videotapes" of movies and track the demographics of their audience in a more precise manner. The mailing- list business will be the reverse of today, with customers chosing which lists to be put on.

Entirely new possibilities could arise. Information researchers or "Cybrarians" could scan the Internet for data relevant to their clients. The buying and selling of information itself could be done through information brokers, who could package the data in specific formats for different clients. Any of these businesses can be set up in a bargain –basement or top-floor fashion, depending on how much one wants to spend.

The Internet is a tool of improvement that unleashes creativity, fosters greater communication and catalyses world peace. There are pragmatic ways to use the Internet as a weapon in your company's arsenal of marketing tools.

The first is your Web site. The most obvious way to increase the value of your Web site is to use it to recruit advocates or evangelists. More Web sites waste a great opportunity because they provide only information such as prices and specifications. Web sites can do much more. A simple four-step process to win over evangelists with your Web page are:

1. Put yourself in the frame of mind of training sales people.
2. Create a part of your Web site where you provide information such as competitive analysis, sales techniques and case histories.
3. Provide an easy way of people to obtain your hard copy promotional material in large quantities for them to distribute, not just to read.
4. Get out of their way and let a thousand flowers bloom as your believers help you in ways your never imagined.

A second way to use the Internet as a weapon is to start a mailing list for supporters and advocates. A mailing list is a broadcast medium. It builds a sense of community among your fans because they share information about your company or product. There are not many better ways to promulgate news throughout the world than E-mail. For example, Apple maintains a mailing list for fans of Macintosh. The list has 33,000 subscribers, and a rule of thumb is that for every direct subscriber, seven people get the E-mail forwarded to them. This means more than 200,000 people read the propaganda that Apple sends out. This helped counter the gloom-and-doom stuff about Apple that permeated the media in the year 1996. The Internet should do more for you than repackage the status quo. It should take your marketing efforts outside conventional lines.

The Internet is set to shake-up the business world because the electronic commerce it generates melts traditional boundaries. Supermarkets can offer banking services, banks sell life insurance, entertainment and shopping. In 1997, more than 60 million people around the world and nearly 20 million computers were linked over the Internet. This is growing at about 50 per cent a year.

The Internet creates chaos because it opens the door to new ways of doing things. When the dust settles, lasting competitive advantage will lie with the companies that have managed to find a new way of doing business. Telecommunications companies must fundamentally re-invent themselves if they are to exploit the huge commercial potential of the Internet. Imaginative new companies are already using the Internet to sell long-distance calls for the price of a local call, undermining traditional fat profit margins. By 2003, over 25 per cent of international call minutes are forecast to be carried over the Internet, by which time the IP (Internet Provider) telephone market will be worth at least $7 billion. This is the reason why AT&T (Corp), Deutsche Telekom (AG), GTE (Corp) and MCI (Communication Corp) are entering the IP telephone market.

Login Windows 98

Microsoft's Window 98, in its present form, is sure to be a hit with avid Net suffers. This is because the Operating System (OS) contains a host of features not available on its predecessor, Windows 95. Windows 98 users have the option of choosing the look and the feel of the desktop by selecting the Web-style desktop option, in which, the mouse pointers turns into the familiar "hand" whenever it passes over a folder or program icon and opens them with a single click. One can, for example, view live updates on the weather or stock quotes without actually spending too much time on the Net.

Table 9.6. Daily Cost of Consumables in the USA for 3 years usage Compared to Microsoft's Latest Windows 98 Package

S. No.	*Items*	*Daily Cost*
1.	Coffee	$1.35
2.	Cable TV	$0.98
3.	Wall Street Journal	$0.75
4.	Candy Bar	$0.50
5.	Cereal	$0.32
6.	Windows 98	$0.15

Folders now open in the form of a Web page interface with their own back and forward buttons. Microsoft claims that the operating system can be run even on a 486/66 MHz machine (with about 200 MB of hard disk space) also. The final version may include Nets-cape's browser, or shipped (separately) without Explorer. The foundation of Windows 98 is the facile integration of a Web browser with the OS.

Windows 98 supports major Net standard-Java and their own Active-X, in addition to bringing streaming data, including digital audio and video, to the desktop. Users can make their online newspaper into the wallpaper. With Windows 98, Microsoft has practically torpedoed the partition between a browser and an OS. It will support new varieties of hardware devices like DVD drives and digital audio speakers, and standards such a Universal Serial Bus (USB) and IEEE 1394, thus making it easy to add serial devices.

Windows 98 will create an even higher bond between operating system and browser, making it even more difficult for competitors. The world of personal computing, telephony and television are coming together. Advances in the industry that allow computers to move faster and use a variety of external devices, are including digital video disc technology, for which the Windows system is key. Providing Windows in the platform for all of these advances to build on. Windows 98 is far simpler to use than the Windows 95 version, which has 150 million copies in use by 1997. Computer makers are expected to use this system as the 95 version quickly become obsolete. Windows 98 is a very obvious move up from Windows 95. It is a straightforward refinement with a lot of neat new things.

Table 9.7. Cellular Phone Subscribers in Delhi, Mumbai, Calcutta and Chennai during 1997.

S. No.	*Months*	*Total Number of Cellular Phone Subscribers*
1.	Jan. 1997	279,892
2.	Feb. 1997	301,985
3.	March, 1997	327,967
4.	April	348,605

Table 9.8. Radio Paging Subscribers in 1994.

S. No.	*Country*	*Number in Radio Paging Subscribers*
1.	United States of America	25 million
2.	China	12 million
3.	Japan	9 million
4.	South Korea	4 million
5.	Taiwan	2.5 million
6.	Hong Kong	2.0 million
7.	Singapore	1.5 million
8.	Britain	1.0 million
9.	Germany	0.8 million
10.	Netherlands	0.7 million

Table 9.9. Growth in Global Telephones, Cellular Subscribers and Internet.

(in million)

S. No.	*Category*	*1991*	*1996*	*2001 (Forecast)*
1.	Telephone Main Lines	545.0	741.1	1,000
2.	Cellular Subscribers	16.3	135.0	400
3.	Personal Computers	123.0	245.0	450.0
4.	Internet Host Computers	0.7	16.1	110
5.	Estimated Internet Users	4.5	60	300

The USA federal government has accused Microsoft of planning "an illegal conspiracy" with rival Netscape to divide up the Internet browser market. On Netscape refusal to go along with Microsoft's plan in 1995, the latter allegedly used its monopoly in Windows operating system to block Netscape's access to the browser market, by offering its own browser free with the Windows operating system, and extending business favours to software companies in exchange for switching from the Netscape browser to its own. With companies increasingly building applications for the Internet, from e-mail programmes to big Web sites that allow online stock trading, the fight for control of the browser market has become intense. Netscape Sun Microsystems and Oracle are promoting a set of technologies that would enable people to bypass Microsoft technology. The danger to Miscrosoft lies in such alternative technologies catching on. And hence its "predatory" business practices that have, according to US regulators, stifled competition, harmed consumers and undercut innovation.

Conclusion

America Online, the largest US Internet online service, grew to 10 million subscribers by 1997, including one million outside the United States, causing gridlock as users have flooded the circuits. Aol and its business partners manage Internet online services in Britain, Germany, France, Canada and Japan. Users in Austria, Switzerland, Sweden and Australia also access Aol services.

Non-business computer usage in the United States averages from five to nine hours per week, and the number of people who telecommute for some part of each week is estimated at 20 to 40 million.

The explosive growth of the Internet poses a life or death challenge to telephone companies. The Internet, the worldwide network of personal computers connected by telephone lines, threatens a call of phone companies which fail to meet the demands of the new technology.

THE INSTITUTION OF ELECTRICAL ENGINEERS, LONDON HONOURS THE "FATHER OF THE WORLD WIDE WEB"

Tim Berners-Lee, the originator of the World Wide Web, was made an honourary Fellow of the IEE, London on 26th March, 1998.

Also Berners-Lee was presented with the 1996 Mountbatten Medal and the 1997 Foundation of Science and Technology's Lord Lloyd of Kilgerran Prize. University of Essex awarded an honourary doctorate degree to him.

Berners -Lee is an Oxford Physics graduate. Working as a software consultant at CERN in the late 1980s, he developed the hypertext-based database search tools that evolved into today's Web browsers, precipitating the worldwide explosion in Internet activity. Berners-Lee is currently based at MIT's Laboratory of Computer Science, as Director of the World Wide Web Consortium (WWWC).

The Shortest Internet Year

Ever since the birth of the browser in 1994 and the explosion of Web crawling things have changed very fast in a wired world. While it took 38 years for radio to garner 50 million users in the USA and 13 years for TV to get 50 million viewers, the Internet reached that number of users in just four years.

An Internet Glossary

Address: Code by which the Internet identifies you. The format is username @ hostname, where username is your username, login name, or account number, hostname is the name of the computer or Internet provider you use. The host name may be a few words strung together with periods.

America Online: A public Internet provider. If you have an account on America Online, username @ aol. com is your internet address, where "Username" is your America Online account name.

Anonymous FTP: A way to use the FTP program to log on to another computer to copy files when you do not have an account on the other computer. When you log on, enter anonymous as the username and your address as the password. This gives you access to public—available files.

Advanced Network Services (ANS): ANS runs one of the largest, high-speed networks on the Internet. Run by Merit, MCI and IBM.

Archie: A system that helps you locate files located anywhere on the Internet. After Archie locates the file, you can use FTP to get it. Archie is both a program and a system of server computers that contain indexes of files.

Authentication: Verifying the identity of a person or computer process.

Backbone: A high-speed line or series of connections that forms a major pathway within a network. The term is relative as a backbone in a small network will likely be much smaller than many non-backbone lines in a large network.

Bandwidth: How much "stuff" you can send through a connection. Usually measured in bits per second. A full page of English text is about 16,000 bits. A fast modem can move about 15,000 bits in one second. Full-motion full-screen video would require roughly 10 million bits per second, depending on compression.

Bulletin Board System (BBS): A computerised meeting and announcement system that allows people to carry on discussions, upload and download files, and make announcements without being connected to the computer at the same time. There are several thousands of BBSs around the world. Most BBSs are very small and run on a single IBM clone PC with one or two phone lines.

Browser: A client program (software) that is used to search through information provided by a specific type of server. Netscape and Mosaic are examples of browsers. A browser provides an easy to use interface for accessing the information on the WWW.

Chatting: Talking in real-time to other network users from any and all parts of the world.

Client: A software program that is used to contact and obtain data from a server software program on another computer, often across a great distance. Each client program is designed to work with one or more types of server programs.

Com: When these letters appear at the end of an address, they indicate that the host computer is run by a company rather than a University or Government Agency. It also means that host computer is most likely located in the USA.

Compuserve: An online information provider (sometimes abbreviated as CIS) that gives some Internet access. If your Compuserve account number is 7123,456 your Internet address will be 7123.456@ Compuserve. Com. Note that the comma in the Compu Serve address becomes a period in the Internet address.

Cyberspace: A virtual universe of computers, programs and data.

Delphi: An online information provider that includes access to Internet services. If you have an account on Delphi; your Internet address in username @ delphi: Com. Where username is your Delphi account name.

Domain Name: The unique name that identifies an Internet site. A given machine may have more than one domain name but a given domain name points to only one machine. It is also possible for a domain name to exist but not be connected to an actual machine. This is often done so that a group or business can have an Internet e-mail address without having to establish a real Internet site. In these cases, an Internet service provider's machine must handle the mail on behalf of the listed domain name.

Edu: When these letters appear in the last part of an address, e.g., info @ mit. edu, they indicate that the host computer is run by an educational institution. It also means that the host computer is most likely located in the U.S.A.

E-mail: Electronic mail messages, usually text, sent from one person to another via computer. E-mail can also be sent automatically to a large number of addresses by use of a mailing list.

Frequently Asked Questions (FAQ): The best way to find one on a subject you are interested in is to use one of the search engines available on the Web.

File Transfer Protocol (FTP): A method of transferring one or more files from one computer to another on a network or phone line.

Finger: A program that displays information about someone on the net. On most UNIX systems, this command tells you who is logged on right now. On most Internet hosts, it tells you the name, and possibly some other information based on the person's Internet address and the last time they logged on.

Firewall: A filter for messages. A system that has a firewall lets only certain kinds of messages in and out from the rest of the Internet. If an organisation wants to exchange mail with the Internet, but does not want other Internet members "telnetting in" and reading those files, its connection to the Internet can be protected using a firewall.

Gateway: A computer that connects one network with another when the two networks use different protocols. The UUNET computer connects the UUCP network with the Internet, providing a way for mail messages to move between the two networks.

G-Enie: An online service run by General Electric. If you have an account on G-Enie and your mail name is ABC, your Internet address is ABC @ genie, gies. com.

Graphic Interchange Format (GIF): The file format commonly used to distribute graphics files on the Internet.

Gopher: A system that lets you find information by using menus. To use Gopher, you usually Telnet to a Gopher server and begin browsing the menus.

Home Page :- The page that is first seen when a requested web site comes up on your computer monitor. The term "home page" is also used for a single document within a web site that represents an individual user.

Host: A computer on the Internet that you may be able to log on. You can use FTP to get files from a host computer, and use other programs (such as Telnet) to make use of the host computer.

Hypertext: A system of writing and displaying text that enables the text to be linked in multiple ways, available at several levels of detail. Hypertext documents can also contain links to related documents such as those referred to in footnotes. Hypermedia can also contain pictures, sounds and video.

Hypertext Mark-up Language (HTML): This is used for writing pages for the World Wide Web. HTML allows text to include codes that define fonts, layout, embedded graphics and hypertext links.

Hypertext Transfer Protocol (HTTP): The method by which World Wide Web pages are transferred over the network.

Internet: The vast collection of inter-connected networks that all use the TCP/IP protocols and that involved from the ARPANET of the late 1960s and early 1970s. The Internet connect over 60,000 independent networks into a vast global Internet.

Internet Protocol (IP): The transport layer protocol used as a basis of the Internet. IP enables information to be routed from one network to another in packets and then reassembled when they reach their destination.

IP Number: A four-part number separated by dots (e.g. 165.113 254.2) which uniquely identifies a machine on the Internet. Every machine that is on the Internet has a unique IP number, if a machine does not have an IP number, it is not really on the Internet. Most machines also have one or more Domain Names that are easier for people to remember.

Internet Relay Chat (IRC): A system that enables Internet users to talk with each other in realtime over the Internet rather than in person.

Integrated Services Digital Network (ISDN): Basically, a way to move more data over existing regular phone lines. ISDN can provide speeds of 64,000 bits per second over a regular phone line at almost the same cost as a normal phone call in the USA.

Jughead: A program that helps you find specified information in Gopher directories, similar to Veronica, but more focused.

Local Area Network (LAN): A group of connected computers, usually located in close proximity (such as the same building or floor of the building) as data can be passed between them.

Leased Line: Refers to a phone line that is rented for exclusive 24-hour, 7 days a week access between your location to another location. The highest speed data connections require a leased line.

Listserv: A family of programs that automatically manage mailing lists by distributing messages posted to the list, adding and deleting members automatically.

Login: It can be used as a noun or a verb. If it is used as a noun, it means the account name used to gain access to a computer system. Unlike a password, the login name is not a secret. When it is used as a verb, it means the act of entering into a computer system, e.g. "Login to the WELL and then go to the CBN conference".

Message: A piece of e-mail or a posting to a news group.

Mirror: An FTP server that provides copies of the same files as another server. Some FTP servers are so popular that other servers have been set up to mirror them and appeared the FTP load to more than one site.

Modem: Modulator, Demodulator—a device that you connect to your computer and to a phone line to allow the computer to talk to other computers through the phone system. Modems convert the computer's digital signals into analog signals that can be transmitted over standard voice telephone lines. Modem speeds are measured into bits per second (bps) or sometimes in kilo bits per second (kbps).

Mosaic: A Windows-based, Windows Sockets-Compliant program that lets you access information on the World Wide Web.

Name resolution: The process of a mapping a name into its corresponding address.

Net news: Another name for Usenet, often refers to Usenet News when being received via the Internet or via NNTP.

Netscape Navigator: A Windows-based, Windows, Sockets-Compliant program that lets you access information on the World Wide Web. This is an improvement on Mosaic.

Network: Anytime you connect two or more computers together so that they can share resources you have a computer network.

Connect two or more networks together and you have an Internet.

Network News Transfer Protocol (NNTP): A protocol defined for distribution, enquiry, retrieval and posting of news articles.

News-Group: A distributed bulletin board system about a particular topic. Usenet news (also known, as net news) is a system that distributes thousands of news-groups to all parts of the Internet.

Netiquette: Network etiquette. Prescribed social behaviour and manners on computer networks.

Node: A computer on the Internet, also called a host. Computers that provide a service, such as FTP sites or places that run Gopher are also called servers.

Online Service: America online, Compuserve and Prodigy provide Internet access, but are more or less restrictive in the interfaces they provide. In addition they host private services for the use of their members only. Access rates are modest or reasonable for low-volume users, but prohibitive for high-volume users. AOL is now available in from India.

Packet: A chunk of information sent over a network. Each packet contains the destination address, the sender's address, error-control information and data.

Page: A document, or collection of information, available by way of the World Wide Web. To make information available over the WWW, it is organised into pages. A page may contain text, graphics, files, video and/or sound files.

Ping: A network management tool that checks to see whether you can communicate with another computer on the Internet. It sends a short message to which the other computer automatically responds to the Ping, you usually cannot establish communications.

Point of Presence (POP): A physical site in a geography where a network access provider, such as UU Net, has equipment that users connect to. The local phone company's central office in a particular area is also sometimes referred to as their POP in that area, e.g., AT &T's POP for the Seattle area is in downtown Seattle.

Post Office Protocol (POP): A system by which a mail server on the Internet lets you grab your mail and download it to your PC or Mac. Most people refer to this protocol with its version number, i.e. POP2, POP3, etc. to avoid confusing it with Point of Presence.

Point to Point Protocol (PPP): A scheme for connecting two computers over a phone line or a network link that acts like a phone line. Similar to SLIP.

Prodigy: An online system run by IBM and Sears. If you have a prodigy account, username @ prodigy, com is your Internet address, where username is your Prodigy user name.

Router: A special purpose computer or software package that handles the connection between two or more networks. Routers look at the destination addresses of the packets passing through them and decide which route to send them.

Secure Transaction Technology (STT). The STT specification is a software technology designed to provide a secure method for handling credit card transactions across electronic networks.

Server: A computer that provides a service to other computers on a network, e.g. an Archie server lets people on the Internet use Archie.

Simple Mail Transfer Protocol (SMTP): A protocol used to transfer e-mail between computers.

Simple Network Management Protocol (SNMP): The Internet standard protocol developed to manage nodes on an IP network.

Serial Line Interface Protocol (SLIP): A software scheme for connecting a computer to the Internet.

Socket: When your computer is on the Internet via a SLIP connection, a socket is a conversation which your computer is having with another computer elsewhere on the net. You may have one socket for an FTP session, another socket for a Telnet session and another socket taking care of getting your mail.

Surf: To surf the net means you fire up you browser and cruise over to splash around in the ocean of WWW info.

Transfer Control Protocol/Internet Protocol (PCP/IP): The system networks use to communicate with each other on the Internet.

Telnet: The command and program used to login from one Internet site to another. The Telnet command/program gets you to the "login" prompt of another host.

Terminal: A device that allows you to send commands to a computer somewhere else. At a minimum, this usually means a keyboard and a display screen and some simple circuitry. Usually, you will use terminal software in a personal computer, the software pretends to be a physical terminal and allows you to type commands to a computer somewhere else.

UNIX: A computer operating system (the basic software running on a computer, underneath things like word processors and spreadsheets) UNIX is designed to be used by many people at the same time (it is "multi user") and has TCP/IP built-in. It is the most common operating system for servers on the Internet.

Uniform Resource Locator (URL): The standard way to give the address of any resource on the Internet that is part of the WWW. A URL looks like this: http://www.matisse,net/seminars, html. The most common way to use a URL is to enter into a Web browser program, such as Microsoft Internet Explorer or Netscape Navigator.

Usenet: A system of thousands of distributed bulletin boards called news groups. You read the messages by using a program called a news reader.

Very Easy Rodent Oriented Net-Wide Index to Computerised Archives (Veronica): A programe that uses word searches to locate articles in Gopherspace. Developed at the University of Nevada, Veronica is a constantly updated database of names of almost every menu item on thousands of gopher servers.

Viewer: A program used by Gopher, WAIS or WWW client programs to show files with contents other than text. You would use a viewer to display graphics files, play sound files or display video files.

Wide Area Network (WAN): Any Internet or network that covers an area larger than single building or campus.

Website: A collection of related hypertext documents administered by a single organisation. A website has Home Page which serves as the root document for the entire collection of documents.

Windows Sockets: Windows Sockets is a standard way for Windows-based programs to work with TCP/IP. You can use Windows Sockets if you use SLIP to connect to the Internet.

World Wide Web (WWW): A hypermedia-based system for accessing information on the Internet.

Yahoo!: A popular website that is a directory type listing of tens of thousands of Internet sites. It also provides a search facility.

10

Personal Computers

What mankind can dream of today, technology can achieve tomorrow. The birth of the personal computer (PC) is not clearly documented. Many of the ideas used in the PC originated at Xerox's Palo Alto Research Centre. However, what propelled the device from the laboratory to the market was a cover story in the January 1975 issue of "Popular Electronics". It offered a minicomputer kit called Altair for "anyone with $400 and a soldering iron who wanted to build his or her own computer to rival commercial models". Therefore, the birth of a PC can be considered in the month of January 1975.

Compared to today's PC prima donnas, the Altair was primitive. Its Intel 8080 chip was far too ponderous to support the windows, the mouse and the sophisticated software developed at Xerox. It was the Altair which inspired Steve Jobs and Steve Woznaik to build the Apple Computer in a garage. Bill Gates and Paul Allen were similarly enthused to write software for the Altair with a newly formed company called Microsoft.

With microprocessors doubling in speed every 18 months today's Intel P6 chip contains 5.5 million transistors as compared to the paltry 2300 transistors on Intel 4004, the world's first microprocessor. According to Larry Ellison, Chairman of Oracle, the personal computer is a ridiculous device and PCs are set to decline in much the same way as mainframe computers ceased to be the centre of the computing business 10 years ago. He predicts that the PCs would be succeeded by cheap and simple terminals costing $500 which would replace televisions and telephones in the home and office. But Bill Gates, Chairman microsoft, disagrees with Ellison's vision. Networks such as the Internet will, no doubt, play a leading role in the future.

What are some of the promising buds on the PC's family tree today? Many of them call for a transformation, with the PC "threatening to disappear into the fabric of everyday life" only to reappear into an "intelligent" wonderland.

The first of these "buds" is Wearware being developed at MIT's Medical Laboratory. This involves wearable computers like tiny computers embedded in tie, wristwatch, shoes, etc., all communicating via radio and a weak body current with computers placed into the smart environment. The Media Lab scientists have already made a wearable device that enables two people to exchange business card information automatically even as they shake hands. That is still far away from having a drawing room wall that massages your ego with soft whispering after a hard day at the "office" which may be on your wrist. There is pseudo-wetware, neural network circuits that mimic the brains-network and "learn" as they go along. The Media Lab experts have also made PCs that can "read" what your hands are doing. This involves building "smart" tables with electrodes and sensors that communicate with the PC. So when you turn your hands on the table as if to turn a page, a document on the screen of the wired-up PC also flips accordingly. Scientists foresee a PC that has "complete knowledge of the physical state of a person, so that you can ask how you want gesture to control things".

Big Step Towards Compatible PC

Computer giants IBM and Apple joined high-tech company Motorola in November, 1994. They have agreed on a common standard for personal computers, ending a longstanding problem of incompatibility. The agreement covers personal computers using a power PC micro-processor developed by the three companies. The first of the new PCs are scheduled to come on the market by the end of 1996.

Table 10.1. Top Selling PCs in 1992

S. No.	*Company*	*PCs sold*	*Market Share (in per cent)*
1.	Apple	1,550,000	13.2
2.	IBM	1,374,600	11.7
3.	Compaq	675,820	5.7
4.	Packard Bell	624,000	5.3
5.	Dell	440,000	3.7
6.	Gateway 2000	428,180	3.6
7.	Tandy	329,870	2.8
8.	AST Research	320,000	2.7
9.	Toshiba	242,950	2.1
10.	.Zenith Data Systems	165.000	1.4
11.	All others		47.8

Table 10.2. Top Ten Selling PCs in 1993

S. No.	*Company*	*Market Share (in per cent)*
1.	IBM	11.8
2.	Apple	10.0
3.	Compaq	9.2
4.	NEC	5.4
5.	Dell	3.7
6.	Toshiba	2.8
7.	AST Research	2.3
8.	Gateway 2000	2.2
9.	Hewlett Packard	2.0
10.	Packard Bell	1.7

Note: Market share percentage figures reflect annual sales.

Table 10.3. Top Selling PCs in China in 1992

S. No.	*Company*	*Sale in China (in million dollar)*	*Percentage*
1.	AST Research, USA	118	26.9
2.	Compaq, USA	81	18.5

S. No.	Company	Sale in China (in million dollar)	Percentage
3.	Great Wall Group China	49	18.0
4.	Legend Computer Group, China	28.7	11.2
5.	Acer, Taiwan	26	6.5
6.	IBM, USA	23	5.9
7.	Lang Chao Group, China	19	5.2
8.	Chang Jiang Group, China	15.4	4.3
9.	Others (less than 3 per cent each)	79	3.5

Note: China's strong economy and the prospect of reduced trade barriers with the USA have prompted USA companies to stake a claim in the PC market in the world's most populous nation. So far, the market is tiny compared with the 12 million PCs sold in the USA in 1991. PC sales in China in 1992 totalled $439.1 million, with 190,000 unit sold. Black market may account for 30 per cent additional sales.

Experts, however, described that the triumvirate would not succeed in dethroning the Microsoft-Intel tandem in the computer market. Microsoft windows is by far the world's most popular personal computer software system, present in more than 80 per cent of current models as compared to 10 per cent for Mac OS.

The three companies said in a statement, "We are creating a new industry standard. The objective is to achieve 100 per cent compatibility with current power-based hardware and software application products, while creating a new base standard that offers advanced function future capability".

Power PC will enable the companies to offer personal computers which could use Apple's Mac OS operating software, IBM's OS/2 and AIX and Microsoft's Windows. The three companies said that "each company intends to take technical and financial responsibility" for bringing the new system onto the market in its own computers. However, they also said that the agreement covers only personal computers capable of working with various types of operating software, and not the software itself. Industry analysts said that if the two computer giants wanted to break Microsoft's hold on the software market, and Intel's dominance on the personal computer sector, they would have to resolve this problem.

The power PC will provide end users to have been locked into a limited number of hardware and software alternatives for years, a higher degree of choice.

In fact personal computer no longer just connect systems but people too. And to exploit this potential has become the priority of the world's leading computer network solution providers. Networks connect people to other people and the information they need, enabling them to act on it anytime, any place. Novell's initiatives outlined by its Chief, Mr. Robert J. Frankenbert, include Advanced Client Services, a graphical set of user and application program interfaces to network services, and Netware Connect Service, providing access to public networks and electronic commerce. Pervasive computing will change the way we govern, work, play and educate.

Table 10.4. The Size of Asia's PC Markets, 1994

S. No.	*Countries*	*Sales in million $*
1.	Philippines	0.2
2.	Malaysia	0.3
3.	Singapore	0.3
4.	India	0.3
5.	Indonesia	0.3
6.	Thailand	0.3
7.	New Zealand	0.3
8.	Hong Kong	0.4
9.	Taiwan	0.5
10.	China	0.6
11.	Australia	1.2
12.	South Korea	1.4
13.	Japan	3.3

Note: PC sales are booming in Asia (including Australia and New Zealand) and the market is expected to grow by 20 to 30 per cent annually.

Table 10.5. Percentage of Small and Mid-size Companies using Computer in 1995

S. No.	*Users of Computer*	*Percentage*
1.	All office workers on PC	59
2.	System upgrades planned	30
3.	PCs linked by network	24
4.	On-line/Internet access	22
5.	No computers at all	19

Note: About one in five small and mid-size companies do not use computers.

Table 10.6. PCs Penetration into Industrialised Countries (Survey in 1995)

S.No.	*Countries*	*PCs in Home (in per cent)*	*Plus Modems (in per cent)*
1.	Austria	15.0	14.6
2.	Benelux	31.5	17.2
3.	Denmark	31.6	14.9
4.	France	14.9	9.1
5.	Germany	28.6	10.9
6.	Japan	7.4	42.9
7.	United Kingdom	25.0	14.2
8.	United States	37.0	46.3

Novell will deliver pervasive computing to the customers with products that are powerful, easy to use and manage, and accessible everywhere, from the office to the home and on the road. A new breed of network applications will give everyone the ability to use the network without knowing how it works. Novell will build on the large installed base Net Ware and UNIX technology, enabling revolutionary personnel and organisations productivity through the evolution of users' systems.

NEST, Novell's embedded networks initiative, is central to its objective to make the network pervasive by inexpensively extending the network to all intelligent devices like : office equipment, computer peripherals, intelligent telephones, TV set-top devices and personal digital assistants.

Sony Electronics officials say they have become a dominant "rulemaker" in the PC business. The initial two home PC models brought in the market by them include a variety of multimedia features such as high quality audio and video, and an easy to use software interface.

PCs do the Most Exciting Things

Today computers are taking over many parts of our lives. From playing cupid-matchmaking using Cyber-astrology to designing clothes, from nose jobs to mushroom farming, from credit card payments to special effects in cinema, computers are making inroads into areas which once specifically required human intelligence and sensitivity. What's made this transition possible is the ability of the easy to use PCs which are installed on many a desk to turn the wildest of ideas into virtual reality. Instead of merely speeding up technical functions like accounting, or data processing, the computer is now being used for creative applications. Moreover, the revolution is taking place not just in the technologically advanced west, but also right here in India.

A Bombay–based book distributor plans to introduce books that can be read on the computer screen in the Indian market which are called CD-ROM books. These books come to life when a CD-ROM is inserted into a computer. A CD-ROM book has an advantage as it is more interactive and has long life. Unlike audio books (presentation of a book on a set of cassettes), which are priced upwards of Rs. 200, a CD-ROM book will set one back by at least Rs. 500. The target consumer will understandably be up-market computer buff. These books will be sold through IBD's existing country-wide network of retail out-lets but if the trend catches on, then some exclusive out-lets might be selected as in the USA market. A CD-ROM can be best described as "a round plastic and metal wafer", and is different from any other medium like TV, movies, video, slide, audio, books or a personal computer, as it is a combination of all these. Based on the multimedia technology, this is one of the best options available in the "electronic publishing" industry. For example, it has 1000 times more storage capacity than an ordinary floppy. Companies like Philips manufacture CD-ROM books for USA and UK markets. Like IBD which is importing from USA, Delhi-based Rupa & Company, is planning to enter this segment soon.

Software maker, Gainax Co. Ltd., came out with the first version of Japanese software called Princess maker in 1991. Princess Make-2 followed in 1993 and a third one is now in the works. In Japan, provocative images of young girls are a staple of male entertainment, and Princess maker is no exception. The girl character is depicted in sexy, wide-eyed coming-book style, and can be programmed to dress in lingeric or sun-bathe naked. Still by the standards of Japanese late-night TV or widely read adult comics, Princess maker is tame. The game, however fanciful, could tie into a trend towards men getting more involved in family life as job insecurity frays traditional loyalty to companies. Magazines give men parenting advice, and a TV show features a single father who struggles to balance the demands of job and parenthood. Princess maker-2 takes place in a medieval fantasy world, where the player is presented with an adopted daughter, aged 10. He names her, picks her birthday, even chooses her blood type which, some in Japan believe, determines character traits.

The player picks the girl's classes and jobs, and the two can have short conversations about how she's doing or how she feels about her studies. The girl, who blossoms physically as the years pass, is constantly monitored in about two dozen categories, including sexiness, strength and smarts, which help determine the game's outcome.

Even with the player making all the decisions, the girl character sometimes rebels. She can make unsuitable friends, run away from home, even get arrested. If she does not get a big enough allowance, she snaps at the player "Cheap". But in the end, the father's programing has the last word. A successful outcome means a future as a queen, a warrior, or a government official. If the player does not score well, "the daughter" might face a future as a bar hostess who giggles as she holds up a slinky dress. Some see the game as a sign that Japanese men would rather deal with feminine fantasy-figures than real-life women. According to Etsuko Yamashita, Professor of Woman's Studies at Japan Women's University in Tokyo, the popularity of Princess maker and similar spin offs is all the more disappointing because most players are college age-group or high school students. "You might think that the younger generation has a better sense of gender equality", she said. "But this game proves it's not necessarily true".

U.S. President Bill Clinton, calling for computers in every classroom by the year 2000, on 16th Feb., 1996, promoted creating of a \$2 billion federal matching fund to foster public-private efforts to bring technology to schools. He said, "When we complete the work of bringing the information super highway to all education and to all our people, it will empower everybody and it will enable us to use these great new forces of the modern world". He visited the Columbus School because it offers a dramatic example of the potential he believes computer technology offers in shaping the nation's future. The Bell Atlantic Corp became involved with the school in a multi–million dollar project in which curriculum was based around computers. Classes now consist of small clusters of students working at computers, while the teachers are free to walk around assisting each group. He signed the Telecommunications Act in Feb. 1996, which includes provisions aimed at establishing computer capabilities at all schools in the United States by requiring carriers to provide significantly discounted rates to schools and libraries.

Computer–literate consumers in the USA are switching from mail order to PCs to do their shopping from home. A growing number of shopping sites is appearing on the Internet, the worldwide network of computers linked by Telephone lines.

Computer shopping is fast becoming a threat to conventional shopping malls. New "virtual" malls, such as Shop INC of San Mateo, California, and the London-based Barclay Square, are creating shopping facilities including services such as travel, banking, book shops, wine and flowers.

Microsoft offers a range of services with its windows 95 computer operating system including on-line newspapers and financial services. More prosaic services are offered by companies such as Peapod, of Evanston, Illinois, which takes orders for groceries on-line and delivers them.

PC owners will be able to browse through merchandise on offer throughout the world and find unheard of bargains.

Retailers will be able to offer huge amounts of goods, 24 hours a day, seven days a week, without the expenses of property or staff. Stocks will be zero as goods are ordered directly from the manufacturer. For the first time, retailers will have a precise record of their customers and what they bought. This will allow files to build up on customers to enable stores to target sales of new products precisely.

Customers in places such as Europe, where prices are high, will be able to fight back. Computer shopping will mean they can by-pass local suppliers and buy from the USA, Taiwan, Argentina, or anywhere.

"International electronic retailing is now in the midest of enormous expansion", said Bud Margolis, international electronic retail industry consultant. He says, "We have the ability to offer a much higher level of service round the clock through the Internet. The consumer wants convenience, choice, information and value. It saves them time and should save them money. By 2010, up to 55 per cent of shopping by Americans will be conducted on line".

Sales generated by the WWW (on the Internet) are expected to grow from $436 million in 1995 to nearly $46 billion by 1998.

Important components would be the real estate sales, computers, software, travel, audio and financial services.

In 1994 the first survey estimated that 31 per cent of all American households had a computer and 26 per cent of all adults used a home computer at sometime. In 1995 it has increased to 36 per cent of all households having a computer and 32 per cent of adults having used one. Besides more than one in four have had on-line sessions lasting 3 hours or more and one in four have an on-line buddy they have never met.

PCs of the Future

What will the future of multimedia PCs look like? No one knows for sure, but an early look at Panasonic's new Galileo Media Explorer provides some clues. The Galileo Media Explorer is what Panasonic calls a "modular multimedia display system". Essentially, it is a cabinet housing a large (17"), high resolution colour monitor with slender speakers built into the side panels of the display. Above and below the screen are slots that hold many types of audio, video and storage devices. The top slot, called Quick Bus, holds one of any number of cartridges, including ones that add a TV tuner, speaker phone, video camera, or cordless headphone interface. The bottom slot, dubbed Quick Bay, holds a variety of removable drives, including CD-ROM, PC Card, and magneto-optical drives. There are also connectors for external devices such as a mouse, keyboard, game controller, camcorder, VCR, and bass booster. The only thing not contained in Galileo is the computer itself. It is designed to work with any type of Windows PC. It is expected to cost about $1000 for the basic unit, including the monitor, speakers, and perhaps a CD-ROM drive. Most Quick Bus and Quick Bay options will cost extra, however.

Database software giant Oracle Corp. has designed a $500 PC that can provide instant connectivity with multimedia capabilities through large computer networks. The computer will use a RISC (reduced instruction set computing) processor and will have a four megabyte DRAM (dynamic random access memory), multimedia audio/video facilities, E-mail, keyboard, colour monitor and local and wide area network capabilities. It will not have any hard disk or CD-ROM facility. The computer industry has been searching for such a computer, especially in the home and small business segments. For instance, with the new PC connected to a wide computer network through a telephone line, one can easily browse through the voluminous data flowing through the Internet. The computing capabilities will be provided by medium-sized computers called servers which facilitate smooth flow of information between inter–connected PCs. Oracle's new software will reengineer the information distribution channel enabling one to one narrow-cast over the Internet as well as using local and wide area networks.

Table 10.7. Ownership of PCs is the Highest in the High Income Group (Survey in 1995)

S. No.	*Annual income*	*Percentage ownership*
1.	More than $50,000	55
2.	$40,000 - 49,999	38
3.	$25,000 - 39,999	28
4.	$15,000 - 24,999	12
5.	Less than $15,000	8

Table 10.8. Nearly 80 per cent of Small-Business Owners whose Annual Revenue is under $5 Million are using their Computers for :

S. No.	*Purpose*	*Percentage of Small Business Owners*
1.	Bookkeeping	87
2.	Analysing Finances	70
3.	Tracking/analysing sales	57
4.	Creating ads, brochures	53
5.	Tracking inventory	40
6.	E-mailing customers/vendors	31

Table 10.9. Percentage Household Subscribers of Computer On Line Service in USA (Regionwise)

S. No.	*Region of USA*	*Percentage subscriber*	*Total Number*
1.	West	15.2	
2.	North-East	14.2	98 million
3.	South	12.5	
4.	Mid-West	9.5	

In a step towards blending the personal computer and the Internet with broadcast television, Intel Corp. and several of the United States personal computer makers and television broadcasters announced in October, 1996 a new technology that would allow broadcasters to deliver computer data along with their television programs.

Intercast would allow broadcasters to transmit data in the portion of the television signal known as the vertical blanking interval at speeds almost four times as fast as the fastest available modems now used to send personal computer data to the home.

For several years, some PCs have come with peripheral attachments which enabled them to display pictures. Intercast, however, is promising an industry-wide standard that adds an element. Instead of simply reproducing television images, the new system would allow broadcasters and advertisers to provide text, still images and graphics. For instance, while broadcasting a murder mystery, a network could send clues such as photographs of the murder weapon or the victim's telephone logs. Advertisers might send a software driving simulator to accompany a car commercial, or an interactive catalogue to accompany clothes or consumer electronics ads. The data would be transmitted in the blank lines now visible to viewers only when their sets are on the fritz. This bank of 10 or so lines is isolated at one end of the television image, and out of the frame of a television set that is operating normally. Each of these lines can be used to transmit data at a speed of 9600 bits a second. Although the system is based on a one-way broadcast model, and the television signals would be pulled in by a standard television tuner, the data would be delivered in the form of worldwide web pages, permitting interactivity through conventional Internet access.

Twelve concerns are endorsing the standard Packard Bell and Gateway 2000, which plan on including the hardware to receive Internet signals in computers they will sell in 1996 the broadcasters NBC, CNN, QVC and WG-BH, the Boston PBS station; the cable operators Viacom and Corncast; the online service provider America on-line and the software developers Asymetrix; En Technology and Netscape Communications. This is an important first step to get television broadcasters thinking about the richness of the Internet. Right now, computer usage is an individual experience, but we do not know where the computer will be in five years. Mr. Mc Gready vice-president and general manager of Intel's Internet Technology Lab, said Intel would become a standard part of all PCs by 1998.

The world's first computer weighed over 30 tonnes and occupied an entire room. Today, a mere 50 years after the historical unveiling of that Electronic Numerical Integrator and Computer (ENIAC) in Philadelphia in February 1946, engineers have managed to contain the complex circuitry of that massive machine into a single chip smaller than a finger nail.

Mindboggling as it sounds, however, this feat of miniaturisation is not considered even remotely remarkable in today's context. Indeed, Microsoft's recent prelaunch announcement of Regasus, a software program meant for handheld computers, is seen by many as a heralder of the palmtop revolution. The program will run the basic functions of the personal digital assistants like Apple Computer Incorporated's Newton or the US Robotics Incorporated's Palm Pilot. It will allow a chocolate-bar-sized computer to provide some basic database and communication functions, including fax and Internet connectivity.

Not satisfied with this unprecedented degree of pocket power, researchers at IBM are working at a frantic pace to develop a tiny disk with a diameter of just one inch which will be able to store 1.5 billion characters, a storehouse of memory which is sufficient for an entire reference library. If this dream is realised, it is entirely possible that by the year 2001, those who own palmtop will be walking around with the world, quite literally, in their pockets.

An electronic newspaper that you can roll up and carry under your arm, might be possible by flat screen technology. It is possible in the future that a computer pulls a small computer out of his pocket and unrolls a screen from the top of it, then he presses a button and a newspaper article appears. The leading flat–screen technology is the Liquid Crystal Display (LCD) system which is now used in camcorders and network PCs. LCDs are small, thin, light and use little power. The best LCD screens are controlled by hundreds of thousands of transistors which give very good picture quality. But these active LCDs are difficult and expensive to produce, especially, when the screen is larger than six inches across.

Environmentalism in computers has developed more rapidly and broadly in Europe, where the focus is on recyclable packaging and parts and cleaner manufacturing. But in USA, the Environmental Protection Agency (EPA) has spurred computer makers to focus on the energy efficiency. Computers represent 5 per cent of the nation's commercial energy consumption in 1993 and could double that by the end of the decade EPA estimates. "Green" computers are the latest in PCs. They are smaller more energetic and better for the environment in other ways. These PCs use 3.3 Volt instead of 5 Volt circuit boards and carry power management chips that put idle parts of a computer to sleep. Some of these PCs have a flat-panel screen that uses less energy and emits less radiation than the TV like cathode ray tube. EPA said it would give PCs that use just 30 watts of energy per hour when idle. Apple Computer Inc hit first with the Macintosh colour classic it introduced in February 1993 capable of powering down to 25 watts per hour when idle. IBM corp has unveiled a PC model called "Energy Saver" in March 1993 that goes to 19 watts per hour, when idle and uses less energy at full power than a 60 watt light bulb, about a fourth the amount of a typical PC. The $3000 PC has a flat panel display, recyclable plastic casing and sleep-mode chips. It does not have a fan. Its power supply uses an adapter similar to a portable PC and it is enough to fit in a desk drawer. If two-thirds of the existing PC base meet the energy star criteria by the year 2000, EPA estimates the forecasted annual electric consumption of 70 billion kilowatt hour for computers will be cut by 26 billion kilowatt hour.

With the appearance of Pentium processors, PCs have become very fast capable of executing complex commands in seconds and managing large quantities of data efficiently. Yet this is not fast enough for some of the advanced publishing, graphics and animation software available today. While microprocessor manufacturers are addressing the problem by devising faster microprocessors, a few PC makers like Daystar have adopted a different approach, i.e. combining more than one microprocessors, in a single PC. Daystar's Genesis, which sells in the USA at $10,000 has four Power-PC 604 microprocessors installed to work in, tandem. The draw, paint and special effects commands of animation software that take minutes to execute on the Pentium PC take only seconds on the Genesis. Intel, realising the benefit of this technique, is now supplying special circuit boards to PC makers like Compaq, Hewlett Packard and Dell that allow them to assemble PCs with four Pentium Pro Microprocessors inside.

Toddlers can now use your PC without damaging it or crashing into your valuable data. Compaq and toy giant Frisher Price have joined hands to create a cruiser set that allows toddlers to surf through the concepts of computing and multimedia the fun way. The colourful steering wheel, horn, phone set and joystick on the cruiser allow the kids to "drive" through their game software, while enjoying the feel of piloting the whole trip. As the cruiser is an attachment, the data and software on your PC is unaffected.

Novel PC Software

August 24, 1995 must have been, one of the most eagerly awaited days in the infotech world. The attention of the entire industry was focused on the release of Microsoft corporations Windows 95. Across the world there are 70 million windows users and of this 20 per cent are expected to purchase Windows 95 while millions of the users will get it preloaded with their new PCs.

The release of this major upgrade to the windows OS is expected to give a significant boost to hardware and software sales. Over the years, Microsoft has acquired a cast-iron hegemony over the market for PC operating systems. The developed software controls the computer hardware and on which applications like word-processors, spreadsheets, games etc. run. Microsoft's hold is so strong that today, virtually all PCs that are shipped come pre-loaded with Windows. The Graphical User Interface (GUI) has the ability to interact with the computer using easy to understand images rather than memorising cryptic commands.

Windows 95 is a 32–bit operating system which means that it can handle more data at a time. It has longer file names so that the users need not remember the cryptic filenames of yore, and runs even those applications developed in 1981. It is easier to use and customise. So is the task of adding peripherals and using several applications at the same time. It is expected to make life easier for the average PC users.

To take advantage of Windows 95's enhanced capabilities, a large number of software vendors have written new versions of their software and expect a major buying spree as a result. Hardware vendors too expect that the higher hardware requirements of the product will spur PC sales.

Table 10.10. Top Ten Indian Software Exporters during 1994–95

S. No.	*Company*	*Sale in Rs.Crore*
1.	Tata Consultancy	286.00
2.	Tata Unisys	83.50
3.	Pentafour Software	55.26
4.	Silverline	51.42
5.	Infosys Technologies	50.96
6.	Digital Equipment	44.54
7.	Fujitsu - ICIM	42.00
8.	Square D Software	38.16
9.	Patni Computer	35.20
10.	NIIT	32.42

Table 10.11. Electronics, Telecom Equipment and Computer

S. No.	*Items*	*1994-95 (in Rs. crore)*	*1995-96 (in Rs. crore)*	*% Increase*
1.	Computer Software and Services	1474	2650	80
2.	Computer Hardware	647	965	49
3.	Telecom Equipment	101	305	202
4.	Consumer Electronics	366	485	33
5.	Electronic Component	324	525	62

Bill Gates has marketed Windows to saturation point and he has come close to his original vision of "putting a computer on evey desk". Now he has extended his sights to "putting a computer on every desk, pocket and car". In a presentation titled "information at your fingertips" in Germany in 1995, he outlined how the information highway (I-way) will be the next major era of the information age. The I-way will bring video-on-demand, home banking, and a host of other services to users. According to gates the PC is the best way of hooking on to this I-way and the best way to do this is to have it built into the operating system. Gates says so far seven per cent of the American PC users have hooked on to the I-way and the market is large enough for all. Gates has displayed tremendous foresight backed up his ideas with relentless zeal.

Employees at Internet-empowered companies are logging onto the web to follow their favourite sports teams, read movie reviews, ogle this month's "playboy" centerfold, Oh yeah, and get a little work done. All of which has corporate executives worrying that too much extracurricular web surfing could cut into productivity, or worse, lead to legal liabilities.

Corporations are just starting to understand what their needs are, and what Cyberloading is all about. Micro-systems sells a web blocker program called Cyber Patrol for families and schools, and another program, Cyber Sentary, for maintaining company networks. The company plans to combine elements of the two in one Corporate Web blocker. Webster's solution is Web Track, a program that lives on a company's computer network server and blocks more than 26,000 Web sites. Surf Watch blocks children from accessing adult material on line.

System aids has tied up with Frontier Technologies Corporation of the USA to bring to India the latest in cyberspace software for networking communication and Internet application. Super TCP suit 1996, the latest of all-inclusive Internet, X-Windows, networking application software, had complete networking communication capability. The software, which runs on windows, could be installed in a minute using a single CD.

Job Opportunities in Computer Hardware Industry

The computer industry is one of the fastest growing industries today and offers ample job opportunities in computer hardware. The workforce in this industry increased from 46,000 in 1990 to 1.2 lakh in 1994. This increase can be attributed to the discovery of India as a potential market, the liberalisation policy announced by the government, and the availability of highly skilled manpower which has resulted in a large number of foreign multinational companies landing in India for market and support their systems.

Table 10.12. The Required Qualification for Computer Hardware Professional

S. No.	*Category*	*Qualification*
1.	Junior Level	B.E./B.Tech.
2.	Middle Management	M.E./M.Tech.
3.	Senior Management	M.E./M.Tech.

Table 10.13. Annual Remuneration of Different Categories of Computer Professionals

S. No.	*Category*	*Annual remuneration (Rs.)*
1.	Sales Executive	95,000
2.	Maintenance Engineer	1,00,000
3.	R&D/Mfg. Engineer	1,00,000
4.	Software Engineer	1,05,000
5.	Sales Manager	1,50,000
6.	R&D/Mfg. Manager	1,85,000
7.	Marketing Manager	2,00,000
8.	General Manager	3,50,000
9.	Vice-President/Director	4,20,000
10.	President/M.D.	5,00,000

Source : Computers and Communications.

This globalisation of operations will generate more jobs for hardware professionals and create an excellent working environment with many new challenges. The hardware engineer can find employment with computer manufacturing companies, selling and supporting agencies, companies undertaking AMCs as well as in the user organisations, like-offices, hotels, banks, railways, etc. which have a large network of computers for their activities. As the market for workstations, PCs and networking systems is expanding, the growth area and demand for hardware professionals is also increasing. Skilled technical specialists are very much in demand and this field offers many exciting and rewarding opportunities. The jobs are as customer/systems support engineer, technical support engineer (consultant), training engineer, R & D engineer, resident engineer, LAN support engineer and marketing executive. One could go on to become the marketing manager or Vice-President after around eight years of experience, depending upon the organisation and one's potential. The hardware professional can even start his own AMC training or manufacturing business which are equally lucrative. The required qualification for computer hardware professionals is given in Table 1.

Annual remuneration of different categories of computer professionals is given in Table 2.

Computer Maintenance Corporation (CMC), a government organisation, set up in 1975, dealing mainly in computer support and hardware maintenance, has a large number of technically trained personnel in different parts of the country working for several large projects, like : modernisation of UTI, the Bombay Stock Exchange, IDBI, the insurance sector and bank automation.

Top PC manufacturing companies, like : HCL, HP, Wipro, Digital, and PCL recruit fresh engineering graduates' and groom them in-house.

India Gains from PC Boom

The information revolution which is likely to sweep the coming generations fuelled by the PC boom, will lead to an enormous need for software programs to make full use of the computer's powers. India's software industry today wooed the world's top computer professional to come to the country. Many of the world's leading computer companies have set up facilities to develop software in India. These companies such as IBM, Texas Instruments, Motorala, Digital Equipment Corporation, Verifone, Novell, Oracle, Hewlett Packard and Bull, were attracted by the high quality of technical manpower and cheap labour costs in the country. One of the country's key foreign exchange earner, the software industry netted $330 million in 1993-94. The export earning is likely to touch the one billion dollar mark by 1997 and increase to four billion US dollar mark by 2004. The National Association of Software and Service Companies (NASSCOM) plans to seek financial help from the Asian Development Bank to facilitate joint ventures between companies in India and in the ASEAN (Association of South East Asian Nations) to develop computer software in the country. Through the Indian government's efforts, a NASSCOM India-European Software Alliance has been set up with financial help from the European Commission to identify partners in Europe. NASSCOM has decided to assist all its 256 members to get ISO 9000 certification on quality by the year 2000. About 55 of NASSCOM members got this international quality certificate in 1994.

Indian offices are changing rapidly. Modems and fax machines are allowing people to travel less and earn more. In 1997, about 800,000 PCs are expected to be sold in the country. Technology is changing rapidly. TVs, computers and telephones can now be integrated. The PC can stand in for the TV, work as an answering machine and a fax.

The need for computerisation in various organisations of the government was recognised long before 1991. Already over 650 districts are connected by satellite and network information on health, population figures, agriculture, land records, legal cases and other government departments. Besides, information is now stored on floppy discs and CD-ROMs. The full potential of a computer is yet to be realised. A majority of government offices use them only for standard office work. Cheque book dispensers and readers and advanced ledger posting machines are now a reality in most Indian banks.

With 4.5 lakh units sold during 1995-96, the PC market in India has grown by a whopping 80 per cent, in contrast to sales of 2.5 lakh units and a growth rate of 67 per cent during 1994-95. Acer topped the list of foreign brands, while PCL was the local brand leader, with the survey showing that in value terms, the share of PCs in the hardware industry remained steady at 50 per cent. The grey market fell 5 per cent to 20 per cent, while local brands constituted 50 per cent of sales.

The Indian computer hardware and software industry has registered a compound average growth rate of 35 per cent and notch up an annual turnover of Rs. 5769 crore for 1994-95, according to the apex body, Manufacturers Association for Information Technology (MAIT).

According to Mr. Gopal Shrinivasan, MAIT chief, India's booming infotech industry can reach global market levels and also emerge as a major offshore manufacturing base, if there is a government-industry partnership.

To achieve a world size market, India needs to focus on reduction of excise duties, simplify and further rationalise import tariffs, and make IT products freely available by allowing for high depreciation as an incentive.

The Indian IT industry is 0.6 per cent of the global IT industry and

India's spending on infotech product is only 0.7 per cent of the gross domestic product compared to 3 per cent in advanced nations. Domestic production accounts for 40 per cent of the market. The prices of domestic products without excise duty are on a par with international levels.

The IT hardware sector is on a path of unprecedented growth. The market is expected to grow to Rs. 27,800 crore by 2001 from Rs. 4400 crore in 1995-96. PC sales volume is expected to reach global scales of three million units by 2001/2002. Exports would grow to Rs. 5926 crore from Rs. 775 crore in 1995-96. The government revenue on account of the hardware industry would grow to Rs. 4375 crore in 2001/2002 from Rs. 734 crore in 1995-96.

Bangalore, the IT capital of India, which boasts of highest E-mail accounts in the country, has the maximum leased lines for software exports in the country. It also has the highest concentration of PC users.

HCL - Hewlett Packard (HP) had launched the "Vectra" series of PCs in 1992. The move was a well planned one aimed at maintaining the top ranking in the PC market. HCL-HP "Busybee" range of PCs had topped the sales in the country in 1991. IBM-Tata joint venture had started manufacturing PS/2 range of systems in 1993. The specifications of HCL-HP PCS are quite similar to the PS/2. This range, based on Intel's 386 SX upwards micro-processors, have imported monitors and keyboards. Apple's Macintosh computers have started coming out of Digital Equipment India's assembly line in 1993. PCL had tied up with Dell computers of USA in 1992.

Conclusion

A multitude of PCs have flooded the market. There is no PC that is perfect for everyone, though choices and possible combinations are endless.

PC is no longer a static device. It adapts and evolves quickly. With the "information high way" which can carry billions of bits of data, voice, graphic and video images, taking shape through the worldwide network of computers, the PC has emerged as the ultimate communication device. This phenomenon is termed as the Info-Structure Spiral which is stimulated by the new applications using computers and communication.

The role of PCs has been growing rapidly. They are in use just about everywhere. Software specialists are much in demand. And so are hardware engineers who can maintain expensive machines.

A company sells a computer with a warranty. But in addition to that there is need for in-house engineers who can be used both for preventive maintenance as well as for times when there are breakdowns.

11

Computer Networks

Necessity is the mother of invention.

During the twentieth century, the key technology has been information gathering, processing and distribution. As our capability to gather, process and distribute information grows, the demand for more sophisticated information processing grows even faster.

The old model of a single computer serving all of the organisations computational needs is rapidly being replaced by one in which a large number of separate but interconnected computers do the job. These systems are called computer networks.

The term "Computer Networks" means an interconnected collection of autonomous computers. Two computers are said to be interconnected if they are capable of exchanging information. The connection is made by copper wires, lasers, fibres optics, microwaves and satellite earth stations. If one computer can forcibly start, stop or control another one, the computers are not autonomous. Neither one control unit and many slaves is a network nor a large computer with remote card readers, printers and terminals is a network.

Network Goals

Two forces are causing centralized computer systems to give way to computer networks. The first goal is to make all programs, data and other resources available to anyone on the network without regard to the physical location of the source and the user. Load sharing is another aspect of resource sharing. A second goal is to provide high reliability by having alternative sources of supply. With a network, the temporary loss of a single computer is much less serious, because its users can often be accommodated elsewhere until service is restored. For military, banking, industrial process control and many other applications, a complete loss of computing power for even a few hours due to some catastrophe, natural or otherwise, is completely intolerable.

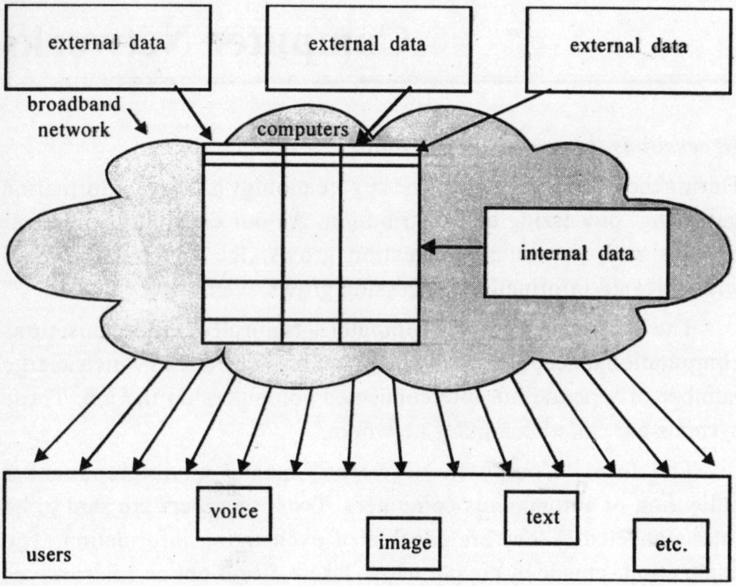

Fig. 11.1. The Integrated Broadband Network.

A computer network can provide a powerful communication medium among widely separated people. In the long run, the use of networks to enhance interpersonal communication may prove more important than technical goals such as improved reliability. The other main force to connect computers in network is the superior price/performance ratio of small computers over large ones. Main frames are roughly ten times faster than the largest single chip microprocessors, but they cost a thousand times.

Applications of Networks

The availability of a computer network makes many new applications feasible. Some of these new applications may have important effects on society as a whole.

Some possible uses of computer networks are, access to remote programs, access to remote data bases, value added communication facilities, etc. A software house that has produced a valuable program may allow their clients to log in over the network and run the program. Having the customer log in on the software house's machine rather than selling the program outright is especially attractive when the program is large, written in an exotic language, machine dependent, or embedded in a web of liberties, special system calls, and other non–portable environmental features. Another major area of potential network use is access to remote data bases. It may someday be easy for people sitting at their terminals at home to make reservations for airplanes, trains, buses, boats, hotels, restaurants, theatres and so on, anywhere in the world with instant confirmation. Home banking and automated newspaper are also possible by these computer networks. The use of networks for calling up a distant computer is cheaper than calling it directly. Computers networks can be used as a communication medium. More than half of all first class mail consists of computer-generated bills. Most of this could be eliminated by electronic funds transfer systems, providing a huge savings to business and their customers. With teleconferencing, widely separated people can conduct a meeting by typing messages at their terminals. International contacts by human beings may be greatly enhanced by network based communication facilities. Using a computer network as a sophisticated communication system may reduce the amount of travelling done, thus saving energy.

Methods of Networking

In order to connect computers which are located in different rooms of the same building or within a small campus, they can be connected through standard input/output ports like RS 232 C or by the use of Local Area Networks (LAN). To connect computers located at different parts of a city or different cities or countries, public switching telephone lines are used with additional hardware and software. The advantages are twofold. First, it is already existing and available almost everywhere in the world and second, it is inexpensive to use. The user has to do dial a number and he gets an actual physical connection to the called party. This is the major use in the world today. Computers cannot be connected directly to the public switching telephone lines. This is because the digital data coming from a computer does not fall within the frequency range of voice signals which the telephone network is designed to handle.

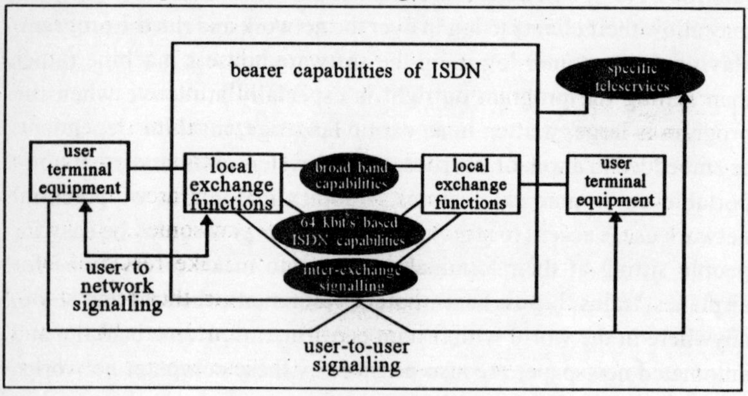

Fig. 11.2. Architectural Model of Integrated Services Digital Network.

By using modems, the digital signal is manipulated electronically in order to transmit it over long distances by using the existing telephone networks. Each modem has a capability of modulation and the demodulations. However, the transmitting end works as a modulator and the receiving end modem works as a demodulator. When the direction of data flow changes the two modems interchange their roles.

Many terminals transmit and receive data at a relatively very slow rate. The keying rate may be as high as 3 characters per second or 30 bits per second. The present telephone networks in India are capable of transmitting 1200 bps or even 2400 bps. If we connect one terminal per line then the line utilization will be very very low. To achieve the maximum line utilization it is necessary to connect several terminals on the same line, thereby reducing the cost of transmission per unit of information. Concentrators and multiplexers are used to achieve maximum line utilization.

Software package COMNET II.5 uses simulation to predict WAN and LAN-WAN performance. It is available for most PCs, workstations and mainframes. It can be used to analyse communication network which uses circuits, message or packet switching.

Alternate routing and adaptive shortest path routing algorithms are built-in as well as CSMA/CD, token passing and other link level protocols.

Typical applications include SNA, DEC net, X.25, SS7, TCP/IP and LAN-WAN capacity planning and analysis.

Global Banking Networks

India has joined the Belgium based Society for Worldwide Interbank Financial Telecommunication (SWIFT) network. Twenty-six of the country's leading banks and eleven branch offices of foreign banks are being linked to the SWIFT global computer network that allows financial institutions around the world to do business with each other using standardised message types that provide a common language.

This network carries more than 1.5 million messages a day that relate to a wide range of banking transactions, including customer and bank transfers, documentary credits and travellers' cheques. With SWIFT network, Indian banks will join more than 3000 financial institutions around the world. Presently the State Bank of India has been connected to this network. The local SWIFT telecommunication centre in Bombay is linked via satellite and by land and sea lines to the system's operating centre in the United States. India is the 74th country linked to the SWIFT network since 1977.

Satellite Lines for Indonet

The department of telecommunication has approved the use of satellite communication, VHF radio and dial up access for its national computer network, Indonet. Coverage of Indonet would increase from 8 to 35 cities. The state of art technique (TDM/TDMA) would lead to optional use of satellite space.

This technique, together with the use of the three metre roof-top earth station, would lead to a cost effective and highly reliable backbone network.

Table 11.1. Different Companies having Internet Access in 1996

S.No.	*No. of employees*	*Internet access*	*No. Access*
1.	100 or fewer	8%	79%
2.	101 to 100	25%	53%
3.	1000 and above	51%	28%

Table 11.2. Percentage of Public Liabraries Accessing Internet

S.No.	*Years*	*Internet access*
1.	1994	21%
2.	1996	44%
3.	1997	67%

Data transmission would take place at 64000 bits per second a thirtyfold increase over what was currently available.

CMC is using "digital packet radio" technology. In this technology inexpensive radio-cum-data equipment are being used. By this system many users can simultaneously utilise a single VHF radio frequency for two-way data communications.

Use of dial-up facilities in cities like Bombay and Delhi would allow infrequent users to utilise Indonet services as charges would be levied only on the basis of each call.

Today, a large number of public and private sector organisations are utilising Indonet, e.g., Oil and Natural Gas Commission, Shipping Corporation of India, The Steel Authority of India Ltd., Coal India Limited, etc. The State Bank of India is using Indonet for its foreign exchange operations.

Computer Supported Telephony

Computer Supported Telephony (CST) is gaining ground. It now promises to be one of the boom markets of the 90s in end-users telecommunication equipment.

The physical realization of a computer supported telephony application involves connecting a computer with a telephone system by a signalling or data link, which supports a protocol to carry command and status information between the two systems. In principle any computer can support the CST protocol and the telephone system may be a PABX, an automatic call distributor, a key system or any other telephone switch. Existing or new systems can be linked by CST.

Real world system does not consist just of a telephone switch and a computer. Computer systems often comprise a large number of PCs linked by local area networks to a common file server. The telephone system itself may provide data links to PCs, integrated voice and data terminals and so on.

In a real world application, a PABX may be linked to a common server which connects to two LANS. If the computer network has well-structured control and addressing mechanisms then CST applications can be implemented in such an environment. The telephony applications will then be available at all terminals and the computing functions available, in principle at least, at all telephone.

CST straddles the telephone system and the computer, bringing the two together functionally. The idea of "straddling" suggests a bridge. The bridge allows information to flow from the telephone system to the computer and vice versa. At the heart of any modern telephone system, there lies a computer. CST links that embedded computer to a less specialised one.

Conclusion

Computer networks now form part of most organizations. The term networking refers mainly to the interconnection of computers and computing devices which may be in many locations throughout an organization. PCs and other computing devices can communicate with each other and to the mainframe computer so that the information each department generates can be used by other staff in the organisation efficiently and effectively. The reason that networking has become so important is that, in today's environment, business can use information and information handling techniques to gain a competitive edge.

Networking also implies the sharing of capital and operating cost between all users as a method to control the per user cost of information handling and processing. Networking has a direct impact on the company's ability to exchange thoughts, messages and information.

The merging of computers and communications has had a profound influence on the way computer systems are organised.

CST is the cornerstone of functional integration. As such, it will impact upon much of the evolving communication technology. Fortunately, it tends to make life simpler for users by bridging the gaps between computer, telephony and voice applications.

12

Computer Software

In the past people used to say "Behind every great man, there is a woman". Now it is true that behind every top executive or scientist or engineer, there is a computer.

It takes strength of mind and imagination to stretch boundaries and do the unheard of. It takes a will to reach near the limiting sky.

The word "program" refers to the sequence of instructions which must be given to the computer for solving the problem. The word "software" is coined to contrast computer programs with the hardware of a computer system. Software programs are stored sets of instructions which govern the operation of a computer system and make the hardware run. Software is a key determining factor in getting more computer power per dollar. Software is used to define the processor programs, library, routines, manuals and other service programs supplied by a computer manufacturer to facilitate the use of a computer. In addition, it may refer to other programs specially developed to fit the users need.

The programer works on a given problem following a step-by-step approach and then writes each step in a language understandable by the computer in the form of a program. The computer accepts binary data at its input consisting of 1's and O's. The computer requires that all the instructions should be written in machine language. In machine language, all commands are written in terms of individual binary, octal or binary coded decimal word. The machine language programing is useful in understanding how the computer performs various operations. It gives a clear picture of data transfer and data manipulation. The machine language programing is also very useful for the design and organisation of a computer. Writing a machine language program is an extremely time consuming process. Fortunately, programs have been developed to allow computers to produce machine language programs from programs written in languages easier for human programers to use. These translator programs are known as assemblers, compilers or interpreters and reside in the computer system. The program that a human programer writes and can read, is known as the source program. The program that results from translation of the source program is known as the object program. Assemblers are used when programing is done in assembly language. It was found that if mnemonic abbreviations are used in place of binary numbers then the programing job can be performed by the user without familiarization with the machine language of a particular computer. A number of advanced languages have been developed which allow commands to be written in a form suitable to the user. These commands and statements have been taken from English. Symbols and notation have been borrowed from mathematics. A single statement in a high-level language can perform the same operation that would require several lines of assembly or machine code to perform. As such, high-level languages are normally easier to use than any assembly language. But programs written in a high-level language require more memory and execute slower than assembly language programs performing the same function. These high-level languages are translated into machine languages by the language compiler. High-level languages are designed with uniformity in mind.

Software Scenario

A breakthrough in computer software has been achieved by the Advanced Software Development Centre of the Hindustan Computers Limited (HCL) to meet the individual requirement of computer users abroad, particularly in the South-East Asian regions.

The new software technology called CAPTO (Computer Aided Programing Tool) or CAMPO (Computer Aided Modular Programing Organisations), employs the computer to analyse unique programing requirements of a user and turn out the most suitable program package to meet them.

More than one thousand computer users in the South-East Asian Region have already taken to the computer generated programs designed by Indian experts. Now CAPTO and CAMPO technology has also been offered to the users of about 3000 HCL computers within the country.

The advanced software development centre of HCL also provides complete support for software development and training to computer installations at 300 locations across the country.

A computer software park has been set up in Pune city in 1988.

In software, Tata Consultancy Services (TCS), started in the sixties, has today become the largest software company in the country. The Tatas have also links with IBM through TCS. At present, TCS develops system software for almost every IBM platform. This includes system 3090, RISC 600 and AS 400, among others.

Lotus Development Corporation has appointed ITC Ltd. as their new marketing and distribution agent in India in place of TCS. The two partners plan local reproduction of Lotus software for distribution in India. According to Mr. Ganesh Krishnamurthy, country manager, Lotus India, "The objective of Lotus is to provide worldwide standard products at affordable prices". With this new arrangement, it is hoped to make the software available at prices which will be amongst the lowest in the world.

Apple and IBM have worked on technology alliance. There is a proposal from Apple for IBM to licence and to help in the development of basic software for a new line of Apple computers that will be a successor to its Macintosh family. IBM has been trying reduce its dependence on Microsoft Corp. of Redmond, Washington, for the basic operating system software that runs IBM personal computers. Using Apple software could be one way to do it. The operating system of the Macintosh, with a screen display that makes the computer relatively easy to use, is considered one of the machine's major advantages in the market place.

In September, 1990, Microsoft broke with IBM over the role of Microsoft's increasingly popular windows program which allows a user to control a PCs with a mouse pointing device and runs several programs simultaneously. IBM preferred to develop OS/2, an operating system designed to take advantage of the new more powerful generations of computers. Since then, these two companies have been in a race to determine which approach would become the standard for future PC systems.

IMR (Information Management Resources), India was incorporated by Mr. Sanan in June, 1990, to address the immediate software development and programing needs of IMR-US (a company of Mr. Sanan) having businesses with several Fortune 200 companies. According to Mr. Sanan, worldwide information services investment is expected to reach US $ one trillion annually by the year 2000. USA firms account for over 70 per cent of world's investment in information services.

As per a report, a PC-based software product which enables industrial organizations to get international quality standard, "ISO-9000" accreditation, has been released by a Madras-based company.

The software package "KI-OMS" from Sundaram Information System (SIS), is a knowledge integrated quality management system which helps organisations set quality systems in accordance with ISO-9000 requirements and maintain documentation pertaining to those systems.

This package consists of three models, namely, (1) quality system-audit module, (2) quality system-documentation module, and (3) a deviation module.

Every year national awards are presented for excellence in electronics. These awards are instituted by the Department of Electronics (DOE). Awards in computer software were given to the Tata Consultancy Services and Digital Equipment India for the year 1991-92.

Software Export Potential

The Indian computer software industry is one of the few industries in the country where sales abroad are larger than sales at home. The Indian computer software business in 1991-92 was estimated Rs. 730 crore of which domestic sales accounted for only Rs. 320 crore. The growth in the value of exports in 1991-92 compared to 1990-91 was over 64 per cent in rupee terms. According to the National Association of Software and Service Companies (NASSCOM), Tata Consultancy Services (TCS) had single-handedly contributed 32 per cent of India's total software exports and 10 per cent of domestic sales. Tata Unisys was a distant second in exports with a 9.5 per cent share. Pertech computers was second in the domestic market with a 3 per cent share of the domestic market.

The third international conference organised by NASSCOM was held in Bangalore between December 5 to 6, 1991. The theme of this international conference was globalisation of software development. The globalisation concept could deflect the focus of exports from the USA which accounts for 70 per cent of Indian software exports and bring into focus new markets like Western Europe. According to president of NASSCOM, the potentials offered by this sunrise industry to Indian exports are immense. Software exports had attained one of the highest growth rates of 43 per cent among all Indian exports during 1990-91. It rose from Rs. 175 crore to Rs. 250 crore in 1990-91. Finland's software market in 1990 was worth $2183 million and India's contribution to that was a mere $100 thousand. India has good scope for software export to Finland.

Table 12.1. Top Ten Indian Software Exporters during 1993-94

S. No.	*Company*	*Sale in Rs. crore*
1.	Tata Consultancy Services	200.00
2.	Tata Unisys	75.00
3.	HCL	40.50
4.	DEIL	37.10
5.	ICIM	32.25
6.	PCS (Computer Division)	31.00
7.	Wipro Systems	30.19
8.	Pentafour Software	28.30
9.	Silverline Industries	27.70
10.	Infosys Technologies	27.42

Table 12.2. Export of Computer Hardware and Software

S. No.	Items	1993-94 (in Rs. crore)	1994-95 (in Rs. crore)	1995-96 (in Rs. crore)
1.	Electronic Hardware	1078	1507	2400
2.	Computer Software	1020	1474	2650
3.	Total Foreign Exchange earned	2098	2981	5050

The software exporters of Bombay, Bangalore and Delhi will have the facility of reliable, high speed, international data communication links. The exporters will be provided with the international connection from VSNL, Bombay, and the link with the exporters' premises will be provided by Department of Telecommunication (DOT). Initially this facility will be offered to 45 software companies in these three cities, which among themselves account for almost 90 per cent of the total software exports from the country. Madras will be the fourth city to get this facility. Later on, it will be extended to other cities. Providing the link to the exporters, premises is significant as many exporters are reluctant to set up a separate facility at a distant location. Overseas client are wary of giving turnkey contracts to be executed entirely in India as they fear lack of control in the absence of a reliable network. This also takes away from the Indian developers a chance to access overseas computers for their development work.

The Indian Government is allowing Cesia, the French public sector undertaking in the field of IT, for promoting export of Indian software to France through a closed user group network. Cesia will take care of the French end of the network and will also help market Indian software as well as encourage collaborations between software companies in the two countries.

Citicorp Overseas Software Ltd. (COSL), the SEEPZ-based software development subsidiary of Citibank, has clinched the first order for its retail banking software, "FINWARE", within four months of its international launch.

In a deal worth over Rs. 2.5 crore, Bank Kerjasama Rakyat Malaysia Bhd., Malaysia, has selected COSL's package solution for its bank-wide technology upgradation project. After this success,

COSL is now hopeful about marketing the product in more countries in South-East Asia and has also started marketing activities in Europe. The more important aspect of this deal is that the company has been able to export a "packaged" product.

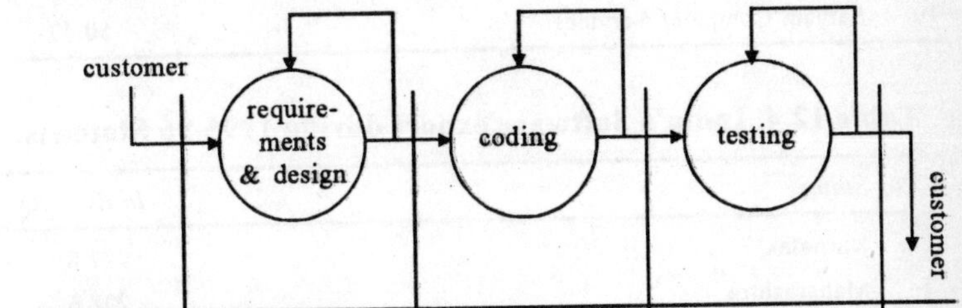

how is the process defined?	requirements and design	coding	testing
who is the customer?	the coder	the tester	the customer
what is to be measured?	internally generated change requests	number of software versions required	number of defects per release
why measure this?	it indicates the correctness from the coder's perspective	it indicates the correctness from the tester's perspective	it indicates the correctness from the customer's perspective
how can these measures be affected?	training, use of diagrams, prototyping	right first time, inclusion of comm-ents, code walk throughs	number of tests performed

Fig. 12.2. Possible Configuration for Statistical Quality Control Applied to Software Projects.

Table 12.3. Top Ten Indian Software Exporters during 1995-96

S. No.	*Company*	*Sale in Rs. Crore*
1.	TCS	420.52
2.	Wipro	163.90
3.	Pentafour Software	102.03
4.	Tata Unisys	94.00
5.	Silverline Industries	81.49
6.	Infosys Technologies	80.65

S. No.	*Company*	*Sale in Rs. Crore*
7.	Fujitsu-ICIM	66.46
8.	Square D Software	62.10
9.	Patni Computer Systems	56.00
10.	Satyam Computer Services	50.47

Table 12.4. India's Software export during 1995-96 Statewise

S. No.	*States*	*In Rs. Crore*
1.	Karnatak	727.8
2.	Maharashtra	708.6
3.	U.P.	347.7
4.	Delhi	326.3
5.	Tamil Nadu	311.7
6.	A.P.	93.1
7.	Haryana	63.0
8.	W. Bengal	54.7
9.	Others	17.1

India's software export revenue is speedily increasing every year. World Bank is very hopeful about India's software export. World Bank has suggested some valuable recommendations.One of the recommendations is the setting up of a Software Development Board (SDB) with representation from both government and industry. The objective of this board will be to refine and coordinate the strategies, plans and activities of other organisations. It suggests that, SDB should be given specific responsibilities for marketing. This includes general promotion, liaison offices for functions in target market countries, attracting development service centres to India, and by providing market information, counsel and assistance to banks and companies. On the manpower training front, SDB can help by fostering academic-industry collaboration in curriculum development, in-service training programmes, interchanges of personnel, and research. Suggestions on financing include establishing a credit line through a financial institution to meet industry's debt financing needs. It estimates that this would require almost $250 million during the period 1992-96. It also recommends that a three-year depreciation should be allowed on hardware and software development platforms. This study also tried to identify potential markets for the software exports. Strategies of competing countries like Ireland, Israel, Mexico, China and Singapore were also examined in detail.

High Level Programing Languages

The first high level language to be widely used was Fortran (an acronyn for Formula Translator). The first specification of the language was published in 1954 and was the product of an effort headed by John Backus. It was first used in 1956 on an IBM computer. Fortran is primarily oriented towards mathematical computation and is still widely used today on mainframe systems. It is used to a far smaller extent on microcomputers. Another significant early language was ALGOL (Algorithmic Language), a joint effort of the Association of Computing Machinery and several European Computing Organisations. This language was first released in 1958. ALGOL achieved some use in Europe but never was widely utilised in the USA. However, several elements of ALGOL were incorporated into future languages such as Pascal.

The U.S. Department of Defence undertook in 1959 the development of a common language for business working under contract to the Department and other government agencies. The result was COBOL (Common Business Oriented Language). A COBOL source program can usually be read and understood by non-programers. COBOL programs are also largely self-documenting, making them easy to revise and update. Several versions of COBOL have been developed for micro-computer use.

BASIC (Beginner's All-purpose Symbolic Instruction Code) was developed by Professors Thomas Kurtz and John Kemeny at Dartmouth College in 1965. BASIC has strong interactive facilities making it possible for a user to converse with a BASIC program as it is executed. This also makes it possible for a BASIC program to ask a user for additional input, make choices, etc. The various implementations of BASIC are used by various micro-computers today.

Professor Niklaus Wirth of the Technical University in Zurich, Switzerland, developed a significant new language in 1971 known as

Pascal (after Blaise Pascal), the well-known seventeenth century mathematician. Pascal is a block-structured language. Pascal programs are divided into sections or blocks, to accomplish specific functions and alterations can be made to one block without affecting the others. Data structures (such as lists and tables) can be easily manipulated. Data typing is extensive and programers can define their own data types. Pascal also includes several restrictions built into the language. All variables and constants must be declared, for example. The order of certain items is also important. Constants must be declared before variables. Pascal does not allow assigning a character to a numeric variable and vice versa.

Dennis Ritchie of Bell Laboratories developed C Language in the early 1970s. It is a portable assembly language which is efficient in memory use and execution speed. It allows programers a great deal of control over system hardware. Like assembly language, It's freedom allows programers to write elegant and efficient programs. It is a difficult language for most users to learn. It has become popular in applications with micro-computer operating systems.

Both compilers and interpreters are used with micro-computer implementation of high level languages. There is no standard as to which should be used, and some languages (such as BASIC and C) come in both compiled and interpreted versions. Interpreted versions generally require less memory while compiled version execute more rapidly. If available memory is not a problem, the compiled version of a language will usually be the preferred choice.

Popular artificial intelligence languages are LISP (LIST Processing) and PROLOG (Programing in Logic). America is betting on LISP and Japan on PROLOG. Both these languages have inductive capacities to a large extent which would allow them to take decision on their own when required. Computer engineers believe that both these languages hold equal promise as tools for intelligence and integration in future.

The list of the presently used programing languages is given below:

Ada, Algol, APL, AWK, BASIC, C Language, COBOL, COMAL, Forth, PC Forth, Fortran, LISP, LOGO, Modula-2, Pascal, Pilot, PL/1, Prolog, RPG, Small talk, SNOBOL, Hyper Card.

Operating Systems

An operating system contains the information that tells the computer how to handle its basic functions such as receiving information, displaying information, storing and retrieving information and printing or telecommunicating information. All personal computer operating systems have these functions whether they are loaded from disk, tape cassettes or on plug-in ROMs. ROM-based operating systems were common on smaller machines such as the Commodore PETs and today on many laptop computers. Tape driven operating systems were also common in the early days of personal computing but they were slow and sometimes unreliable because of the low sophistication of the cassette units themselves.

Steve Wozniak, one of the founders of Apple, is credited with developing the first floppy disk-driven operating system for the Pc. Disk operating system (DOS) offered a more powerful way to move data back and forth from the disk to the computer and provided a quicker access to files. Disk unlike tape cassettes, used both sequential and random access file structures. Sequential files saved disk space, while random access files allowed the computer to find the file almost immediately by reading the disk memory map and following the pointers which told the computer where on the disk the actual file was located.

By the early 1980s, most PCs were configured to use floppy disk systems because the technology had become inexpensive enough to be included in the package. Besides Apple, Tandy's TRS series, Heath/Zenith, the Altos, the North Star, and the Commodore series 4000 and 8000 had operating systems that were implemented on disk drives. At that time, Apple DOS and TRS-DOS were specific to the Apple II and the TRS 80, respectively, and CP/M had become an early business standard because of its sophisticated file handling and portability. Through 1983, CP/M was the standard, although by 1983 it had become largely replaced by MS-DOS, Microsoft's version of PC-DOS had been developed for the IBM PC. Today, MS-DOS has become a basic standard of the business software industry that has produced application programs for the 16 bit PC and PC compatibles. MS-DOS and CP/M behaved very similarly and users found that the transition from CP/M to MS-DOS was not at all jarring.

Apple DOS 3.3 also resembled MS-DOS in some respects, a similarity that reveals it in early origins. Apple DOS 3.3 has since been replaced on proDOS, designed to run on the IIe, IIc and IIgs and resembled MS-DOS in its ability to support file paths and subdirectories. This made data storage and retrieval on the Apple much more efficient, especially for application programs such as APPLE-Works which required large amounts of data storage. ProDOS was also designed to support Apple's 5-M byte hard disk as later versions of MS-DOS were designed for the hard disk of the IBM XT and compatibles.

The development of large storage hard drives in the mid-1980s and of multiuser and local area networks provided a flexible and powerful medium for upgraded operating systems. Gradually, more and more system developers began to integrate the functions of AT & T's UNIX into their product lines to enable to handle large scale business applications software. UNIX was originally developed at Bell Laboratories for internal use within the company. It provided for multiuser, multiterminal applications as well as the concurrent processing of different applications on the same system. UNIX and its look-alikes such as XENIX have had a great influence upon the business community. This influence is likely to grow as business PCs become more powerful, address larger amounts of RAM and expand their range of applications.

In UNIX, the operating system itself supports many operations that were traditionally confined to application programs such as word processing and editing, screen formatting, terminal to terminal communications and even typesetting. The housekeeping functions of UNIX alone make it more like an integrated applications package than a straightforward operating system. This, however, is what makes the system difficult for novice users to master. Because UNIX, like C, the language in which it was developed, is essentially a programer's tool that does not provide easy access, developers have constructed UNIX shells or communities of commands that allow users to detour the core command structure of the system and avail themselves of subsets of routines that accomplish a specific group of procedures.

Because of the large library of both UNIX applications for larger machines and MS-DOS applications for PCs and personal system computers, the business market is pushing the two operating system together. In fact, OS/2, the latest operating system for the 80386-based computer, makes use of a UNIX-like structure for multiuser networks and multitasking front-end environments. Many third party developers are also offering UNIX-to-DOS bridges for older ATs and 80286 compatibles.

The appearance of the Xerox Star, the LISA and ultimately the Macintosh environment brought with it a totally different type of operating system for personal computers. These icon-based machines differed from the command-based IBM environment in their use of graphic symbols which were dragged across a screen and command menus that could be opened by physically pulling them down or popping them up from header or footer bars. The earlier implementations of this system in 1984 were primitive but helped introduce the graphics-based user interface. Within three years after the Mac's introduction, however, the development of the more powerful Macintosh SE and Mac II with their respective large megabyte hard drives has necessitated the release of multitasking operating systems (called "Finders") for the Macintosh as well. Currently, system applications such as Microsoft's Windows and other graphics environments for the IBM AT, personal system/2, and high-end 80386 computers have created Macintosh-like interfaces for the traditionally command-based PC as well.

Operating systems are still in the process of evolution because the hardware that they will drive continues to evolve. The promise of CD-ROM technology and voice recognition and synthesis hardware means that operating systems will soon become personalised to the individual user by means of user-created query and command languages and voice instructions. As the personal computer continues to evolve into a desktop information appliance, the result will likely be a merging of today's single-application programs into a coordinated and integrated operating systems menu, similar to the Macintosh Multifinder, which allows for the concurrent foreground/background processing of data in different applications at the same time while its direct system functions.

Application Software Packages

One of the most instructive ways to understand and appreciate the structure, design, logic and execution of computer programs is to evaluate the way professional software publishers and their designers and programers adapt their product to the demands of the market and the professional user environment. The aim is to evaluate the products as comprehensive programs within their respective applications market places to see how the market is defined and how the programs fit into the markets. The software will be examined as examples of programing as well as examples of consumer products that satisfy professional needs within a very tightly defined market. Each application has defined a separate market in today's personal computing environment and has itself been defined by a definite set of expectations. Presently application software packages are used for word processing, integrated software, graphics programing, computer aided design and drafting systems, desktop publishing, artifical intelligence, neural networks, robotics, music and composition, games and simulations, etc.

One module of the integrated software package should be able to read data created in any other module without requiring the user to make any modifications to the data. For example, a data base module should be able to be import text created in the spread sheet module, the word processor should be able to read text created in the database and the spread sheet should be able to cross-load data from the database or the communications module. In addition, the entire program should share a common command structure and style through all the modules, integrating the way the software looks to the user and works its data files, in order to cut down the learning time and speed up product use. All the modules of the integrated software should be available at any given time once the program is loaded into RAM. Accordingly, users should not have to return to the operating system in order to use a different module. In the most advanced packages such as Framework, Enable, Jazz, Excel, the integrated software should appear as it has its own pseudo operating system so that the operator can use the related modules concurrently, moving back and forth between screen with one or two key strokes.

A computer user does not have to know the computer languages to become a good computer user. He may just have a good working knowledge of some very useful software packages like Lotus 1-2-3, Excel, d-BASE, FOX BASE or Wordstar depending on his needs. Most software packages are user friendly. It is important to select the right software for the required work. For most executives, a spread sheet program such as Lotus 1-2-3 or Excel is good enough.

The market for legal copier of Lotus is currently around Rs. 4 crore. Lotus has drawn up a scheme to legalise individual purchases of pirated software, through the Lotus Vserb club for a paltry US $69 to be obtained from the Reserve Bank of India against the market purchase price of Rs. 16,000 upwards.

Computer Virus

The Michelangelo Virus is lurking in PCs across the USA. Companies, government agencies and schools are taking precautions but every computer cannot be examined in time therefore the invader will do some damage. With the help of special software it is possible to destroy this virus.

According to a report, the computer virus Michelangelo made an advance appearance in India, but software engineers detected it early and destroyed it before the virus could wipe out computer data. Software engineers said the virus was found lurking in computer systems of the Engineers India Limited in late January, 1992 and subsequently in computers of a multinational bank and a private company in Delhi.

A Bangalore based company, produced the cure for Michelangelo and all systems found infected so far have been cleaned of the virus. This virus can spread very easily through computers. Michelangelo was detected using special virus search programs. Software scientists say some 24 families of virus have surfaced so far in India since a virus called "C Brain" showed up in computers in Madras in 1988. Michelangelo wipes out all stored data irretrievably in just ten minutes.

A system engineer of the Metallurgical Consultants India Limited, Bangalore has developed a Vaccine to eradicate the dreaded DIR (Directory)-2 virus. This DIR-2 virus is very difficult to detect compared to Boot Sector and EXE (executive) and COM (Command) files virus. It spreads very fast. To eradicate this virus, first the computer is booted to a clean floppy then the user should scan the disk, utilising tools such as Norton utilities, for the last two sectors and look for a starting signature like "BC00060006EB043" in hexadecimal. If found then it has to be replaced with blanks or any other character. In the next step with the clean bootable floppy, the system command should be executed to transfer the clean boot files to the hard disk and then a copy of a clean command to the hard disk. This would eradicate the DIR-2 virus from the medium.

Are Algorithms Patentable?

The issue of whether algorithms are patentable has arisen since computer programs are functional statements which use algorithms to solve problems.

Uncertainty over the scope of patent protection of computer software in the USA is being further compounded by legal technicalities which can be illustrated by a recent case involving M/s Refac Technology. M/s Refac Technology, without producing any software, acquired a five per cent ownership interest in many software patents, by promising that it would bring infringement actions. To procure its portion of all the royalties, the firm filed about 2000 patent infringement suits against both big and small software producers for current and retroactive royalties. The court rejected Refac's claim on the ground that the firm's "slight interest" in the patent was void for having been obtained solely for the purpose of bringing "abusive litigation".

In the USA, much litigation has been pending over the copyright protection of both computer operating systems and computer screen displays, with firms. In Apple's suit against Microsoft and Hewlett Packard, the court saw that the alleged infringing use of Apple's visual displays was covered by Apple's software licence to the defendant. Rank Xerox's suit against Apple is pending further hearing. Xerox did not bring allegation of infringement; it simply sought to have Apple's copyright declared invalid.

There is a controversy over a recent decision on extending copyright protection to the menu command structure of a popular spreadsheet program. In this suit Lotus Development Corporation and Paperback Software Intnoel are involved. The most troublesome is the protection of input command words such "move", "copy", "print".

Software theorists in the USA fear that strong intellectual property protection might trigger fierce patent or copyright races because of the "potentially large returns in developing a broadly used interface standard", as a result of which an excessive amount of resources may be devoted to this activity.

Conclusion

Perhaps not everyone needs to know how to write a computer program but by acquiring that skill one will surely learn about computers. Practicing that skill and learning about computer applications that affect all of us are pedagogically sound means for becoming knowledgeable about social impacts of computers.

The operating systems act as the resident hosts for application programs. The high level languages serve as development tools as well as applications such as integrated software and word processing, music, artificial intelligence, computer aided design and desktop publishing.

Software has emerged as the second fastest growing export item for India with an annual compound growth rate of 56 per cent in the last few years. It had a turnover of $164 million in 1991-92. India will be able to export 11.5 per cent of the total world software requirement worth $660 million by 1996 with the existing infrastructure. The World Bank study has recommended the need for enhancing the number of trained, experienced computer professionals in India to maintain the growth trend.

The world software market is now at Rs. 30,000 crores and ever growing. It is recommended that Indian software industry should tap it by taking advantage of this favourable business climate. It is a rare opportunity indeed for the discerning investor.

REFERENCE

1. Microcomputer Applications Handbook by William J. Brines, McGraw-Hill Publishing Company, New York, 1989.

13

Hardware and its Maintenance

The computer is an extremely useful tool for management of information, data handling and decision making. Rapid development in computer technology in India and abroad has put computers within the reach of even the smallest organisation.

A simple digital computer consists of four main blocks namely the memory unit, the Central Processing Unit (CPU), Control Unit and Input/Output devices.

The memory unit generally consists of random access type of memory. It is used to store both the sequence of instructions needed by the control unit to carry out a given task and the data needed by the control processing unit to make the computations.

The CPU consists of a set of registers and logic system. The control unit does two main functions. First, it controls the order in which the instructions are carried out and second, it controls the operation of the CPU and other parts of the system during the execution of a particular instruction.

The input/output devices serve as interface between the system and the outside world. Sometimes input/output information flows through the CPU while at other times the information transfer takes place directly between the input/output devices and the memory unit.

General Design Approach

The design of a digital computer may be divided into three phases, namely system design, logical design and circuit design. The system design takes into account many factors such as cost, size, operating environment, type of applications, reliability and maintainability. A number of decisions have to be made regarding the design objectives, design philosophy, speed of operation, types of operations to be performed, error checking provisions and facilities like interrupts etc.

The logical design of the computer consists of logical design of the subunits of the computer to perform specific tasks in an integrated manner. For logical design, decisions have to be made regarding the word format, computer configuration and machine instruction. The logical design ends with the logical expressions or a detailed logical diagram.

The last phase of design is to implement the logical equations and/or diagrams by actual circuits. The actual design of the logic circuits, input-output devices and the circuits for memory and control are to be designed during this phase. The most important consideration is the selection of proper devices to satisfy the conditions of reliability and minimum failure rate.

The choice of the components used in a computer and the way in which they fit together, is determined by its architecture. Computers built to conform to the PC architecture, even if they are made by different manufacturers, should all run the same software and produce the same results. This is known as PC compatibility.

A computer is made up of system unit, the keyboard and the monitor. The power supply converts the AC mains to the stabilised DC voltages at plus and minus 5 and 12 volts needed by the electronics of the computer. Large circuit board holds the expansion slots into which other circuit boards fit. This is known as the motherboard. On most PCs the motherboard contains the CPU, the main memory, serial and parallel I/O ports, disk controller and video display adapter. The advantage of this is that the motherboard can then have fewer expansion slots. This allows the manufacturer to build a small computer. Components mounted on the motherboard and expansion cards are integrated circuits (ICs). Each IC is made up of hundreds of thousands of transistors, all etched on to a single wafer of silicon. These ICs with seven or eight metal legs on each of the long side, are known as dual-in-line-package (DIP) ICs. Earlier these ICs were the basic building blocks of a computer. Advances in technology have made it possible to build larger, more complex circuits on a single chip. This technique is called Very Large Scale Integration (VLSI). Use of VLSI chips gives many advantages. The system board can be made smaller, hence the overall size of a computer is reduced. It is quicker and cheaper to manufacture. Power consumption and heat dissipation are lower. It gives better reliability. On the latest board designs, components are soldered directly to the board. These are known as Surface Mounted Devices (SMDs). It is not possible to repair these SMD faulty boards. The faulty boards can only be replaced by good boards.

Computer Scenario

Zenith Computer Ltd. has embarked on expansion plans to set up new and modern production facilities for the manufacture of computer system including PCXTs, ATs and LAN and other cards. The company has tie-up arrangement with Texas Instrument, USA for notebook computers and laser printers, Racal Interlan for net-working products, Retixinc for Open Systems Integration (OSI) Products, Eicon Technology for connectivity products, 3 Com corporation for internetworking products, Microtest INC for networking products and Umax Inc for scanners.

Apple computer is planning to repackage its Macintosh series in a less expensive line. These machines would offer an optional built-in CD-ROM player in an effort to jump-start the home market for multimedia software which can combine audio and video with more traditional computer applications. CD-ROMs are optical disks for playing back such software.

The new line, named the performa series is listed at $1000 to $3000 but is likely to be priced for lower at a wide variety of department stores, discount shops and consumer electronics outlets.

In 1992, at the Consumer Electronics Show, Apple previewed a new category of handheld computers which are the dubbed version of the Newton. Such systems are more powerful versions of the Sharp Wizard personal organiser and they will be available commercially soon.

American Information System Inc unit of Toshiba Corp. has recently introduced the T4400C notebook computer with colour display and 486 microprocessor. This unit costs $3999.

As per a report from Britain, a new computer system being developed in Scotland will offer a new voice to thousands of people who have no speech. The computer-based system, developed over the last five years at Dundel University, is the first to use a rapid text facility to allow users to conduct a conversion and crucially alter its speech mode to reflect mood. It is designed to allow a user to retrieve phrases and words stored in the computer memory at speed, so that a near normal conversation can be conducted. Built into a system are voice patterns reflecting anger, sadness, happiness, grief, disgust and fury. The operator uses a computer "mouse" to call up phase indicators on the screen menu.

A Japanese company has developed a new computer system called, "neuro-computer" resembling the human brain which is capable of learning certain functions without complicated software programs. This computer uses Large Scale Integrated (LSI) chips to achieve a processing speed four times faster than a supercomputer and about 500 times faster than a typical engineering workstation.

Astrophysicists at the University of Wales in Cardiff have produced computer simulations that show, for the first time, how stars are formed by the gas in intersteller space.

Like in all other fields, computers have entered astrology in a big way. Computers have revolutionised the ancient system of astrological calculation providing accuracy and speed.

Indian Computer Industry

In the emerging world order, developed countries are increasingly tightening controls on technology transfer to developing ones. Technological advancements are much greater today than in the pasts. If India is even five years late to assimilate an emerging technology, the chances are very likely that it will remain behind forever in that field. As resource constraint is a major consideration, available resources have to be carefully allocated to various technology areas on a priority basis. In order to increase the use of information technology and increase software exports, the government should consider undertaking missions on computers, software and hardware within a specified time-frame. Developing countries should have more technological interaction among them. There has to be greater emphasis on exploring what is available in other developing countries. This would open up more markets for the developing world.

In the past five-six years one of the most rapidly growing industries in India is the computer industry and in particular the PC industry. Though the computer industry has shown tremendous growth it still has tremendous potential to be used in our country and in that sense it may be considered to be still in its infancy. In spite of this growth lately the computer industry has suffered a setback in terms of overall growth. Giant companies like Hindustan Computers Limited have had to change their market strategy and have been forced to merge with internationals like Hewlet Packard, to stabilise their position in the market. The computer industry had a growth rate of 60 per cent in 1987-88, 44 per cent in 1989-90 with an annual turnover of Rs. 1675 crore and 24 per cent in 1991-92 with a turnover of Rs. 2075 crore. The IT industry is basically an import-oriented industry. Due to the devaluation of the rupee and the subsequent cuts in Government expenditure, the computer industry is the worst suffer since the price factor is playing a decisive role.

Another factor which is influencing the market is the entry of fly by night operators who use smuggled components. These assembled computers are therefore much cheaper than sold by the established companies and hence more popular than products developed by the organised sector and pose a serious threat to the computer industry at large.

The Government has recognised the tremendous importance of the computer industry and has started "industrial parks" where industry would be allowed to take root.

Another industry which has grown as a consequence of the computer industry is the computer education industry, like NIIT and Uptron.

The outlook for the future shows a scenario which is promising in spite of the current recession of the computer industry.

Some Indian computer hardware industries are given below:

1. Lipi Data System. This company manufactures all types of printers. Their principals are Mannesmann Tally of Germany, Olivetti of Italy and Data Products of USA. Lipi technology was obtained under licence from Data Products Corporation USA. Lipi's line printers provide hard output in mega industries and services like airlines, railways, banking, insurance, education, steel, coal and mines, power generation and other core sectors. Lipi's printers are easily compatible with all computer systems being manufactured in India.

2. Mudra Electronics Private Limited. This computer firm is five and a half years old. It is the supplier of 486, 386, 286, XT and PC systems. Mudra Electronics provides solutions custom tailored for each client on a variety of hardware configurations. Communications between the clients requirements and computer is their motto.

3. Appollo Computers Private Limited. This company supplies hardware, software and computer peripherals. The customer can avail of a maintenance contract supplied by this company.

4. Uptron. This is a Government of India undertaking, a computer education company. It offers Master's diploma in Software Engineering and a Post Graduate diploma in Software Engineering. It meets the standards set by DOEACC (Department of Electronics Accereditation of Computer Courses).

5. Modi Olivetti. It supplies printers manufactured under license from Olivetti of Italy.

6. Data Pro. A Tata Unisys Company, it was founded in 1976. It is a diversified company which supplies software, hardware and computer peripherals.

7. Intercom (India) Limited. It supplies NEC printers, Japan.

8. Moser Baer India Limited. It produces magnetic media and supplies floppy disks.

Innovation in Computer Hardware

Physical computer equipment like mechanical, magnetic, electrical and electronic devices, is called the computer hardware.

A hand-held device, separate from a keyboard, used to control cursor position on a display screen, is called the mouse. As the mouse rolls along a table top, its relative position approximates the position of the cursor. Introduced by Xerox in the Star 8010 professional workstation in 1981.

Laser printers are the stars of non-impact technology. A laser beam is used to draw characters directly onto a photosensitive drum. The full page image is then transferred electrostatically to the toner and paper. After that the toner is melted into the paper. Laser printers offer higher speed of about eight pages per minute, a tremendous variety of type faces and 300 dots per inch graphics over a full page. The laser beam creates closed packed dots or pixels to provide high resolution text and graphic images. In a single horizontal scan line of the laser beam, pixels are generated every 0.0033 inch, thus creating the approximately 300 dots, per inch. By performing 300 scan lines every inch vertically, the beam achieves a resolution of 90,000 dots per square inch. The older standard is Hewlett Packard's PCL (Printer Control Language) developed for the first desktop laser jet printer of Hewlett Packard. The other major standard is Adobe System's Postscript, a page discription language. Apple became the first manufacturer to adopt postscript. In future faster and less expensive laser printers will be available in the world market with increased resolution and multicolour printing.

Intel Corp., the leading maker of the "brains" in PCs has announced the latest version of a micro-processor that runs twice as fast as its predecessors. By doubling the chip's internal "clock", Intel says the microprocessor can speed up the PC's processing by 70 per cent, even though the rest of the computer continues to operate at its usual speed. Intel's new 486 DX2 chip runs internally at 66 MHz but it sends and receives data from the rest of the computer at 33 MHz.

A new 16 Mb memory chip has been developed by Matsushita Electric Industrial Co. Ltd. which operates at very low voltage, thereby extending the amount of time a battery can be used on one charge. The developers claim it to be the world's fastest 16 Mb Dynamic Random Access Memory (DRAM) chip. These new chips will replace the earlier 1 Mb and 4 Mb DRAM chips in computer equipment. This chip will also keep pace with the present speed of the Central Processing Units.

The future lay not much in more speed but in building different software tools to inspire creativity on the part of the engineers and scientists who use the computers. Computer users should wait for the next generation of supercomputers which would drastically shorten the time it took engineers to design products like cars and aeroplanes and master problems that now defy solution.

Personal communicators combine the functions of a cellular phone, computer, fax and electronic organisers. Apple corp. was the first to develop the prototype of a personal communicator. By using a special pen it is possible to write on the screen of this device. This device is called Newton and it is able to recognise the hand-written words, figure out what they mean and store that information in its proper place in its memory. When connected to a telephone line, Newton can send or receive faxes. An attachment will link it to the wireless communication networks.

Computer Hardware Exports

The total global computer and peripheral market stands at around $200 millions which traditionally has been catered to by the manufacturers from USA, Japan, Taiwan and Singapore.

At present the growth rate of hardware exports has fallen due to loss of a large market in the erstwhile USSR. A two-pronged strategy is required to promote hardware exports from India. First thing is to revive the CIS market and second is to develop markets in other countries.

Traditional links with USA, Japan, Taiwan, Singapore and other buying organisations would also help in reestablishing ourselves as a regular source of supplies. The strategy should be to increase our country's presence in the world market. Areas which need special attention are:

1. Creation of extensive servicing and support facilities.
2. Serious efforts on setting up of new joint venture as well as taking up production in existing ones.
3. Concentrated efforts on packaged solutions.

Very planned and directed efforts have to be made in this direction by the computer industry and with support from Government and other promotion bodies. With this we can hope to make some penetration in the export market.

India's export performance of various electronic hardware items to the European Community market has been steadily improving and is likely to have a quantum jump, says a study. Exports grew by 7.5 per cent to Netherlands due to exports of computer hardware and Spain by 6.8 per cent due to computer and data processing equipment.

The government is seriously considering delicensing the consumer electronics sector. In every year the national awards for excellence in electronics, instituted by department of electronics (DOE), are presented. The award for computer system was given to Wipro Infotech of Bangalore for the year 1992. Tata Consultancy Services and Digital Equipment of India were given the award of computer software.

Dell computers of USA has signed an agreement with Delhi based Pertech Computers Ltd. (PCL) to buy computer motherboards worth

Table 13.1. Export of Computerware from India

S. No.	*During the year*	*Hardware (in Rs. crore)*	*Software (in Rs. crore)*
1.	1992-93	294	740
2.	1993-94	427	1020
3.	1994-95	647	1474

Note: While the export of computer hardware in 1994-95 registered a growth of 51.5 per cent the export of computer software registered a growth of 44.5 per cent during the same period.

The countries to which computerware is exported include USA, Mexico, Belgium, Denmark, U.K., Germany, France, Italy, Netherlands and CIS, etc.

$50 million during 1993-94. A motherboard is the main printed circuit board of the computer system on which the different processor cards are mounted. Dell Computers will supply PCL with the board designs and will help in procuring the required máterials.

The Manufacturer's Association for Information Technology (MAIT) had demanded that duty on finished goods be brought down to 90 per cent, on electronic components to 50 per cent, non-electronic components to 30 per cent, on memory chips and CPUs etc. tö 30 per cent during the budget for the year 1993-94.

Duty on electronic components has come down to the rate demanded (50 per cent) and the duty on finished goods has been brought down to 80 per cent. Duty on non-electronic components as well as CPUs and memory chips, however, has been pegged at 50 per cent and this has not pleased the computer industry. The peripheral manufacturers feel quite let down by the non-lowering of duty on non-electronic components. The computer industry on the whole was disappointed that the government has done nothing about its demand for introducing investment allowance on the purchase of computers. The bright side of the 1993-94 budget was that in spite of the convertible rupee, the product was cheaper for the end user. According to the secretary of MAIT, the product was cheaper by 13 to 14 per cent.

Computer Maintenance

Computer maintenance can be divided into three categories:

1. General Maintenance
2. Watching symptoms of trouble
3. Controlling Computer Functioning

1. General Maintenance: The computer service industry holds an important and unique place in today's business world because it is critical when a business's computer fails. Quick, competent and reliable servicing and repairs are absolute necessities.

Most businesses cannot allow their computers to go down for any period of time. Few decades ago, when computers were first introduced into companies, they were used in only a limited time; therefore, it was not critical if the computer was down for a few days. Today, with the growth of powerful computers in the business world, even few hours of down time is unacceptable.

The traditional computer service process is a straightforward one. A well-trained computer service engineer is sent to diagnose a problem on a computer system and to do whatever is necessary to repair the system. The traditional service call has become increasingly expensive. This is due to the substantial and growing salaries of service engineers and hike in the prices of the spare parts. While the cost of repair of a computer system is rising, the price of these systems keeps falling. These economic pressures have led to the use of a number of new servicing techniques. These techniques take advantage of improved technologies and are designed to lower service costs.

Modern electronics is so reliable that component failures are rare. Most problems are caused by mechanical parts and electrical interconnections. As far as circuit boards are concerned, they must be treated as a single unit. If a fault occurs in circuit boards then these circuit boards should be discarded as a whole. Most boards run forever without a fault.

2. Watching Symptoms of Trouble: The novelty of the function calls for novel ways of monitoring it. However, in the absence of established monitoring parameters, one can keep watch on a few symptoms which manifest themselves when all is not well with EDP (Electronic Data Processing).

Continuous investments will have to be made in EDP to replace obsolete hardware and software and acquire additional hardware commensurate with the growth of the business and the increased scope of computerisation, to develop software for new applications and to develop staff resources. One of the symptoms of trouble may emanate from an analysis of the overall trend of the investments during the last few years.

The second symptom of trouble in EDP that one can watch out for is the proportion of time that the systems personnel spend in development and maintenance work. If a large proportion of their time is dedicated for the maintenance of EDP, it is a sure sign that EDP system is getting old and inefficient.

When things are not right in EDP, routine reports generated on computers do not come in time, mistakes keep recurring in reports and changes/enhancements requested are inordinately delayed.

A periodical age analysis of both hardware and software would provide a clear indication of the state of EDP health. When the hardware is old and out, moded-tit becomes difficult to meet the demand of the users for computing power. Besides, there are frequent breakdowns which upset all schedules. Maintenance of such equipments become difficult as the vendors probably have discontinued the manufacturing of such items. Just as hardware needs to be constantly upgraded or replaced, so does software.

Most systems professionals prefer development activities. They expect to work in a "State-of-the-art" environment or at least in companies that show clear signs of moving towards that. An increasing rate of turnover of systems staff may be an indication that the company is not keeping up with the latest developments.

3. Controlling Computer Functioning: In the case of a computer the asset is not just the computer itself but the software and data too which are its integral parts. The users of a computer have, therefore, to adopt and adhere to certain operation measures for safeguarding these assets. For the smooth functioning of a computer, the following points are important:

(a) Be sure you keep backup. A computer can malfunction at any point of time due to hardware, software or misuse by people. If, due to malfunction the data gets lost then the stored data in floppy disk can be reloaded and the given job can be started without losing time.

(b) Be prepared for possible disaster. Calamities like fire, earthquake, building collapse, etc., have a characteristic that they seldom occur by giving advance notice. If you have any data on the computer or on a backup device which is critical to the business then periodically keep a copy of that data away from the office building.

(c) Beware of viruses. Computer viruses have attracted a lot of attention in recent times. One has to take precautions against these viruses. The important thing to do is to ensure that no one uses an outside floppy on your computer without having it checked for a virus by your engineer. To check for viruses an antidote programme is needed.

(d) Prevent having data forests. Over a period of time, the disk space gets cluttered with unwanted data. Data are not deleted when these have outlived their utility. The solution commonly resorted to is to start grumbling about inadequate disk space. So before filling the disk space, have a look at the existing data on the disk and clear out the unwanted data. Clearing the disk regularly will also save from confusion that arises when one is not able to distinguish between different versions of the same data that may have been stored at different points of time or by different persons.

(e) Keep a tab on software. It is essential that important documents, catalogue and software should have two or more copies. Also ensure that at least one more person is conversant with them. This will be an insurance against bottlenecks that may be created in the absence of the particular individual because using a software when one has never used it before, is difficult. This may also save you from sabotage by a disgruntled employee.

(f) Development of systems: It will be a good idea to develop the systems under the guidance of competent system professionals. The system design and development is a•specialized function which has certain principles and methodologies the an unexperienced man may not be aware of.

(g) Beware of the crooks: Make sure that the confidential data and important programme files of the company cannot be accessed.

obtained or modified by unauthorised persons on computer. Security is implemented by special software and hardware and the computer's operating procedure.

Computer Furniture

Efficient use of computers demand properly designed environment in computer installations. The furniture used for computer installation as well as the surrounding interior should be very carefully designed taking into account various factors, like agronomics, fatigue, free operations as well as pleasant environment.

The following points should be taken into consideration for proper design of computer furniture:

1. The dimensions of the furniture should take into account the most comfortable operating height, legspace, etc. for fatigue free operations.
2. Space and facilities should be provided for easy access to frequently used computer related materials.
3. The operator should be able to supervise and control the entire installation including the terminal, printers, power equipment, etc. with ease and minimum effort.
4. The furniture should be made in building block system to facilitate flexibility in its arrangement.
5. Maintenance like repolishing etc. are highly undesirable in a computer installation and therefore the furniture should be made virtually maintenance free using laminated sheets and modern finishes.
6. The decor scheme of the furniture and surrounding interior should be pleasant and soothing, keeping in view the long hours of complex work in a computer room.

Computer Applications

The important applications are given below:

1. Scientific Applications: These applications require the ability to process arithmetic calculations at high speed with great degree of accuracy. A large primary storage (memory) is required to store the large programme and large quantity of data. Examples of scientific applications are : Seismic data processing, reservoir modelling, process simulations, structures analysis, etc.

2. Commercial Applications: These applications deal with routine aspects of organisation such as payroll, financial accounting and accounting, project management, etc. The commercial applications depend more on input/output operations and hence require large secondary storage.

3. Technical Applications: These applications pertain to the details of parameters associated with basins, reservoirs, wells, equipment, etc. This also requires large secondary storage.

Conclusion

The magnitude of problems faced in India today and the developmental options chosen make it obvious that computerisation has come to stay in India. This is because, from industry to agriculture, medical research to economic forecasting, irrespective of the field, computerisation has something positive to offer. It also holds the key to link India on a technological wavelength at par with the best in the world.

With hardware becoming less expensive and software easily available, computer installations are increasing at a rapid pace in India. Computers have the potential to change the way we live, think and work. Hence, it becomes essential for us to gain a knowledge of computer applications and operations.

The advance of information technology has given rise to a new kind of computer security hazard that is electronic trespass. Today the whole computer industry has grown up around preventing this danger.

Irrational tariff structure has made import of finished goods cheaper than that of subassembly and also capital goods. Government is talking about export thrust but it is hardly visible in this new policy. The new policies have made it easy to sell in India, not to buy from India.

14

Quality Management of Hardware and Software

Quality management is a key issue both nationally and at the level of the individual organisation. It is now one of the central determinants of corporate survival. To understand customer's needs and to respond to them more effectively sustained attention to the management of quality is crucial.

In the 1970s, America, a world leader in economy, was rudely jolted out of its complacency, when customers preferred Japanese and German goods. The American companies woke up when finance measurements were done and turned to Mr. Philip B.Crosly, internationally renowned quality management expert, for help. He provided consultations to the American companies like IBM, Xerox, Corning, Motorola, Chrysler, General Motors and others.

In principle, quality has two separate components. Objective qualities can be clearly named, quantified and measured-objective and subjective. These include functionality performance, cost, reliability, repeatability and flexibility. Subjective aspects are non-quantifiable. These are aspects which people respond to, often unconsciously and rarely open and which can easily dominate their attitudes.

Successful research and development is crucial in achieving high degrees of customer satisfaction and greater market shares which mean more earnings for the country, from exports, royalties and income from overseas operations. Factors which have been crucial in winning leading positions in the selected fields by the successful management of many high-tech long-term projects are:

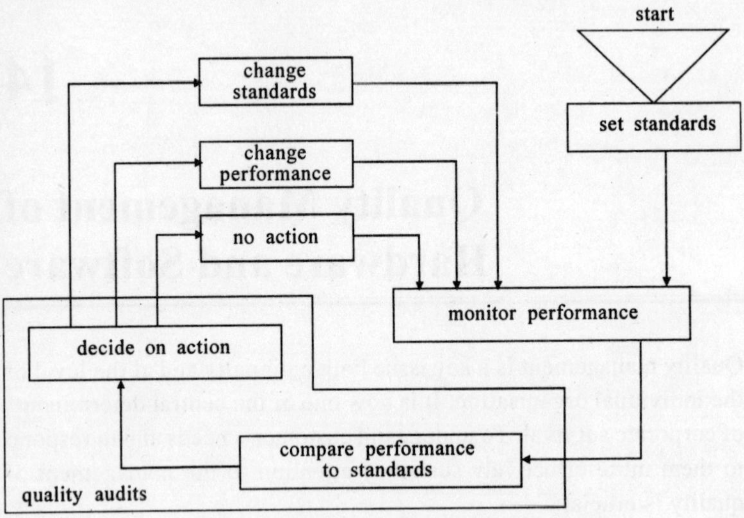

Fig. 14.1. Role of the Quality Audit.

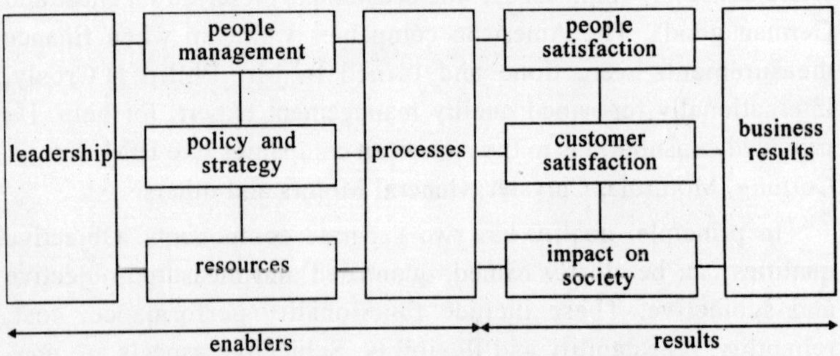

Fig. 14.2. The Total Quality Management Philosophy.

1. A good knowledge and understanding of the selected markets have been always linked with the awareness of, and access to, current and emerging technologies.
2. Careful selection of projects as per the future needs of customers require to provide a steep change in performance, sometimes demanding invention, to extend available technology.

3. Good project teamwork is vital, with strong leadership and detailed planning, exploiting the supporting capabilities of IT.

Building a Technical Strategy

Technology presents competitive opportunities and threats to a manufacturing business. The penalties for making the wrong strategic decisions in this arena are always damaging and can be fatal. Critical technologies offer opportunities for product differentiation and there are substantial differences in competence among competitors. The first step in building a technological strategy is to identify the distinct technologies which are blended together to create the products offered. The second step is to assess the relative competitive importance of the product-market technologies and the competence of the Strategic Business Unit (SBU) in each such technology. The final step is to identify promising new business technologies.

Excellent companies are obsessed with quality and reliability. These characteristics constitute an essential part of the value system and strategy of these organisations.

The concern for quality is not new, but in an increasingly competitive and complex market place that promises to extend beyond our domestic boundaries, it would become imperative to restructure our competitive approach to make quality a load-bearing element in our business strategy. Quality has a direct impact on both market share and profit margins. There is no one factor that can be singled out as a key to achieving quality. Quality is all pervasive. It is an attitude of mind that has to be transformed into organisational culture where it becomes everybody's responsibility.

Those success criteria which cannot be quantified should not appear in any commercial contract because there will be no way of confirming that the requirement has been met. They should nonetheless be taken into account when designing the system because they will affect future relations with the client.

When a system development team starts a project first they define the target system and produce a plan of actions necessary to achieve the desired results. Also they include all the objective and subjective success criteria which they have been able to identify. As the project progresses, they keep track of their progress against the plan, measuring the various components against their targets. The results of these measurements are used to modify the plan in order to ensure that the end result matches the desired result. These methods are well documented in the following publications:

1. Military Standards (AQAP 1 & 13)
2. British Standards (BS 5750)
3. International Standards (ISO 9000)
4. Tick IT Guide
5. Local Company Standards
6. Project management books

Still people do their own thing and projects fail. It is much easier to define success criteria after the event, based on what was actually achieved. The main difficulty is that the real success criteria are not always obvious due to undeclared criteria. The real skill in defining success criteria rests in the ability to identify these hidden features and include them explicitly in the list. These hidden features are given below:

1. Unstated requirements as the customer knows something more is required now but it was not stated in the beginning. The system had been developed in such a way that now it is not possible to add this unstated requirement without a complete redesign.
2. If a project is undertaken with the long-term goal of achieving a greater market share or of preventing a competitor from winning a prestigious contract then the team will be disillusioned for not getting recognition for their development work because they were not aware about it at the time of development.
3. When a project is given to inexperienced people to carry out, but the declared budget and time-scale are suitable only for experienced staff. The project may be successful according to the training criterion, but depressing and unsuccessful according to the declared goals.
4. In the greater world of politics, whole projects may be initiated more for the benefit of few individuals' political status than for any of the declared concrete goals.

Quality Management

Quality is on everyone's lips these days because it can make the difference between success and failure in a very competitive and changing world. Today, quality means more than product quality. In other words, an effort in which everybody and every function in an organisation participates. In the midst of liberalisation and globalisation process, it is perhaps more obvious than ever that a business, if it is to survive and prosper, simply must embrace the philosophy and methodology of Total Quality Management (TQM). Companies which master TQM will triumph and those ignoring it would be swept into oblivion.

Quality management is about organisational culture. Everyone in an organisation has to understand and care about what they do, be supported to do it and be challenged to do it better. Agents for cultural change include role models, quality awards, systematic self-assessment, benchmarking and partnership sourcing. Attention to human factors is crucial. So, too, is an ungrudging commitment of time and other resources. Self-assessment is a thorough experience and periodically repeated self-assessments provide a remorseless measure of whether progress is being made.

Everyone leads by example. Manor customers at the head of a customer/supplier chain are in a good position to influence the quality management practices of their suppliers and they in turn can influence their suppliers. This sets up a cascade of influence along the chain, which can be a powerful agent of cultural change within the sector as a whole.

A further agent for cultural change is education and training. There are some encouraging developments at all levels of the education system, but they tend to be restricted to technology or management disciplines and even these are to be promoted too modestly. There is scope here for a strong lead from the engineering profession.

The first priority is to understand why the organisation wants to control quality and what will be the gain of the management.

It can be seen that people's attitudes to quality defy attempts to quantify it and remain highly subjective. The organisation wants to control quality because there are following benefits:

1. It can have some clear sales benefits.
2. It can provide a mean of limiting technical and commercial risk during a development.
3. It can enable management control of system life-cycle costs.
4. It can provide proof of a disciplined approach which may help avoid or reduce future litigation costs.
5. It can help make the delivered system more pleasant to use.

Once the goals have been identified, management at all levels need to identify their own attitude to quality. It is rarely sufficient to

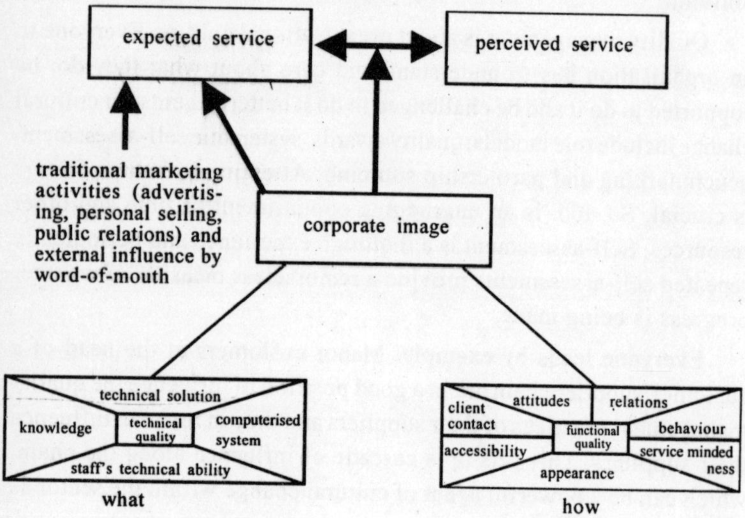

Fig. 14.3. Managing the Perceived Service Quality.

list quality requirements in a company or project quality manual and then expect staff to follow obediently. Management at all levels must demonstrate their commitment to quality in their behaviour towards each other and their staff.

It is important that management avoids giving conflicting messages. This tends to come about when the official line is that quality is important, but once the pressure is on to achieve a deadline it is the quality which is cut first. It is a usual practice on internal projects to postpone the documentation until the end of the project. If it is not important then it need not have been planned in the first place.

When determining the level of quality required for a system, it is necessary to recognise how the different people involved with the system during its life have different perceptions of the meaning of quality. In some cases these perceptions may be incompatible. It is management's responsibility to identify these cases and be prepared to take action to ensure that the quality which is achieved is that which is the most appropriate overall. When performing quality control checks it is important to maintain a sense of proportion. More efforts should, therefore, be put into checking the meaning than the presentation.

Failure to achieve any of the expected quality characteristics is in some way undesirable. The effects of these undesirable characteristics can be described as the cost of failure. Intangible costs of failure are given below:

1. Reduced performance and job satisfaction for users of the system as they struggle to overcome obstacles placed in their way by the system's failure to perform as expected.
2. Loss of reputation or credibility for the people or companies involved in the project. This will then show as increased difficulty in getting further work, leading to the closure of the company.
3. Reduced career opportunities for the development staff. In the extreme case it could result in unemployment if a series of failures are found in the system.
4. Loss of social and family life as staff spend more time at work trying to meet increasingly improbable deadlines because good health and happy marriages have been destroyed by runaway projects.

Quality Through Technology

One of the major problems afflicting Indian industry today, is technical obsolescence. It is unfortunate that we are considerably behind the technological frontiers, and unless urgent measures are taken to modernise, we will only fall back further. High costs and paucity of capital restrict investment in research and development, despite our possessing the third largest bank of scientific talent in the world. Despite adversities, India has made significant progress over the last four decades, and today, is competent enough to manufacture some of the most sophisticated products, albeit at higher cost and often, to lower quality standards. Both the Government and industry acknowledge the urgency of undertaking modernisation programmes to improve quality and reduce costs. We should invest more in R&D to develop our own technologies in order to close the technology gap.

We are witness to a rapid pace of technological growth and development in industry the world over. The current pace of technological progress is bound to create some very difficult issues for business management. The way a company manages technology will have significant implications on its long-term existence. It would be pertinent, while considering technological growth, to examine the choice of technology in relation to the phase of the company's existence. Instead our immediate concern shall lie in the development of key technologies, focussing on process development, product innovation, product improvement and product range. This computer industry, technologically, is a precision industry. The use of complex electronic devices, therefore, is making the technology increasingly more precise and sophisticated. Now the process control equipment ensures consistent quality to the consumer. The revolutionary development of the computer chip permits function enrichment of many conventional products and processes. More importantly, they make possible whole new families of products. The more glamorous areas of IT, such as artificial intelligence, will soon be affecting our lives in a more profound way.

Quality Through Clean and Safe Environment

High quality products cannot be produced in a mismanaged work-place. The investment in upgradation of plant, machinery and production processes must be preceded by the task of achieving a clean work environment.

Similarly, a safe workplace is a prerequisite to quality of human performance. Good safety standards must necessarily be achieved through management attitude and worker education. It is not uncommon to find management giving scant attention to building "safety first" measures into plant, machinery and work practices. Accidents tend to be recorded and explained away rather than avoided through meticulous planning, training and adherence to stipulated practices. Often this would involve keeping the pathways clean, protecting personnel from moving parts of machinery, keeping extraneous parts away from the workplace and giving special attention to movement systems and fire hazards. Managers are tempted to dismiss a zero-accident rate as impossible to achieve statistically, yet the acceptance of anything less tantamounts to tolerating fatal mistakes and an acknowledgement of failure even before having started.

Quality Through People

In a scenario where economic growth is fuelled by technological progress, the effective constraint is likely to be the mismatch between traditional skills and the new skills in interfacing between the machine and the users. The growth of demand for adjustment will be formidably fast. The growth of supply of adjustment through education multi-skill training and reduction in working time is very prompt in the most adaptable and successful companies.

The companies that tend to lead the way are those in which management keeps its employees informed in advance of the options the company faces and involves them in the formation of corporate plans. An enlightened approach to trade union activities, coupled with the active support and cooperation of the recognised unions will significantly contribute towards ushering in the changes which are required in process, plant and machinery work methods and computerisation and upgradation of skills at all levels of employees. Through these enlightened policies and bilateral long-term agreements, a unique relationship will be forged between management and workmen which will give stability and good reputation to the company. One of the emerging trends is the process of transition of the workforce from "loyal employees with traditional skills" to "committed employees with modern skills".

Risk Analysis

Risk analysis is important for management decisions. Risks associated with innovative engineering development are greater today than they have ever been. Over the last few years risk analysis has become a popular subject with industrial managers, and a number of software packages have emerged. However, the issues involved are not simple and no single method or package provides a complete answer.

Risks cannot be avoided. The world is in a state of constant change. To survive, a business must adapt to the changing world around it. Developing new products for sale on the open market is one of the most risky of all business activities, yet companies do it all the time. Despite the risks of failure in the market and the associated losses, the collective experience of manufacturing companies is that ceasing to speculate through the development of innovative products is actually a strategy with greater risks. Thus, a measure of risk taking is essential to success of business in a competitive world. A totally risk averse approach will stifle and in a long run, it will lead to the demise of the organisation. What distinguishes the good risk taker from the poor one is how well the risks are perceived at the outset and the quality of the decisions that are made to handle them. Business risks associated with technology system from investing in developing technological items.

Risk management is the practice of reacting to a perceived risk in such a way as to minimise the adverse consequences that may arise from it. A sound analytical approach to any risk situation should be the starting-point for the management action. The initial decision, whether or not to start in the first place, is the most momentous. This decision encapsulates the whole nature of the risk management problem. The risk analysis techniques can be divided into three broad categories, i.e., invest risks, strategy risks and conditional risks.

In the investment risks the principal determinant will be the expected benefit from the project against the expected cost.

Those techniques that deal with the risks associated with choices about the way that ventures are undertaken, are called "strategy risks". Those methods that deal with the risks associated with the conditions that actually arise during the course of the venture, are called "conditional risks".

"Zero-Defect" Performance

Mr. Philip B. Crosby, an international authority on quality management, is the propounder of the concept of "Zero-defects" which eventually replaced the conventional norm of "acceptable quality levels" in business.

In the USA, the awakening about quality came because of market infiltration by the Japanese and Germans.

Quality cannot be a normal part of a company's operation unless the leader has a personal philosophy of quality management which says, "We will deliver defect-free products and services to our customers and coworkers, on time". Systems such as ISO 9000 and awards such as the Baldridge criteria have little use in creating a quality culture in the company.

The word "quality" means conforming to agreed requirements. Personnel in an organisation, whether manufacturing, service, government, etc., must be able to count on each other to do what has been agreed. The customer can only be made successful by providing what has been promised to them.

"Zero defect (ZD)" is achieved when an organisation takes creating requirements very seriously, selects and trains people to meet them and encourages ZD performance by appreciating it.

The first principle of quality management is prevention and not cure. The vital importance is of focussing on the highest standard of quality. The obsession with "Zero defects" is still an alien notion to most people who are willing to live with a large margin of error and inefficiency. Those who are used to such complacency find it disconcerting to discover that even a margin of error of one per cent can often imply loss of millions . If all professionals pursue the ideal of ensuring ZD the world would be a very different place to live in. Even if that ideal cannot be easily attained in many walks of life, the pursuit of quality as a virtue and a necessity is a message that Indian industries must imbibe. Attitudes to quality cannot be changed through policy statements by the government or any opinion making body. It is a trait and had to be acquired from the earliest stages in one's education. Perhaps, if Indians begin now to cherish the value of ZD in a generation's time, India might succeed in winning the battle for quality.

Software Quality Management

With the progress of information technology, the amount of software products has been increasing and software has become an integral part of many electronic and electric systems. In future software industry will become the important sector of industry the world over. Developing a reliable software would determine the success of future products. National and international bodies such as USDOD, ANSI, BSI, IEEE have been active in production of software engineering standards in order to achieve reliable software. International organisation for standardisation has brought out a document namely ISO 9000-3 as a guideline document for software quality assurance.

Each individual within the world of software systems development is expected to show initiative and not require fresh instructions at every move. If this initiative is to be successful, the individual must understand the goals to which the initiative should be applied. The skill of managing a group of people who are all expected to show initiative involves communicating the common purpose of the group to each member and ensuring that all the individual initiatives coalesce.

The important thing is to identify what is expected from the project and to communicate these expectations to all members of the team. The aim should be to determine what level of quality is required in the system and to establish controls which are appropriate to achieve that level of quality. Given clear goals and appropriate controls, the staff will be far more willing to apply the controls on their own initiative without management stress or pressure.

The perception of quality is very dependent on each individual's own role in the development and use of the system. The developer will be looking for a stable set of clear system requirements so that he knows what is expected of him. He will be looking for areas where he can apply his creative genius to solve system development problems without customer help. Under development the environment should be bug-free and as per the developer expectations. At the end of the development, the software produced by teams developing other parts of the system will be available when it is needed and will work exactly as defined in the specification so that the integration testing will run smoothly.

The buyer would like to explain briefly what he is looking for, how much he has available to spend and when he needs the system. When the system arrives, he expects it to be the one he thought he had ordered.

The user wants the system should be available whenever he needs it. It should match his normal way of working without putting any obstacles in his path. The system should be bug-free and should do everything in the way the user would expect.

The maintainer of the system would also like the system to be bug-free. It will be necessary to change the system occasionally so the maintainer will need to understand how the system works. Once the maintainer has read and understood the documentation, he will be able to design and implement the appropriate changes to the system. After the changes have been incorporated, the whole system will continue to work as expected.

To promote the cause of the Indian computer industry on the whole and to provide comprehensive information under one roof about computer users, hardware, software manufacturers, dealers, R&D and other organisations, computer zone has brought out a national directory of computer users.

Any company can fail if planning is based on projections of the past rather than the analysis of the future. For the success of a software company, there should be clear-cut priorities which are given below:

1. People are the most valuable assets of a company. Therefore respect for the individual is the primary axiom of the company. A work culture and work ethic should be evolved with emphasis on collective innovation and creativity. The management style should be characterised by delegation of authority with responsibility.
2. The company should give continuous training in development of software programs, project management, interpersonal skills and foreign languages. In fact, there should be strict adherence to total quality management.
3. Excellence should be the only criterion in the recruitment drive. Excellent workers should be encouraged by offering the right opportunity at the right time.

The government is formulating ambitious plans for mounting a computer software export drive based on the World Bank funded study of the sector commissioned by the department of electronics.

International Organisation for Standardisation

Since the beginning of 1992, at least 24 surveys of quality management practice have been published in the U.K. The Science & Engineering Policy Studies Unit (SEPSU) has published a report which is based on a careful analysis of large data collected from varied sources. This analysis deals with the standards-based approach to quality systems, i.e., ISO 9000, with TQM, and several other approaches to systematic quality management including some like benchmarking and self-assessment. Both large and small companies, and manufacturing and service sectors, are included. Over 30,000 companies have been registered to ISO 9000 in U.K. (more than in France or Germany). Many customers use ISO 9000 registration as a filter for judging potential suppliers. The most significant benefits of ISO 9000 registration come from its role in stimulating cultural change, both in terms of the internal dynamics of the company and in terms of how the company relates to its suppliers and its customers.

The ISO-9000 series of standards are based on the Supplier's quality system assessment. While ISO-9000 applies to virtually any industry, there are special interpretations of the ISO clauses for software developers. This is the present form of ISO-9000. For example, Datamatics Ltd. was given ISO-9001 Certificate for manufacturing Strategic Business Units and Micro Shoes Company was given ISO-9002 certificate. New authorises of ISO-14000 standards have been started. ISO-14001 Environment certificates were given to INDALIS Dungmenwadi, Loherdaga Mines and Hirakund Power Plant.

A small company has the same need as any big company for an effective approach to quality management. Implementation, however, does need to be simplified with continuous improvement. Successful implementation of a program of quality management demands close attention to company culture and to its changes. Agents for cultural change include role models, quality awards, systematic self-assessment, bench-marking and partnership sourcing. Besides these, human factors, ungrudging commitment of time and other resources are also important. Periodically repeated quantitative self-assessments provide a remorseless measure of progress made by a company. A further agent for cultural change is education and training. There are some encouraging developments in the technology and management disciplines.

The International Organisation for standardisation is worried about the dilution of the ISO 9000. About 45,000 ISO 9000 certifications have already been issued so far all over the world. The Geneva-based federation of national standards institutes has registerd the ISO 9000 family of standards as "registered and protected trademarks" in member countries. Once ISO 9000 is registered as a trademark in ISO's 100-odd member countries, the world body expects to have a better grip on the manner in which it is being used at present. For better control, ISO committees have given task force to Quality Systems Assessment and Recognition (QSAR) group which will lay down stringent norms on the use of ISO service.

The national quality systems registrar, an ISO 9000 certification body in India, has signed a memorandum of understanding with Britain's oldest quality system certification body, the SIRA certification services recently.

The saga of ISO 9000 in India has come a long way. From a mere handful of companies certified in 1990, today there are over 300 companies which have achieved this unique distinction. This elite group includes giant public sector companies, Government owned factories as well as small food processing companies. Initially ISO 9000 used to be seen as a competitive advantage. Gone are the days when the certification used to be a passport for exports into EEC. Today besides this export objective, organisations are very keen to build a strong quality foundation for their business processes. Now ISO 9000 is being seen as a harbinger of the better future. More than 1000 Indian companies are expecting to receive ISO 9000 certification by 1995-96.

Conclusion

For building an organisation based on solid concepts requires a good leadership with an agenda, a philosophy of quality and a comfortability in dealing with people from anywhere in the world. Do not blame the culture. Get your workers to do what you want them to do, help them to achieve it, till defect-free becomes a mindset. Quality has become essential in a competitive environment. Quality does not mean the philosophy of finance but is conformist to requirements. It is necessary to reengineer your strategies continuously and do not get locked in one script.

Quality comes from leadership. The purpose of quality management is to establish an operating practice where all the transactions of the company are accomplished completely and where relationships with the employees, suppliers and the customers are aimed at making these people successful.

Quality management alone and not control, can bring about a change in the mindset of people to accept the concept of ZD quality aimed at doing things right the first time itself. There are four quality absolutes, namely, conforming to the stipulated requirements, prevention and not detection, zero defects and cost saving.

Use of ISO 9000 is much more widespread in the U.K. than in other countries and has grown rapidly in recent years. ISO 9000 can bring real benefits if used intelligently. An infrastructure of assessors, certifiers, accreditors and consultants has grown up around the standard so that customers can be assured about claims made by the suppliers about their quality management. U.K. companies now spend £80 million per year on ISO 9000 certification fees alone.

It is high time to start emphasising on quality of life, in general, rather than confining the concept of quality to the industrial sector. By and large, Indian people are conscious of quality but the problem is in its implementation. Americans talk much more of quality while the Japanese talk less but put in into practice. Indian workers can be motivated to a large extent by a leadership committed to quality.

15

Automatic Control and Robots

The work on the problems of developing and introducing automatic manipulators was started in the late 1940s. However, the robots of 40s and 50s were expensive, technically inadequate and could do only simple jobs. Now the robots are becoming more and more sophisticated.

The first generation robots were programmable and memory controlled. Those of the second generation have hand and eye coordination control through machine vision. Third generation robots will be factory intelligence controllers and could even provide artificial intelligence to help solve problems in factories.

Computers too have become an integral part of the construction industry. They are used to determine the plan best suited for a client, for calculating the shadows cast by buildings, for anti-seismic design calculations, for drawing perspectives and for designing the electrical systems.

Automation and Robot Development

Japan, USA and some other countries in Europe which have rapidly taken to automated manufacturing system have enormously profited from it in the international market. Aided by Computer Aided Design (CAD), Computer Aided Manufacturing (CAM) and Flexible Manufacturing Systems (FMS), the performance of the production systems in these countries, of high quality and cost effective. The CAD, CAM and the FMS systems can produce a much more wide range of products at relatively low costs. The application of these automatic systems in production creates flexibility in the product-mix, versatility in the production processes, lessens the costs and increases the quality of the products by reducing the errors.

In the West, as well as in Japan, robots are fast following computers from the workplace into home. They are already used to entertain children as well as adults. Soon they will be singing, dancing and telling jokes and taking effective control of all electronic entertainment equipment. They will turn on the TV, select the right compact disc, switch on the stereo, turn up the volume, take a phone call, act as a security guard, companion or servant as you wish.

In the USSR (now Russia), the number of robots installed during 1976 to 1980 were over 7000. By 1983, the production of robots grew to 10,700 pieces a year. A report gives the number of robots in use worldwide in 1987 as 1.2 lakh : Japan-67000, USA-14000, West Germany-6600, France-3400, Italy-2700, the UK-2600, Sweden-2400 and Canada-700.

Robots Scenario of India

The Science Advisory Council to the Prime Minister (SAC-PM) in its perspective plan for 2001 AD, states "Industrial robots are being increasingly used in several engineering applications including manufacturing. Tasks such as welding, spray-painting, material handling and assembly constitute the major uses of robots on the factory floor. Recent advances in machine vision and expert systems, and their use in development of intelligent robots have made robots versatile and integrated parts of the automated factory."

Assembly robots, industrial robots, automated guided vehicles, CNC (computerised numerically controlled) machines, conveyor systems, local area networks and communication media are yet to make an impact in most of the industrial environments in the country.

With further advances in artificial intelligence, robots will be eventually able to learn, to reason, and even make decisions. Personal robots will become as common as personal walkmans in the not so distant future. Perhaps, soon robot specialists will out-perform human doctors in cases involving difficult diagnoses.

In 1963, the Hyderabad Science Society put on display WALROBO, the wholly indigenously made remote-control robots. In

1964 two researchers at the Indian Institute of Technology, Bangalore, developed an industrial robot with limited intelligence. This robot could look around and find a particular type of item in a restricted area. The Bhabha Atomic Research Centre (BARC), Bombay developed robot and other material handling equipment for nuclear applications. This robot could move around and perform operations in reactor maintenance, decontamination and decommissioning of nuclear facilities. BARC also gives details of the remote-handling systems developed and deployed at the various nuclear plants manned by the Department of Atomic Energy (DAE). Remote handling systems are imperative in nuclear establishments. The objective here is to build robot-centred plant through indigenous manpower and resources. This will demonstrate the integration of machines, electrical devices and controllers, computer hardware and software, synchronised conveying systems, etc. resulting in automated and readily reprogrammable robot workstations.

TELCO has also developed the industrial robot through imported technology. Electro-Pneumatics and Hydraulics India developed ELECTROROBOT which was the star attraction at the IMTEX exhibition in 1986.

Robot development is definitely a big-money operation. The Indian Machine Tools Manufacturers Association admits that only in giant companies robots can get enough job-feed. BHEL, HMT and BEML have got robot manufacturing licences. Robots development technology and automation will definitely create more challenging occupations.

The Indian Army engineers have introduced a robot for carrying out reconnaissance in the field areas and for detection and destruction of mines and explosives, devices which will minimise sapper casualties. The robot acquired from the UK had proved its mettle during the operation in Sri Lanka to curb the LTTE guerrillas.

An Electro-Mechanical robot innovated by Ashish Panwar, a 16-year old Lucknow student has gained entry into the first international Robot Olympics held in September, 1990. This robot keeps a count on the number of people entering the premises it is guarding. An arm fixed on its head sounds people inside the building when it starts to rain.

Later on this robot will be developed to perform functions as varied as drilling, spray painting, counting, cleaning, preparing horoscopes and even activities across a fast food counter. Ashish's robot was the only Indian entry into Olympics.

Introduction of robots and computers, will not lead to job displacement but generate more employment and boost the economy, especially in the country like India, according to Prof. Robert Ayers of Carnegie Mellon University, USA.

Robots for Fast Progress

If robotisation in manufacturing is not encouraged, foreign competition will make inroads creating problems of industrial unemployment which will later on lead to severe financial crises like budget deficits and adverse balance of payments.

Very logically the growth of robots is encouraged in an environment where there is high growth rate, low level of unemployment, low inflation, low interest rates and shortages of labour and industrial skills.

Robots and computers would increase production, ensure quality, reduce prices, create competition and generate more employment. Apart from industries computer are being employed in banks, airlines and railways, etc.

The Force of the Future

Robots are being used in many industries for some time. Robots are now being introduced in the building trades. They are used to spray cement and other material on steel structures of high-rise buildings to protect them from fire. Many high-rise buildings are using robots frequently in the construction work.

Robots could be used for deep mining, repairing leaks in nuclear power stations, fighting fires and in fuel reprocessing plants and toxic waste facilities.

Cook hamburgers, set and clear a table, make a bed, knit a sweater, tune up a car or fix a simple puncture; these are but some of the chores a future generation robots could do for us.

Man vs Robot

God made the man and man made the robot.

During the last decade, many models of our intelligent biological system have appeared. Each was designed to function the way our brain and nervous system functions. The intelligent biological model is called the artificial neural system model. This module uses a representation of a single human neuron and the interactions between neurons as a basis. In classical artificial intelligence, experts are used to supply their own tested methods and knowledge to give the computer the basis for appropriate answers for a specific domain. A system constructed by the contribution of each expert is called an expert system. A neural system learns directly by interacting with the domain. It does not need any expert knowledge about the domain. Given enough time and experience, the neural system will learn everything about the domain.

The type of programming used to provide a robot with explicit instructions sets for assembly, control, navigation or other tasks must rely heavily on position feedback mechanisms. As a result, sophisticated robot programing languages have finally evolved that can utilise position feedback signals as a form of direct input from within the system itself. The WAVE language is used in controlling two robot manipulators by alternating control from one to the other. In this way, simultaneous movement is emulated. A new language AL is developed which is a combination of WAVE and Algol. This enables programers to control the simultaneous motion of the two manipulators. A more efficient language PAL is developed which provides a refined manipulator movement and a stronger control structure. Today, Pascal has become one of the most popular robot programing languages.

A Japanese company has developed a new computer system called, "neurocomputer" resembling the human brain which is capable of learning certain functions without complicated software programs. This computer uses large-scale integrated chips to achieve a processing speed four times faster than a supercomputer and about 500 times faster than a typical engineering workstation.

The brain of a man promotes creativity, imagination and intuition.

Also it prompts logic and analysis. It is not possible to put all these functions in the man made robot.

Conclusion

Japan and USA have taken to robots manufacturing on a large scale. Several countries in Europe are going on to robots on a massive scale led by countries like Sweden and Germany.

Robotics and robotisation are at the threshold of a very fundamental change in manufacturing and productivity levels, in industrial and management policies. The role and status of the nations in the industrial markets will depend to a significant degree on successful development and installation of systems of equipment for automatic manufacturing.

Robots have become synonymous with high productivity in the industrialised nations. They can venture into deep sea and underground, high altitudes and mountain terrains, cold climates and nuclear reactors.

Appendix A

News in Focus

1. E-Mail Explosion: In 1993, North American businesses sent almost 6 billion electronic mail messages. If each message had 50 words, it would be like sending 1000 manuscripts the length of *War and Peace* everyday.

2. Over 9.6 million go cellular in 1995: More than 9.6 million customers started using a mobile phone in 1995, bringing the total USA users up 40 per cent to 33.8 million. According to Cellular Telephone Industry Associations (CTIA) president, Thomas Wheeler, in one year, we added as many customers as we did in the first nine years of the industry. Annual revenues reached $ 9 billion, up by 34 per cent from a year earlier, and 13 per cent of US citizens are now users.

3. Intelligent Network Services: The Mahanagar Telephone Nigam Ltd. (MTNL) will introducc intelligent network service in Bombay by 1996, to facilitate calls through credit cards among other benefits. The value added high-tech IN services are toll free service, premium rate services, and Virtual Private Network (VPN). Credit card calling facility would enable a subscriber to make a telephone call from any available telephone line (including public call offices) without spot payment of charges. The charges for the call including long distance calls, would be debited to the subscriber's account or to his credit card.

4. Hand-held satellite phone is coming: An important step in that direction has been taken in 1996 with the launching of one of the world's most advanced mobile communications pay-loads in the first of Inmarsat's third generation satellites. Eight times more powerful than Inmarsat's two satellites, the new system architecture enhance the transmission power while reducing the onboard power demand.

A unique feature of the Inmarsat 3 is the seven spot beams in addition to one global beam. A spot beam concentrates power on a small area within the satellite's footprint, depending on the intensity of the telecommunications traffic. The savings on mass and energy, increased transmission power and higher performance means the world is getting closer to the hand-held satellite phone. The new satellite promises more to the existing and potential customers on ships, aeroplanes and on land.

The five third-generation Inmarsat satellites will expand the service and bring down the cost of communication services which will be available through more economical and smaller mobile terminals. Inmarsat-3 will make it possible to introduce Inmarsat-M phones the size of an A4-laptop with new features found in cellular systems such as smart cards, short message service and voice mail.

The international organisation of which India is a member will launch smaller Inmarsat-C terminals for users in peacekeeping, relief work and the news media. One can expect more live TV reports from the battlefronts. It will introduce Aero-1, a new mobile voice and data service using smaller, lighter and less expensive avionics equipment and antennas designed for aircraft. Inmarsat is to launch shortly a new messenger/pager service.

Inmarsat has 79 member countries and uses a global system of eight satellites to provide mobile communications at sea, on land and in the air. More than 59,000 customers in 135 countries communicate via the Inmarsat system. The customer base is growing by 1000 each month. Inmarsat has established a separate company, ICO, to provide services to pocket phones through a system that will use 10 satellites in intermediate circular orbit.

5. Cisco launches Internet Servers: The US-based $2 billion Cisco systems has launched an extended range of Internet and remote access servers and dial-up products (April, 1996).

The products and services offer new "breakthroughs" in remote access for Internet Services Providers (ISPs), telecommunications carriers as well as home users.

6. Apple Computer to Unveil Windows-friendly Macs: Apple Computer Inc. is set to launch a flurry of new products offering greater compatibility with Microsoft Corp's windows operating system (April, 1996). Customers can run more software on Apple than on any other PC.

7. Bell Atlantic and NYNEX Merger: NYNEX Corp and Bell Atlantic Corp agreed to a $52 billion merger to create a "Super Bell" (April, 1996) which will be the second largest USA telecommunications company. However AT & T would remain by for the largest USA telecommunications firm, worth $75-80 billion. The new Bell Atlantic NYNEX would be a dominating force in local telecommunications in the north-east of the United States, reaching from Maine to Virginia. It will have 38 million phone lines in 13 states and the District of Columbia. The two companies hope to exert a global influence particularly in Asia, where NYNEX has a 13.5 per cent stake in Telecom Asia of Bangkok and Bell Atlantic has a 24.8 per cent share in Telecom Corp. of New Zealand.

8. AT & T develops US-Russia fibre-optic link: AT & T Corp is offering point to point fibreoptic communications for private line service between the United States and Russia. AT & T's ACCUNET Digital Service to Russia will be the first point to point terrestrial fibre-optic link from anywhere in the United States to St. Petersburg and Moscow. The service will offer connectivity from 64 Kilobits per second up to 2.048 megabits per second.

9. IBM speech features in OS/2 Warp: IBM will unveil a new version of its OS/2 Warp operating system that allows users vocal commands to their PCs. With its speech technology, a PC user can give commands, dictate memos and even navigate the Internet.

SPACE FEAT BY HANDS

Commonsensical use of base hands by astronauts in times of crisis situations has saved many a crucial space mission from ending in near disaster. Space scientists, engineers and other specialists have no doubt forged ahead by leaps and bounds in space exploration, enabling manned lunar landing and unmanned missions to nearby planets of Mars and Venus. Some artefacts have even been hurtled beyond the solar system itself, but at the back of them all man's hands or rather his manual controls have stood him in good stead. The dramatic rescue of a stranded communications satellite (May 1992) by three space walking astronauts of the space shuttle endeavour once again demonstrated the ingenuity of manual operations over other hi-tech gadgets. For two days the astronauts struggled to retrieve the wayward satellite using the shuttle's 50 ft long robot arm, but to little avail. In desperation the astronauts made a last ditch attempt the third time using only their gloved hands. They not only succeeded in grabbing the 4000 kg satellite orbiting the earth at 17,500 miles per hour, but also managed to propel it after attaching to a rocket motor into its required 22,300 miles high orbit.

This is not the first time it has happened to spaceman. At the time of the momentous first manned landing on the moon in July 1969, the computer on board the lunar module guiding the lander's last stages of soft landing on the lunar surface started showing altitude that appeared at variance with what Neil Armstrong could notice from the window. He was commanding the module and if he had relied on the computer data the module would have ended up landing on a lunar rock seriously damaging the craft and making their return journey impossible. Armstrong's quick reflexes and his use of manual controls to negotiate the soft landing on a plain surface saved the situation at the nick of time. So, too, proved the fate of the jinxed Apollo 13 lunar mission, which could have ended in a certain disaster had not the astronauts improvised many commonsense approaches to bring back the faulty spacecraft to earth. And most of the operations involved the use of bare hands at the most crucial moments.

THE SPIN-OFFS OF SPACE RESEARCH

The space programme has given the world much more than moon rocks and glimpses of Saturn's rings. The earthbound have NASA to thank for lighter tennis rackets, more absorbent diapers and cordless power tools.

The ingenuity that allows astronauts to work in space's extreme temperatures and weightlessness is also responsible for the digital graphics, the cordless vacuum and computer software for makeup applications.

The shiny, metallic material known as Mylar that covers most satellites and other space vehicles was invented to shield against radiation. On earth, sunbathers use it to promote tanning and marathoners wrap themselves in it for warmth after a run.

The composite materials developed for stronger, less cumbersome spacecraft gave the American consumer a lighter, more powerful tennis racket. Boots that Neil Armstrong wore to take the first steps on the moon in July 1969 were bound by a set of interlocking plastic coils that can be found today in millions of running shoes to provide cushion impact to the joints.

Freeze-dried foods like cheese omelettes and sliced peaches that saved astronauts space and weight now perform the same function for hikers.

Computer-enhanced photo maps helped NASA choose a landing site for the first manned lunar mission. The software that assigns numbers to the contours of the surface of the moon now allows cosmetics companies to track the topography of a customer's face for facials and make-up application.

Scientists created a joystick to help astronauts in clumsy spacesuits drive the Apollo Lunar Rover over the moon's surface. Today, paraplegics use the single-handed mechanism in cars for steering, accelerating and braking.

Superabsorbent diapers, scratch-resistant sunglasses, cordless power tools and the household lubricant known as WD-40 are some of the more lucrative spinoffs of space technology.

Satellite Phone

The International Maritime Satellite Organisation (INMARSAT) launched the smallest global mobile satellite phone system in India, as part of its global launch to enable communication between any two places in the world.

Landing on Moon

The history of human endeavour is aglow with barriers that constantly challenge the human spirit to rise, shine and conquer.

Fuelled by the driving force of grit, determination and an all consuming passion to conquer the unattainable, the American Astronauts Neil Armstrong and Edwin Aldrin in 1969, fired the first salvo. The young astronauts broke through every single barrier of the past to land on the moon. On 20th July, 1969, Neil Armstrong said, "That's one small step for a man, one giant leap for mankind". When he stood on the moon, he saw a world without borders.

Cellular Phone

Cellular phone is the power to keep people in touch. In a world where the pace of business is accelerating every minute, one has to be on the move. One cannot afford to miss an opportunity just because he cannot be physically present there. Who says you cannot be in two places at the same time? Cellular phone helps you to be in two places at the same time. Yes, cellular phone gives you Quality Time. Time you had previously written off. Time that is now completely in your control. Therefore, you get the maximum out of every minute of your day.

Microsoft to Launch Internet

The Internet facility enabling customers to increase the effectiveness of their business management systems would be released by the Microsoft in Bombay (PTI news 23rd June, 1996). Intranet, the combination of the Internet and the PCs with existing computing environment, would develop a new generation of more powerful, flexible and cost-effective Intranet solutions. Intranet would have an immediate and dramatic impact on the business over the next few years.

AT & T, Microsoft Announce Internet Alliance

Telecommunication giant AT & T Corp and software superpower Microsoft Corp announced that they would jointly promote and distribute Microsoft's Web browser, Internet Explorer 3.0, and AT & T's internet service, World Net. The alliance was another plus for Redmond, Washington-based Microsoft's effort to displace Netscape Communications Corp's Navigator Web browser as the software for accessing the burgeoning Web, the graphical, point-and-click section of the Internet (27-07-96).

ET on Internet

The *Economic Times* is now available across the globe on the Internet. Situated at htt//wwwp:www.economics times. Com. on the I-Way, The *Economic Times* site provides from July 22, 1996, complete coverage of each day's news as it appears in all its printed editions as well as analyses, features, editorial articles and market quotations. Access to the contact-rich site is being offered free at present. The *Economic Times* is the largest financial daily in the eastern part of the globe and the second largest in the world. From Hong Kong and Singapore to London and New York, international investors are increasingly using ET as a reference point in an increasingly competitive environment.

Microsoft will Modify Software

Microsoft Corporation on 26th June, 1996 announced the introduction of modified versions of many of its popular software programs such as Windows, which will allow existing computer users to access the Internet easily. The focus is on Windows and efforts are on to evolve it into the best platform for browsing information.

The advanced version will incorporate Internet connectivity tools. At present computer users have to buy specialised software such as Netscape, Browser, etc. to get hooked on to the Internet. The Windows Internet platform will unify Web pages and office files over the Internet and simplify connectivity to the network by just a single mouse click.

Indian Software Industry

The Indian software industry recorded an exceptionally good performance during 1995-96, with the total turnover showing an increase of 61 per cent and exports growing at 64 per cent. Total sales for the year 1995-96 were Rs. 4190 crore, while exports amounted to Rs. 2520 crore. The domestic software market sales grossed Rs. 1670 crore. During 1995-96, 104 companies out of the Fortune 500 companies outsourced their software requirement to India. This clearly established how companies around the world derive competitive advantage through alliances with Indian software companies. So far 41 Indian software companies have achieved ISO 9000 standards.

TCIL, Fujikura pact on Optical Fibres Unit

A memorandum of understanding has been signed on August 9, 1996 between Telecommunications Consultants India Ltd. (TCIL), and Fujikura Ltd. of Japan for the manufacture of Optical Fibre Cables (OFC) by Tamil Nadu Telecommunications Ltd. (TTL). OFC are being increasingly preferred for telecom needs in India and abroad.

Achievements of Indian Ministry of Communications (up to 1996)

1. The number of Telephone Exchanges has gone up to over 21,000.
2. The number of villages having telephones has gone up to over 2 lakhs, with about 20 lakhs connections in rural areas.
3. The number of stations connected with STD facility has gone up to over 10,000.
4. The number of public telephones has increased to over 2.9 lakhs.
5. To put Indian business and industry on the fast track, a vast array of value added telecom services are being provided, including ISDN facility in major cities, E-mail, Voice Mail, INET, a Packet Switched Public Data Network and a Remote Area Business Message Network and Gateway to Internet services.

   In addition, with the participation of private enterprise, the Indian telecom network now provides world-class innovative facilities like Cellular Mobile Phones, Radio Paging, Video Conferencing and Data communication using VSATs.
6. In the 9th Five Year Plan, it is proposed to introduce several new services like personal communication services, Home & Tele-banking, etc.

Motorola, IBM launch enhanced chip: Motorola Inc and IBM Corp said they launched enhanced versions of the Power PC 603e microprocessor, including a 24OMHz version. The 240 MHz version is the highest speed volume microprocessor for portable and desktop computers, the companies said. They will be manufactured by both companies. Motorola's RISC microprocessor division said the 603e microprocessors- 240 and 225 MHz-are immediately available. They are priced at $425 for the 240 MHz version and $346 for the 225 MHz, when purchased in quantities of 1,000.

Frontier invests $2 bn in fibre network: Long distance and local telephone company Frontier Corp. said it is up to $500 million in a $2 billion fibre optic network being built across the United States. Frontier said it will be the largest fibre optic network built in the United States as a single project.

Indian IT Undermarketed

The world's leading management consultancy U.K. based Arthur D. Little, in its research on Indian IT industry has highlighted seven initiatives that it considers imperative for making it a world class and competitive industry. The seven suggestions include:

1. To bunch an integrated marketing plan.
2. Implement an industry-wide training and awareness programme.
3. Stream-line export processes and stimulate domestic demand.
4. Encourage industry clustering and collaboration.
5. Attract inward investment.
6. Strengthen transport and communication infrastructure.
7. Employ management information technologies.

India currently manufactures approximately $1.3 billion worth of IT product each year, and accounts for only 0.5 per cent of the total global market. The IT hardware industry currently employes 25,000 workforce and has the potential to employ at least 100,000 by the year 2000 and the total global market for IT hardware products is currently valued at $243 billion.

At present, the country has 350,000 PC's which is 0.6 per cent of world production. The hardware industry exports 34 per cent of its total production.

Videsh Sanchar Nigam Limited (VSNL)

Videsh Sanchar Nigam Limited (VSNL) is India's gateway to the world. In 1986 Overseas Communications Services (OCS) was converted to VSNL. VSNL completes 10 remarkable years in 1996. It has made rapid progress in the field of international telecommunications during these last ten years. As the successor to the erstwhile OCS, VSNL has been directly instrumental in placing India on par with world standards. It is made possible largely due to a deliberate shift in its outlook: That from being a government-owned monopoly to a customer-oriented market performer. Such a change in focus was bound to produce results. VSNL today, provides flexible global connectivity through satellites, submarine cables (optical fibre and co-axial) and terrestrial links. In a short span of ten years, it has become a global player offering one of the most comprehensive range of international telecommunication services which include:

1. International telephony, telex, telegraphy.
2. Home Country Direct Service.
3. Inmarsat "A", Inmarsat "C", Inmarsat "M", Inmarsat "B", Inmarsat High Speed Data (HSD) and Duplex High Speed Data Services (DHSD).
4. Gateway Electronic Mail Service (G-EMS-400).
5. Gateway INTERNET Access Services (G-IAS).
6. Concert Packet Services (CPS).
7. Gateway Packet Switched Services (G-PSS).
8. Gateway Electronic Data Interchange Services (GEDIS).
9. Intelsat Business Services (IBS).
10. International Private Leased Circuit Services (IPLCS).
11. International Television.
12. Video Conferencing Service.
13. Radio Photo.
14. Meteorological Broadcasts.

With an eye on the future, VSNL continues to upgrade existing networks with state-of-the-art technology and enhance its service portfolio through projects like:

1. Global personal hand-held satellite telephone service-1-Co (Inmarsat "P").
2. Inmarsat Mini - M.
3. SEA - ME -WE -3 optical fibre submarine cable system.

4. Fibre Optical Link Around the Globe (FLAG).
5. VSAT services.
6. Metro switches.
7. Setting up new Gateways.

The new decade (1996-2006), indeed augurs well for international telecommunications in India.

Inet

It sparks off a communication revolution by providing cost effective channel of high speed and reliable data communication for business houses, industries, corporate houses, software houses, information providers, banks, hotels, Airlines, Travel and Tourism agencies, importers, exporters, transporters, couriers, stock exchanges, credit card providers, etc.

(a) Types of access available

1. X.25 leased access at 2400, 4800, 9600, 19200 or 64000 bps.
2. X.28 leased access at 1200, 2400, 4800 or 9600 bps.
3. X.28 dial up access at 300, 1200, 2400 or 9600 bps.
4. X.32 dial up access at 2400, 4800, or 9600 bps as back-up to X.25 leased access.
5. "099 Access" (dial up) to INET from any city other than the cities with INET exchange.
6. Frame relay in major cities.

(b) Gateways

INET has both way connectivity to:

1. Remote Area Business Message Network (RABMN).
2. High Speed VSAT Network (HVNET).
3. Gateway Packet Switching System (GPSS).
4. Public Switched Telephone Network (PSTN).
5. INTERNET via VSNL gateway.

(c) Facilities Provided

1. Permanent Virtual Circuit.
2. Closed User Group.

3. Reverse Charging.
4. Fast Select.
5. Global Network User Identification.
6. Additional facilities as per CCITT's X.2 recommendations.
7. PSTN dial out facility for INET customers to call any computer connected to telephone lines on PSTN in cities with INET exchange.
8. Dedicated Dial-up service for creation of virtual private networks within INET.

(d) Applications

1. Electronic Mail Service.
2. Corporate Communications.
3. Information Retrieval.
4. Data Base Services.
5. Remote Job Applications.
6. Credit Card Verifications.
7. Travel Reservations.
8. Electronic Fund Transfer.
9. LAN TO LAN Connectivity.

PROGRESSIVE NETWORKS HUSTLES TO RULE WEB AUDIO

Michelle V Rafter

Progressive Networks wants to rule the world—the Internet world of sound.

The privately held Seattle-based company rose to fame as the creator of Real Audio, a so-called streaming-audio technology people use to tune in to live concerts, radio stations and other audible material on a Web site without having to download enormous sound files.

Although there are other streaming media companies, Progressive Networks is a standout.

Since Real Audio's debut in 1995, people have downloaded 8 million players or the software needed to use the technology available free on Progressive Networks' Web site (http//www.relaudio.com).

Players also come bundled with copies of Microsoft's Internet Explorer Web browser, and are one of the most popular helper applications for Netscape's Navigator browser.

Several thousand Web sites currently air 7,500 hours of programming a week using Real Audio servers, which begin at $500 each and run into the tens of thousands of dollars for systems that 'stream' to hundreds of listeners simultaneously.

None of this is good enough for Rob Glaser, the ex-Microsoft executive who used the considerable cash he made from Microsoft stock options to form Progressive Networks in 1994.

As Glaser learned at Microsoft, successful companies don't live by technology alone, but by combining technical savvy with business smarts.

So Glaser and his lieutenants-including a dozen fellow Microsoft alumni-are attempting to solidify their place in the market by constantly improving their technology base and building relationships with key partners.

It's a mission that's led to a number of announcements over the past few months, including.

* A pact with Netscape, which had also been developing audio standards. On October 14, the partners, and 38 supporters including Apple, Digital, Hewlett Packard and IBM, announced a compromise called Real-Time Streaming Protocol (RTSP) they hope will be adopted as the HTML of audio programming. The parties have submitted the RTSP proposal to an Internet rules body called the Internet Engineering Task Force, which is expected to take about six months to consider the issue.

* A next-generation multimedia technology called Real Media Architecture that, along with sound, will stream graphics, animation and eventually video to an Internet user's Real Media player.

* An upgraded Real Audio 3.0 that eliminates audio drop-outs and allows for near CD-quality sound over ISDN lines, and FM stereo sound over a 28.8 bps modem. Available in pre-release form presently, the final version of Real Audio 3.0 is due by year's end.

* Retail sales of Player Plus, an improved version of the free Real

Audio player that works like a car radio, with buttons that can be pre set to favourite Real Audio sites, and a scanner that trolls through 20 of 110 Web radio stations listed on Timecast (http// www.timecast.com), a Progressive Networks-produced Real Audio broadcast guide.

* Progressive Networks officials are excited about the Netscape deal. On its face, RTSP isn't sexy–"It's all internal gunk," says Progressive Networks president Bruce Jacobsen–but the long-term effect could be substantial.

"Once you have standardisation, all kinds of (content) people will jump in." Glaser said in an interview shortly after the announcement. "In five years, the Internet could have the same number of viewing hours as TV or radio. Someone can now build an Internet Walkman or Internet TV."

Paul Kagan Associates analyst Jae Kim sees RTSP and Real Media Architecture as stop-gap measures before cable modems hit the mainstream.

"Maybe you won't have 30 frames a second coming to your desktop, but you could see an image of someone with closed caption text coming to your PC," he said.

Net Radio CEO Robert Griggs isn't convinced Progressive Networks has the answer. (Reuter)

Appendix B

Abbreviation of Technical Terms

AGRIS : International Information Systems in Agricultural Sciences and Technology

APINESS : Asia-Pacific Information Network in Social Sciences

APINMAP : Asian and Pacific Information Network on Medicine and Aromatic Plants

ASTINEO : Regional Network of the Exchange of Information and Experience in Asia and the Pacific

ACS : Asynchronous Communicator Server

BIS : Bureau of Indian Standards

CRRERIS : Common-Wealth Regional Renewable Energy Resources Information Service

CCF : Common Communications Format

CDS : Computerised Documentation System

CII : Confederation of Indian Industry

CIS : Committee on Institutional Cooperation

CMC : Computer Maintenance Corporation

CTIC : Central Technical Information Centre

CCITT : The International Telegraph and Telephone Committee

CD-ROM : Compact Disc-Read only Memory

DESI-DOC : Defence Scientific Information and Documentation Centre

DEVSIS : Development Science Information System

DIS : United Nations Development Information System

DBS : Direct Broadcast Satellite

DEVINSA : Development Information Network on South Asia

DFS : Document Finding System

DOE : Department of Electronics

DOT : Department of Telecommunications

DST : Department of Science and Technology

ENVIS : Environmental Information Centre

ER-NET : Education and Research Network

GPSS : Gateway Packet Switching Service

INIS : International Nuclear Information System

INSDOC : Indian National Scientific Documentation Centre, New Delhi

INNERTAP : Information Network on New and Renewable Resources and Technologies for Asia and the Pacific

ITIB : Industrial and Technological Information Bank

ISO-NET : The International Standards Information Network, Geneva

ISDS : International Serials Data System

IDRC : International Development Research Centre, Canada.

IODE : International Oceanographic Data Exchange

ITI : Indian Telephone Industry, Bangalore

IIMC : Indian Institute of Mass Communication

INFLINET : Information and Library Network

ISBN : International Standard Book Number

ISI : Indian Standards Institute

ISIS : Integrated Set of Information Services

ISO : International Standards Organisation

ISSN : International Standard Serial Number

JANET : Joint Academic Network

LAN : Local Area Network

MAN : Metropolitan Area Network

NIC : National Informatics Centres

NISSAT : National Information System for Science and Technology

NACID : National Access Centre for International Data Centre

NCLIS	:	National Commission on Libraries and Information Science
NCSI	:	National Centre for Science Information
NDI	:	Network Device Interface
NICMAP	:	National Information System for Machine and Production Engineering
NRSA	:	National Remote Sensing Agency
NTIS	:	National Technical Information Service
OSI	:	Open System Interconnect
PIS	:	Patent Information System, Nagpur
PADIS	:	Pan-African Documentation and Information System
POPIN	:	Population Information Network
PSTN	:	Public Switched Telephone Network
PSDN	:	Packet Switching Data Network
PGI	:	General Information Programme
PID	:	Publication and Information Directorate
PSE	:	Packet Switching Exchange
PSS	:	Packet Switch Service
RAM	:	Random Access Memory
ROM	:	Read only Memory
SIC	:	Sectoral Information Centre
TIES	:	Technological Information Exchange System
TIPS	:	Technological Information Pilot System, Delhi
UNISIST	:	United Nations Information System in Science and Technology
UUNET	:	Unix User Network
WAN	:	Wide Area Network

[illegible] [illegible] Organisation of Library and Information [illegible]

[illegible] National Centre for Science Information

[illegible] [illegible]

[illegible] National Information System for [illegible]
[illegible]

[illegible] [illegible] Science Library

[illegible] National [illegible] Information [illegible]

[illegible] Open System Interconnection

[illegible] [illegible] System [illegible]

[illegible] [illegible] Information [illegible]

[illegible] Population Information Network

[illegible] Public Switched Telephone Network

[illegible] Packet Switched Data Network

[illegible] [illegible] Information [illegible]

[illegible] [illegible] and Information [illegible]

[illegible] [illegible]

[illegible] [illegible] Service

[illegible] Random Access Memory

[illegible] Read Only Memory

[illegible] [illegible] Information [illegible]

[illegible] [illegible] Information [illegible] System

[illegible] Technological Information Pilot System

[illegible] United Nations Information System in Science and
Technology

[illegible] [illegible] Network

[illegible] [illegible] Network

Appendix C

ADDRESSES OF TELECOMMUNICATION EQUIPMENT AND COMPUTERS VENDORS

1. National Panasonic India Pvt. Ltd.
   Systems Business Group
   M-61, Greater Kailash-II
   Commercial Complex
   New Delhi - 110 048
   Tel : 6219002-06, 6226448-50
   Fax : 6219001

2. Air Tel Connect
   A-10, Lajpat Nagar-II
   New Delhi - 110 024
   Tel : 6919700, 6919800, 6919900

3. DSS Mobile Communications Ltd.
   C-22, Richmond Chambers
   Safdarjung Development Area
   New Delhi - 110 016
   Fax : (011) 6969076

4. Essar Cellphone Sale and Service Centre
   South Extension-I
   N-5, Bajrang House
   New Delhi -110 049
   Phone : 4649301
   Fax : 4649300

5. Cambridge Technology Centre,
   Melbourn, Royston, Herts SG-8 6DP
   (UK)

6. NEC Technologies (UK) Ltd.
   Research and Development Centre
   Imperium, Imperial Way
   Reading RG - 2 OTD
   (UK)

7. Siemens Telecom Ltd.
   (A Joint Venture of Siemens and Bharti Telecom)
   Regional Office
   Delhi
   Tel : 011-6834463
   Tel/Fax : 011-6919485

8. PCL
   Nalin Chaudhary
   Access Manager
   Delhi
   Tel : 6446935, 6444358

9. Hewlett Packard Ltd.
   Cain Road, Bracknell
   Berkshire RG-12 IHN
   (UK)

10. Shape Technical Centre
    P.O. Box. 174
    2501 CD The Hague
    The Netherlands (Holland)

11. Philips Telecom Private
    Mobile Radio
    P.O. Box-24
    St. Andrews Road
    Cambridge CB-4 IDP
    (UK)

12. Compuaid Enterprises
    Communication Centre
    48 - M Block Market
    Greater Kailash - II
    New Delhi - 110 048
    Tel : 6462309, 6463068, 6482673
    Fax : 6444169, 6473018

13. TGK (India) Ltd.
    406-408, International
    Trade Tower, Nehru Place
    New Delhi - 110 019
    Tel : 6464441, 6472161
    6426433, 6465496
    Fax: 6466157

14. Punwire
    M/s. Karsun International Pvt. Ltd.
    B-338,CR-Park
    Delhi
    Tel: 6221445, 6475686

15. Akai Service Centre
    Baron International Ltd.
    36, Community Centre
    Basant Lok
    Vasant Vihar
    New Delhi - 110 057
    Tel: 6884142, 6883079, 6884447
    Sales: 6884445

16. Bitek Monitors
    Batra Electronics Ltd.
    302 Kirti Mahal
    19 Rajendra Place
    New Delhi
    Tel: 5745201
    Fax: 5740844

17. Synergy Systems
CB - 385 A, Ring Road
Naraina, New Delhi - 110 028
Tel: 5422278
Fax: 5703574

18. Stabiline Systems
D-15, Sector - 7
Noida, U.P.
Tel: 89-20413, 89-29153

19. Orbit Peripherals Pvt. Ltd.
C-29, Sarita Vihar
New Delhi - 110 044
Tel: 6910218, 6827007
Fax: 6820166

20. FSL, Delhi
Tel: 6418325, 6467829

21. Microsoft Corporation
Paharpur Business Centre
21, Nehru Place
New Delhi - 110 019
Tel: 6460694, 6460767, 6460813
Fax: 6474714

22. Indocon Micro Engineering Ltd.
A-5, Naraina Industrial Area
Phase-I, New Delhi-110 028
Tel: 5454245, 5438003
Fax: 5462841, 5472572

23. Adhite Electronics Pvt. Ltd.
C-37, Okhla Industrial Area
Phase-I, New Delhi - 110 020
Tel: 6814663, 6814665
Fax: 6814663

24. Macro Multimedia Systems Pvt. Ltd.
    A-36, Chittaranjan Park
    New Delhi - 110 019
    Tel: 6410206, 6411838
    Fax: 6468518

25. Moser - Baer (India) Ltd.
    63, Ring Road
    Lajpat Nagar - III
    New Delhi - 110 024
    Tel: 6844106, 6844109, 6832762
    Fax: 6838238, 6849544

26. Apple Computer
    Odin Computers India Ltd.
    Delhi
    Tel: 6857717, 6856701
    Fax: 6863306

27. E-Mail Service
    Indonet Manager, CMC Ltd.
    New Delhi
    Tel: 4623111-4
    Fax: 3746025, 6844652

28. Ericsson Telecommunications Ltd.
    Ericsson House
    New Delhi 110-062

29. Essar Cellphone Sales & Service Centre
    Barakhamba Road
    Ground Floor
    DCM Building
    New Delhi - 110 001
    Tel: 3716195, 3716197
    Fax: 3739942
    Mobile: 98-110 -90113

30. Motorola India Electronics Pvt. Ltd.
"The Senate"
No. 33 A, Ulsoor Road
Bangalore - 560 042
Fax: 91-080-5598660

31. Software Technology Group
International Ltd.
176, Gautam Nagar
Opp. Gulmohar Park
New Delhi - 110 049
Tel: 6965646, 6855669
Fax: 6963559

32. Escotel Mobile Communications Ltd.
23/7, Mathura Road
Ballabhgarh
Faridabad - 121 004
Fax: 232326

33. Siemens Telecom Ltd.
15th Floor, Devika Tower
6, Nehru Place
New Delhi - 110 019
Tel: 6448957, 6448959, 6463687, 6415769
Fax: 011-6462016

34. Infocom Network Ltd.
C-3, 2nd Floor
Main Shopping Centre
Vasant Vihar
New Delhi - 110 057
Tel: 600714, 679443, 6117499
664427, 6856178, 6515487
Fax: 6116213

35. Sunsoft
Tata Consultancy Services
Bangalore
Tel: 2260353, 2203323
Fax: 2250108

36. Trans American Information Systems
Kumar House No. 201
Central Market
D-Block
Prashant Vihar
New Delhi - 110 085
Tel: 7269911, 7268734
Fax: 7862033

37. Micro Processor Engineering
133, Hill Lane
Southampton, S01 5-AF
(UK)

38. Fibre Transmission Installations Limited
43, Sir Thomas Longby Road
Medway City Estate
Rochester, Kent ME-2 4DP (UK)

39. Oscar Quality Systems
Freepost RM-388
Rochford
Essex SS4 1-BR (UK)

40. SGS Yarslay
Quality Management Services
SGS House, Johns Lane
Tividale, Warley B-69 3-HX
(UK)

41. ABS Quality Evaluations, Inc.
16855 Northchase Drive
Houston, Texas 77060
(USA)

42. Quest Quality Consulting Ltd.
The Manor House
Farncombe Hill
Godalming
Surrey GU-7 2-AR. (UK)

43. Hewlett Packard India Ltd.
Paharpur Business Centre
21, Nehru Place
New Delhi - 110 019
Tel: 6472311, 6472328-30

44. Tata Consultancy Services
Lotus House
6, New Marine Lines
Sir Vithaldas Thackersey Marg
Mumbai - 400 020
Tel: 2039136
Fax: 2016689

45. RPG Paging Services Ltd.
4th Floor, Sangam Cinema Complex
Sector IX, R.K. Puram
New Delhi - 110 022
Tel: 6111025/6/7/8
Fax: 6111029

46. Dixon Utilities and Exports Ltd.
C-33, Sector - 57
Noida (U.P.)
Tel: 528624, 527814, 552234
Fax: 552880

47. CMS Computers Ltd.
CMS House, Plot No. 91
Street No. 7, MIDC Maro-l
Andheri (East), Mumbai - 400093
Tel: 022-8340041
Fax: 022-8364954

48. Internet Consortium India
59/9, Kalkaji
New Delhi - 110 019
Tel: 6477310, 6482027, 6215507
Fax: 6464229, 6215507

49. Videsh Sanchar Nigam Ltd.
Videsh Sanchar Bhawan
M.G. Road, Mumbai - 400 001
Tel: 91 (22) 2624020 , 91 (22) 2619632 (DID)
Fax: 91 (22) 2624027
Telex: 81(11) 82429 VSNH IN
Internet: helpdesk @ giasbm 01.Vsnl.net.in

50. Department of Telecommunications
Ministry of Communications
Government of India
Sanchar Bhawan
20, Ashok Road
New Delhi - 110 001

51. Mahanagar Telephone Nigam Ltd.
Jeevan Bharti Building, Tower - I
12th Floor
124, Connaught Circus
New Delhi - 110 001

52. Telecommunications Consultants India Ltd.
Chiranjiv Tower, 3rd Floor
43, Nehru Place
New Delhi - 110 019

53. Siemens Ltd.
Private Communication System Division
B-8, Jungpura B, Mathura Road
New Delhi - 110 014
Tel: 4694093, 4632379/2389
Fax: 4697281

54. Alcatel Business Systems (India) Pvt. Ltd.
Laxmi Complex
38/3, Lal-Bagh Road
Bangalore - 560 027
Tel: 91-80-2244721, 2276706
FAx: 91-80-2241684

55. Telerex Communications India Pvt. Ltd.
H-18, Masjid Moth
G.K.-II, New Delhi - 110 048
Tel: 6429811, 6445354, 6222153
Fax: 91-11-6460968

Appendix D

CAREER OPTIONS IN INFORMATION TECHNOLOGY

In the field of information technology (IT), there are numerous opportunities. The IT industry is growing at a very healthy rates of over 40 per cent and to make IT a key area in terms of our day to day operations, we need people who can understand the implications of IT and how it can be used in various facets of our lives. For this, we need skilled professionals who appreciate the use of IT, open-minded and perserving, and willing to put in hard work to see the results of implementation of IT.

In an open, liberalised environment, IT plays a very key role in organisations where, as organisations become flatter, it serves as a key differentiator by which organisational communications happen faster. It helps in faster decision making and improves overall effectiveness and reduces waste in the system thereby making our country a more globally competitive player.

IT can play a key role in transforming the Indian economy to be a globally competitive one. It is playing a key role in improving efficiency and effectiveness of our organisations. It is only possible when we have capable people manning key positions in the IT industry.

To ensure that for the next decade we have adequate number of skilled people we need to invest now in infrastructure relating to IT and also to in new emerging technologies. We need to focus on proper training methodologies so that people can start using IT in a more impactful manner.

To get ahead in the IT profession, people have to constantly be on the learning mode to learn developments in technology as well as software processes. They should have a mindset to constantly reskill themselves and also understand business issues on how IT can be used to leverage business advantage.

Professionals who are likely to succeed in the IT business are people who are analytical, persevering, and people who can put in high number of work hours per week.

Training methodologies which are the best are job oriented methodologies. It is not only critical to teach the concepts but it is fundamental to apply these concepts and learn on application intensive projects. Hence training methodology which combines conceptual knowledge along with application of the concepts in job oriented environments is the best.

The role of IT is to significantly change the common man's life. With consumer electronics, computers and communication technologies merging, there is going to be a whole lot of areas where computers will impact a person in his day to day life. Also new developments like Internet which is a global network of computers will change the whole way in which we communicate with the outside world and this will pose a lot of challenges for the IT professional in the coming decades.

Fourth generation language followed by object oriented programming has led to an unprecedented revolution. Multimedia usage has also led to unlimited possibilities of use of computers.

Technology and process in the IT industry change drastically, hence it is critical for a professional to learn and learn new methodologies. Corporate training is becoming an important part of activities with liberalisation.

There are gaps, particularly in the areas related to development methodologies and software quality process. These are addressed by software companies through in-house training programmes since some of the areas might be very specific to that organisation.

Each student who is entering the field of IT should be prepared to constantly learn and unlearn since technology as well as knowledge and skills become obsolete quite fast.

Career options in IT are software development, marketing, various support services and teaching.

Marketing of both software and hardware is a high growth area and requires technical skills as well as salesmanship. Teaching is an option that has vast opportunities in India. The most important attributes for a successful and effective teacher are presentation and behavioural skills.

If one wants to go in for software development, he has to be a team player, since software is generally developed in teams. One has to have excellent communication skills, and a proficiency in English, since most of computer literature is in English language. Among mental attributes, analytical ability and logical thinking are essential. For marketing jobs in IT, one naturally needs to be outgoing and confident, besides being technically up-to-date.

Appendix E

DEPARTMENT OF TELECOMMUNICATION (MINISTRY OF COMMUNICATIONS)

Telecom services have been recognized the world over as an important element in the socio-economic development. Accordingly DOT has formulated developmental activities for accelerated growth of the telecommunication services to the tune of 15 per cent to 20 per cent in the urban areas to meet the growing demands and taking the services to rural areas as a part of infrastructure development.

The main functions of the DOT include planning, engineering, installation, maintenance, management and operation of voice and non-voice telecommunication services all over the country. In addition, the department is also responsible for frequency management in the field of radio communication in close coordination with international bodies. It also enforces wireless regulatory measures for wireless transmission by users in the country.

Till March 1996, 980 new telephone exchanges were added. The switching capacity and direct exchange lines have been increased by 26.02 lakh lines and 21.83 lakh lines respectively. DOT has now achieved a network of more than 21152 telephone exchanges with 119.78 lakh telephone connections. Besides, new and value added services, such as Fascimile, Remote Area Business Message Network, Packet Switching Data Network, Electronic Mail, etc. have been further enhanced. A long distance transmission network consisting of over 1,68,756 RKMs of microwave, UHF, coaxial and optical fibre now serves the country. The objective of the department is to connect all the villages totalling about 603.6 lakhs. During the year 1995-96, connectivity has been achieved in respect of 31,496 villages. DOT has provided STD connectivity practically to all the District Headquarters and it is planned to extend the same to cover all the Sub-Divisional Headquarters. The network is getting automated rapidly.

The two basic thrust areas of the 8th plan (1992-97) are:

1. Rapid expansion of telecom network.
2. Transforming telecom network into a modern and most efficient one.

National Telecom Policy 1994 paved the way for private sector participation and funding to help achieve the objective of universal coverage at affordable prices by the end of 8th plan. The guidelines for private sector entry into basic telecom services have been announced. Companies providing basic telephone services will have to provide telecom service in rural areas also. Letters of Intent (LOI) have been issued to companies registered in India for providing basic telecom services in 5 service areas. Value added services have also been opened to private sector.

It is proposed to set up a statutory Telecom Regulatory Authority of India (TRAI). An ordinance for its establishment was promulgated on 27th January, 1996. A second ordinance was promulgated on 27th March, 1996.

In the area of consumer satisfaction, three main concerns are billing, fault repair and redressal of consumer grievances. This calls for attitudinal change in telecom functionaries and enforcement of action plans at the field level under the strict supervision of Area Managers.

SHOWING EXEMPLARY SPIRIT OF SERVICE SINCE 1947, DOT AND VSNL HAVE BEEN PROVIDING INTERNATIONAL TELECOMMUNICATION SERVICES FROM INDIA TO OTHER COUNTRIES OF THE WORLD

The Commitment Continues

With a spirit of service to the nation, DOT and VSNL have been constantly updating and expanding the telecommunication network thereby providing telecom facilities to every nook and cranny of India. The idea is to enable greater socio-economic interaction for every Indian citizen in the emerging global village.

Milestones Achieved

	1947	*1997*
• Telephone Exchanges	321	More than 21,000
• No. of Telephones (DELS)	0.82	130.33 lakh
• LDPCOs	338	Urban PCO about 4 lakh VPTs 2.28 lakh
• Rural Telephones		24 lakh
• Trunk Automatic exchange capacity	Nil	7.31 lakh lines
• STD Stations	Nil	11,697 with full coverage of Distt. Headquarters and 1142/1205 of Sub-Divisional Headquarters. i.e. about 95 per cent
• Type of Exchanges	Mostly manual and a few Electro-mechanical Automatic Exchanges	No manual telephone exchange. Mostly (96 per cent) Electronic Automatic
• Long Distance connection mode	Only telegraph messages	A variety of facilities, in addition to STD phone service, such as Telex, FAX, E-mail and Data Communication with global Access

A faster growth in telecommunications took place three decades after independence. In 1977 the number of telephones in the country was about 15 lakh which rose to 35 lakh by 1987 and it almost quadrupled in the next decade to reach 130 lakh.

There has been a tremendous transformation from the primitive manual and electromechanical systems of telephone exchanges to electronic analogue and digital systems with further advancement with the introduction of Integrated Services Digital Network and scores of value added services such as * Radio Paging * Cellular Mobile Telephone Service * Electronic Mail Service * Voice Mail/ Audiotex Service * 64 Kbps Data service using VSAT * Videotex Service * Video Conferencing * Public Mobile Radio Trunked Service * Credit Card Authorisation Service.

Long Distance Services

* Subscriber Trunk Dialing * Trunk Services.

Achievements of VSNL

Services

* Basic Services * Telephone * Country Direct Services * Telegraph Services * Specialised Services : Leased Line Services * Television Transmission * International networking via VSNL * Satellite Networks * International Business Services * Intelsat Internet Services.

INMARSAT Services

Submarine Optical Fibre Cables.

Value Added Services

* Data Services * Electronic Mail * Electronic Data Interchange * Easynet Service * Managed Data Services - GNS * GNS Dedicated Services * GNS Dial-Up Services * GNS Protocol Support.

INTERNET Services

New Services

* Frame Relay Services * Universal Connect

Glorious Five Years of VSNL at a Glance

Description	*1991-92*	*1992-93*	*1993-94*	*1994-95*	*1995-96*	*percentage (over previous year)*
INTERNATIONAL TELECOMMUNICATIONS						
Telephone Paid Minutes (million)	473.9	614.2	742.82	942.00	1147.56	21.82
Transit Telephone Paid Minutes (million)	0.098	0.31	1.39	4.64	6.70	44.40
Telex paid minutes (million)	42.1	38.67	30.99	24.19	20.40	(15.67)
Telegraph words (million)	44.8	39.77	28.84	24.47	21.14	(13.61)
Photo Telegraph in sq. cms. (million)	0.24	0.20	0.44	0.28	0.34	21.43
Television traffic (in minutes)	70955	55748	62159	99811	116683	16.90
Bureaufax (Pages)	190502	184000	133143	104233	80356	(22.91)
Data Transmission (GPSS)						
Minutes (in 000s)	1977	3522	4868	8673	7725	(10.93)
Segments (million)	100.75	182.5	215.0	439.33	560.86	27.66
Inmarsat Traffic						
Telephone ('000 mts)	-	754.25	1808.49	2249.82	2597.28	1[illegible].44
Telex ('000 mts)	-	346.57	770.04	929.53	982.52	5.70

GROWTH OF INTERNATIONAL CIRCUITS

Telephone Circuits	3331	4789	8520	11525	12873	11.70
Telex Circuits	1124	936	1039	1064	1128	6.02
Telegraph Circuits	39	39	39	38	38	Nil
Leased Telegraph Circuits	142	130	120	114	102	(10.53)
Leased Voice/Data Circuits #	98	91	81	72	54	(25.00)
Leased High Speed Data Circuits*	2	38	85	161	245	52.17
Satellite Circuits	2465	3749	6937	7702	8573	11.31
Cable Circuits (IOCOM, Gulf & Sea-Me-We-2@)	866	1040	1583	3781	4300	13.73

Including IBS circuits.

* Commissioned on 7.2.1992, 64 KBPS & above.

@ Commissioned on 1.6.1994.

Performance Indicator

	Items	Unit	1985-86	1986-87*	1987-88*	1988-89*	1989-90*	1990-91*	1991-92*	1992-93*	1993-94*	1994-95*	Percentage change over previous year
1.1	Direct Exchange Lines (DEL)	(000)	3165.8	3486.4	3800.8	4166.5	4589.5	5074.7	5809.9	6796.7	8025.6	9795.3	+22.05
1.2	Telephone Waiting List	(000)	985.7	1124.6	1287.1	1419.6	1713.4	1961.0	2287.0	2845.9	2496.8	2152.9	–13.77
1.3	Registered Demand	(000)	4151.5	4611.0	5087.9	5586.1	6302.9	7035.7	8096.9	9642.6	10522.4	11948.2	+13,55
1.4	DELs added annually	(000)	268.0	320.6	314.4	365.7	423.0	485.2	735.2	986.8	1228.9	1769.8	+44.01
2.1	Number of Telex Working Lines	(000)	30.5	34.0	37.3	41.3	44.5	46.7	48.6	49.1	47.2	43.9	-6.99
2.2	Telex Waiting List	(000)	2.8	2.8	3.5	2.5	2.5	2.8	3.3	2.4	1.6	0.8	–50.00
2.3	Registered Demand	(000)	33.3	36.8	40.8	43.8	47.0	49.5	51.9	51.3	48.8	44.0	–8.40
3.	Number of Telex Metered Call Units	(Lakhs)	2813.4	3583.5	3597.8	3887.0	4345.2	4704.6	4511.7	3886.1	3373.6	2875.0	–14.77
4.	Number of Telephone Metered Call Units	(Crores)	1382.4	1648.4	1933.4	2027.6	2153.9	2389.7	3060.3	4013.0	4672.4	5860.0	+25.42
5.	Number of Effective Trunk Calls	(Crores)	21.8	22.9	20.9	20.4	22.0	22.4	20.6	20.6	16.2	12.2	–24.69
6.	Number of Inland Telegrams Booked	(Lakhs)	761.0	742.2	735.1	690.9	704.5	641.0	651.3	645.8	605.5	577.1	–4.69

	Items	Unit	1985-86	1986-87*	1987-88*	1988-89*	1989-90*	1990-91*	1991-92*	1992-93*	1993-94*	1994-95*	Percentage change over previous year
7.	Long Distance Circuits ends Speech (Equipped capacity)	(000)	133.2	150.9	163.3	179.8	189.7	198.6	208.7	247.1	294.5	297.2	+0.92
8.	Revenue Rs.	(Crores)	1309.31	1770.39	2424.07	3405.58	4013.15	4447.43	4966.58**	6198.91**	8205.18**	10206.39	+24.39
9.	Expenditure Rs.	(Crores)	1112.33	1409.50	1758.44	2190.48	2532.43	3041.22	3535.58	4158.56	5660.38	6832.49	+2.74
10.	Revenue Surplus Over Expenses Rs.	(Crores)	196.98	360.89	665.63	1215.10	1481.10	1406.21**	1431.00	2040.35	2544.80	3373.9	+32.58
11.	Capital Investment during the year Rs.	(Crores)	850.03	982.32	1353.01	2047.47	2596.13	2772.22	3400.26	4605.85	5579.12	5815.86	+4.24
12.	Progressive Capital Investment (at the end of the year)	(Crores)	5387.64	6389.96	7742.97	10020.94	12312.75	15112.68	18512.94	23118.79	28697.91	30439.63	+6.06
13.	Personnel (at the end of the year)	(000)	345	349	350	362	370	375	373	385	395	419	+6.07

* Includes MTNL. ** Excluding network charges received from MTNL.

Includes Analogue and Digital long distance circuits Ends Speech (Equipped Capacity in 000's) 188 and 166 respectively.

ORGANISATION CHART

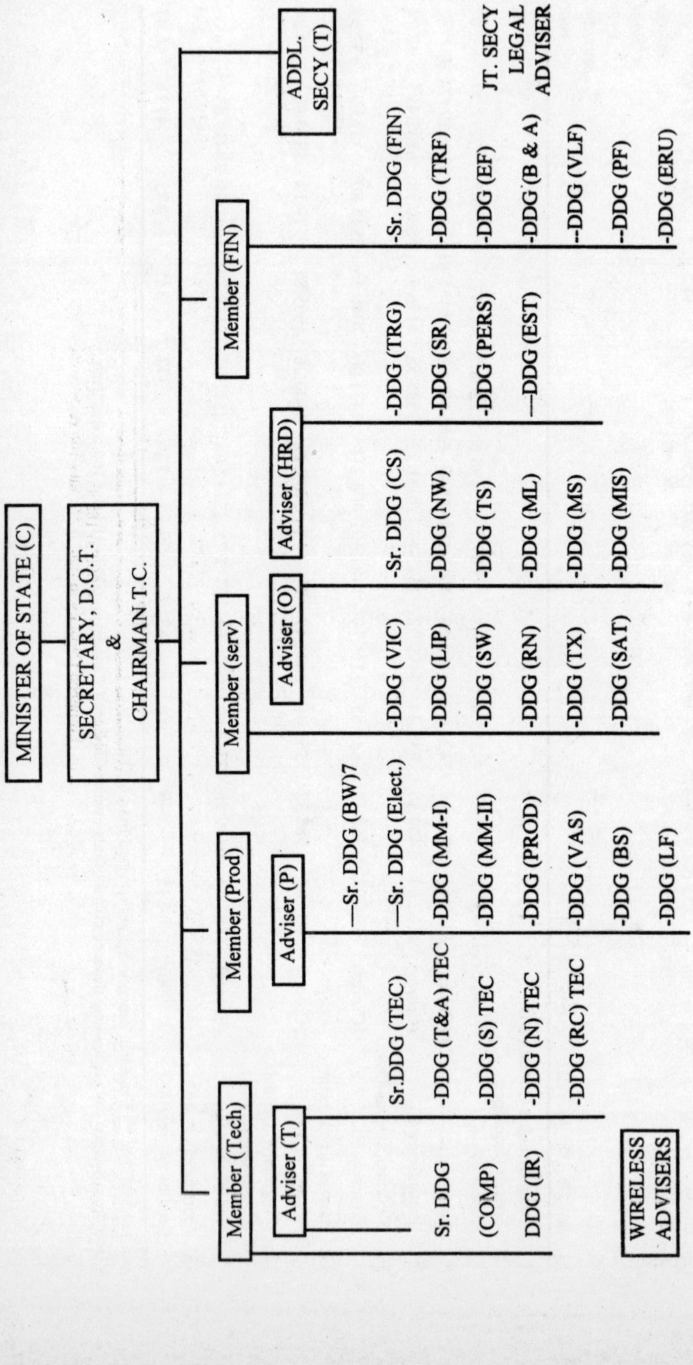

Appendix F

FUTURISTIC DEVELOPMENTS IN INFORMATION TECHNOLOGY

Plan for Ultimate Internet

Quantum leaps in communication technology, especially Internet, have phenomenally increased the size and scope of business transactions. A party in Bangalore can now place orders directly with a firm in Japan on behalf of a second party somewhere in the USA and authorise its bankers in yet another continent to release immediate payments. An intercontinental deal worth millions can be clinched in a matter of hours, a process which otherwise would take several weeks to complete.

The corporate manager plays a vital role in utilising infotech as a tool in solving problems and enhancing output by synergising different components of production like administration, accounting and manpower and resource management.

Cable Internet technology aims at overcoming bandwidth restriction by sending data from Internet server to desktops through the same cable which carries video information at speeds ranging from 2 to 10 mbps. Here the transmissions are bi-directional between server and home PCs. The digital data which is modulated/demodulated rides atop one of the many TV channels without any interference.

Beginning in 2000, rockets all over the world will begin carrying Volkswagen-sized satellites about 700 km. above the earth. Over the course of two years, 840 of them will be gently dropped into place, fanning out to form a constellation that covers the globe.

Put a geostationary satellite at a height of 36000 km. and it takes only one to beam television to all Asia. The signal takes half a second to bounce up to a satellite and then find its way back down to earth. A half second delay works for a TV signal because it is continuous and the viewer does not know or care when the original picture was sent. But on the Internet, it is a nightmare. That is because the basic building block for the Net is called TCP-IP (transmission control protocol-Internet protocol). As a message is sent, each bit of information is checked to make sure it got to where it was going. Pulling up a page on the World Wide Web (WWW) means thousands of messages sent back and forth, with the computers having a conversation. It would fall apart if there is a half second delay between those check-backs, which is why the Teledesic satellites have to be so close to the ground. To get the service, users will buy or rent antennas about the size of a pizza disk and signal decorders that plug into their computers or telephones. With that set up, they will be able to do high speed data transfers like video conferencing from anywhere in the world.

IT tools have already done away with the tedious paper-ridden processes at the offices. The next on their list are the offices elimination.

Sony Corp plans to launch desk-top personal computers in Japan in the 1997-98 business year and is considering selling notebook PCs in the USA in the future.

Colour TVs

Of the 30.55 million colour TVs units sold across Asia in 1996, India accounted for 1.9 million and China for 18.5 million. Recent surveys estimate that the Asian market will grow to 46 million units by 2001, or roughly one-third of the global market, with sales expected to increase by an average 8.5 per cent annually. Within Asia, it is China that is all set to become the world's largest buyer to colour TV sets, with the projected sales figure pegged at 25 million units.

Money-clip

Recently a group of companies have announced that they have developed new technology which can turn almost any PCs into an Automatic Tellers Machine (ATM). This new technology is called Moneyclip and it will allow its users to perform virtually an ATM transaction from the comfort of their homes. Consumers can buy devices now that attach to a PC and allow them to check an account balance, pay bills, transfer funds between accounts, or download electronic cash onto a smart card. This smart card, a plastic card embedded with a silicon chip, can then be used to make a purchase over the Internet or as cash at merchants that accept them. Moneyclip is a portable diskette that carries a smart card and the software necessary to access a bank account. It can be fed into the floppy drive of any PC. In order to use moneyclip, a PC has to be already loaded with online banking software, and the user has to have an account at a bank that offers online banking.

New Supercomputer

The Centre for Development of Advance Computing (C-DAC) is developing a teraflop open-frame architecture machine that would be a thousand times more powerful than any of the present computer system. It would be capable of performing 20 billion mathematical operations in the blink of an eye. An open-frame architecture implies the capability to put together a supercomputer using commercially available off-the-shelf components.

Insat

Insat-2D, fourth of India's second generation communication satellite, will be launched from French Guyana on May 29 by a European Ariana-4 rocket. It has a weight of 2070 kg. Insat-2D would increase the effective isotopic radiated power in some of the channels and it would provide more redundancy to enhance the reliability of the payload. Insat-2D would carry 10 normal C-band channels, two C-band channels to provide expanded coverage, six extended C-band transponders, mobile satellite service and KU-band transponders. Insat-2E would be launched in 1998. INSAT-3, series will begin in 1999.

Augment of Intelligence

If we want to augment our intelligence further, we can only do it by linking ourselves to machines and computers. Brain size is limited by the capacity for blood circulation, as are the links between neurons. Even with memory enhancing drugs, etc. brain improvement is marginal perhaps 10 per cent. Silicon based machine or computers offer the best route through direct and indirect connection with the brain.

Fibre Optic Cable

Demand for fibre optic cable is 10 per cent ahead of world production. It has greater capacity and is more efficient than traditional copper phone lines. Fibre optic cable installed in 1995 was 10 million miles and be the end of 1998 it will be 20 million miles. It will be approximately 35 million miles in 2001.

Global Language

As many as 90 per cent of the world's languages may disappear in the next century, due to the ability of IT to create a global culture. Global computers networks are reinforcing English as the dominant international language, and it may become the most common second or even first language for most people around the world.

GLOSSARY

Alogorithm

A step by step procedure for carrying out a numerical or algebraic operation.

Authority File

A set of records that establishes authoritative forms for headings or access points for a set of bibliographic records.

Asynchronous Transmission

A mode of telecommunication transmission in which each character or small block of data is synchronized. The gap between transmitted characters may be of unequal length.

Analog

A continuous physical variable which bears a direct relationship to another variable so that one is proportional to the other.

Bandwidth

A measure of frequency use or capacity. Voice transmission requires a bandwith of 3 to 4 KHz.

Batch Processing

A type of computer processing in which similar operations or problems are stored and put in batches to be processed.

Boolean Logic

A form of symbolic logic, devised by George Boole (1815-64)

which provides a mathematical procedure for manipulating logical relationships in symbolic form.

Bearing

The horizontal direction of one point with respect to another, usually measured as a clockwise angle. True bearing is with respect to true north.

Binary

Composed of only two elements. A number system in which two digits, 0 and 1 are used.

Binary Gain

A gain control system in which amplification is changed only in discrete steps by factors of 2.

Bit

A binary digit, the smallest unit of information.

Bench-Mark Problem

A problem used to evaluate the performance of computers relative to each other. A flow chart that is coded for execution on various systems is often used so that the problem-solving ability of different systems can be compared under similar circumstances.

Compler

A programme for converting a source program in symbolic language to an object program in machine language independent of the running of the source program. An interpreter involves the conversion concurrently with running the programme.

Compatible Software

The ability of software to run on different computers without modification. Also, a feature that enables different application programs, such as framework and Word Star, to share common conventions and rules so that they can be run together as one coordinated package.

Computer

A device capable of solving problems or manipulating data by accepting data, performing prescribed operations on the data and supplying the results of these operations. Various types of computers are: analog and digital.

Communication

Transfer of ideas and information from one mind to another mind is called the communication. Man is a communicator of information. It is this capability of communication of very complex ideas from man to man which has led to our present state of civilisation.

Cordless Phone

It consists of a base unit and a handset. The handset can be used only within a specified range, up to a maximum distance of 100 m from the base unit. A cordless phone unit is connected to land lines and underground cables.

Cable Television

A transmission system using a broadband cable (coaxial cable or optical fibre) to deliver video signals directly to television sets, in contrast to over-the air transmission.

C-Band

Portion of the electromagnetic spectrum in the 4 to 6 GHz range used for satellite communications.

Data

Information represented in a formal manner so that it can be processed, stored, manipulated, and transmitted by computers or other equipment.

Data Base

An automated body of information that is systematically recorded, retrieved or updated.

DBM-S

Database Management system is a special kind of a program that permits users to examine and/or rearrange data-bases in special ways.

Disk Drive

A circular, metal plate with magnetic material recorded on both sides continuously rotating for reading or writing by one or more read/write heads mounted on fixed or movable arms.

Digital

Representation of quantities is discrete units. A digital system is one in which the information is contained and manipulated as a series of discrete numbers.

Down Link

An earth station used to receive signals from a satellite the signal transmitted from the satellite to earth.

Disk Operating System (DOS)

An operating system that uses disks for its secondary storage medium. Typically, the disk operating system regulates space allocation, keeps track of files, saves and retrieves files and manages other control functions associated with disk storage.

Ethernet

A type of LAN based on CSMA/CD technology developed jointly by DEC, Xerox and Intel.

Ethernet Cables and Bus

Run at a much higher speed and send information in packets. Ethernet bus is a coaxial cable which is routed round the station, enabling new modes to be added, without cutting the cable but just screwing on a connection box. The speed of communication through this coaxial cable is 1 MBps.

Electronic Mail

The electronic transmission of letters, messages and memos from one computer to another.

Electronic Spread Sheet

A software package for variable calculations. The screen display consists of an accountants spread sheet of up to 60 or more columns and over 250 or more rows. Any element in the display grid can be a numeric value, a formula or an arithmetic calculations, any item can relates to and/or affect any other element.

Ernet Mail

It was established by the Department of Electronics during the Seventh Five Year Plan (1986-91) to provide academic and research institutions with electronic mail facilities. It is currently used by DSIR labs, research centres and academic institutions.

Flow Chart

A diagram showing the operations involved in a process. Often used to show a computer program or computer processing steps and their sequence.

Fourier Transform

The formulae which convert a time function into the frequency domain representation and vice versa.

Floppy Disks

Storage devices in the form of small flexible disks used for random access requirements in controllers and CPUs and as a compact substitute for punched cards. A typical floppy disk provides capacity for about 300,000 data bytes. Floppies were originally developed for low cost, low capacity data storage and relatively low data transfer rates.

Facsimile (Fax)

A system of telecommunication to transmit images for reproduction on hard copy. The original image is scanned and converted to an electrical signal and the electrical signal is subsequently converted to a replica of the original image at the receiving terminal.

Gateway

A protocol translating interface between a given LAN and the external communications environment which uses a different protocol.

Global System for Mobile Communications (GSM)

It is a Pan-European standard and is the latest in cellular technology worldwide. The new GSM technology uses a digital computer language. The digital transmission eliminates background noise and other interferences. GSM's digital system allows a very large number of calls to occur simultaneously, enabling more people to use mobile phones.

Geostationary Satellite

A satellite with an equatorial orbit 22,300 miles (36,000 km) above the earth. The satellite revolves above the earth in the same direction and with the same speed as that of the earth's rotation (i.e. 24 hours), and thus appears stationary when viewed from the earth.

Geosynchronous Orbit

Synchronous with the earth. An orbit 22,300 miles above the earth's equator where satellite circles the earth once in 24 hours, thereby appearing stationary to an observer on earth.

Hard Copy

A printed copy of data in human readable form.

Hardware

Physical computer equipment, e.g., mechanical, magnetic, electrical or electronic devices.

Host

A system or subsystem in a network that performs actual processing operations against a database and with which other network nodes communicate.

Host Computer

A primary or controlling computer in a network or system.

Hub

A head end for bi-directional (midsplit) networks.

Information Technology

It is the combination of information science, computer technology, communication technology and management science. Information technology is the brain of hi-tech industry and telecom is the heart. IT, at a basic level, is the conversion of human intelligence and logic into software that propels the computer to give the desired output. Telecom provides the wherewithal to send the bytes of information soaring across the country or even to far off countries via satellite uplinks.

Information Theory

Information theory is the body of statistical mathematics which has developed out of efforts to understand and improve the communication art. The modern theory of information is based largely on the theories of Shannon. The basic principle adopted is that any message which has a high probability of occurrence conveys little information. Most information is conveyed by the least likely message. Thus information theory is based on probability. Meaningful messages can appear by sheer chance.

Inmarsat

The International Maritime Satellite organisation, which provides satellites for maritime and aeronautical communication.

Internet

Internet was born in 1969 as a pentagon research and development network. Now, half of the Internet domains are outside the United States. Internet is the fast growing network of computers around the world. Connecting millions of users through a simple telephone line.

Integrated Service Digital Network (ISDN)

An electronic superhighway for transmitting digital signals using internationally accepted standards.

Indonet

It is an integrated information management and distributed data processing facility. It is a commercial network with nodes at Calcutta, Bombay and Madras on IBM 4361. It is connected to other cities like Ahmedabad, Delhi, Pune, Bangalore through MUXs/cluster controllers. This network uses IBMs System Network Architecture. It is planned as a geographically dispersed computer network linking scattered organisations in the country. It will be connected through international gateways to GTE Telnet and TYMNET computer networks of USA. Also it will be connected to DATEX-P in Germany and TRANSPAC in France and to the other IR networks. It provides access to remote user terminals.

Infotel

It was established by Informatics India Ltd. in 1989. It is an on-line service centre with access to 1500 international databases tapped through DIALOG or EASYNET.

Layer

Used to define a discrete level of function with a defined service interface.

Link

A communication path or circuit between two nodes or points.

Long Haul Network

A wide area communication facility ranging from a few kilometres to around the globe.

Laser Printer

Laser printers are the stars of non-impact technology. Using a laser beam to draw characters directly onto a photosensitive drum, the full page image is then transferred electrostatically to toner and paper and then the toner is melted into the paper.

Memory

A part of a computing machine in which data can be stored and from which it can later be retrieved. Types of memory include core, magnetic drum, magnetic tape, registers, etc.

Modem

An A/D and D/A conversion device interfacing the data termination equipment and the analog transmission lines.

Mainframe or CPU

The heart of the general purpose computer that controls the interpretation and execution of instructions. Does not include interface, main memory, or peripherals. It also controls input and output units and auxiliary attachments.

Micro-Computer

A complete tiny computing system consisting of hardware and software that usually sells for less than five thousand dollars and whose main processing blocks are made of semi-conducting integrated circuits. In function and structure it is somewhat similar to a mini-computer, with the main difference being price, size, speed of execution and computing power. The hardware of a microcomputer consists of a micro-processing unit which is usually assembled on a PC board with memory and auxiliary circuits. Power supply, control console and cabinet are separate.

Micro-Processor

The central unit of micro-computer that contains the logical elements of manipulating data and performing arithmetic or logical operations on it. A single chip may contain RAM, ROM and PROM memories, clocks and interfaces for memory and I/O devices.

Minicomputer

A small programmable general purpose computer typically used for dedicated applications. The term often refers only to the mainframe, which typically sells for less than $25,000. Usually it is a parallel binary system with 8, 12,16, 18, 24 or 36 bit word length incorporating semi-conductors or magnetic core memory offering from 4 to 64 K words of storage and a cycle time of 0.2 to 8 micro seconds or less.

Mouse

A hand-held device, separate from a keyboard, used to control cursor position on a display screen. As the mouse rolls along a table top, its relative position approximates the position of the cursor. Introduced by Xerox in the STAR 8010 professional workstation in 1981.

Modulation

It is a process by which some characteristics of the information carrier are modified in accordance with the instantaneous value of the input function. Modulation methods serve to improve the transmission reliability.

Multiplexing

The cost of a communication channel is often very high and therefore it is desired to send number of information on the same channel. The technique of transmitting many messages over the same channel is known as multiplexing. In this case, several sources of information are connected to the same transmitter. At the receiving end, the signals are converted back into respective messages.

Mobile Phone

It is a two-way communication device. Through which both, the caller and the receiver can carry out a complete conversation at any time and anywhere. The mobile phone service will also give the facility of "short message services". When one does not want to talk, he can simply receive the message on the display screen of his handset.

Noise

Any unwanted signal.

Nyquist Frequency

A frequency associated with sampling which is equal to half the sampling frequency. Frequencies greater than the Nyquist frequency will alias as lower frequencies from which they will be indistinguishable.

Node

An identifiable point in a design that must be electrically connected to other nodes. A node may or may not be associated with a specific device or topology.

Nicnet

The National Informatics Centre (NIC) was established in 1975 for advanced computer based methodologies, data management techniques, generating specialised manpower and building intracity and intercity computer networks. NIC established NICNET in 1977. It links four regional nodes at Delhi, Pune, Bhubaneshwar and Hyderabad and has established 32 nodes of State and Union Territory levels and 439 nodes at district headquarters. NICNET is based on spread spectrum multiple access techniques and uses C-200 series micro-earth stations.

Network Architecture

A network architecture is the pattern that network components make. It comprises the hardware architecture, distributed applications architecture, applications integration architecture, communications architecture, etc. Each architecture contributes to the development of an integrated environment. The placement of servers, users, clients, hosts and communication hardware in a suitable pattern gives birth to a functional network architecture.

Offline

A system in which peripheral devices operate independent of the central processor.

On Line

A system in which peripheral devices are in direct and continuing communication with the central processing unit.

Operating System

Software that controls the operation of a data processing system and that may provide the following services: determine what jobs are running and what parts of the computer system are working on each job at any given time, impose standards and procedures on machine operation, take care of the numerous little details lumped together as house keeping, and invoking standard troubleshooting actions in case of malfunction. These operating systems are usually very complex and require large amount of machine and disk storage. Sometimes called Supervisor, Executive, Monitor, Master Control Program, depending on the computer manufacturer.

Optical Fibre

A thin, flexible glass fibre the size of a human hair which will transmit light waves capable of carrying large amount of information.

OSI Standards

Open system Interconnect is technically promoted by TC 97, the technical committee of ISO and its other related components. Its work is conducted in CCITT. The important characteristics of OSI are that the systems participating in a network should be open, distributed and heterogeneous. OSI undertakes the job through seven layers. The top three layers cater to users of data and information services, the fourth layer controls the transformation of data between a user and the network. The lower three layers cater to specific functions and are called network layer, data link layer and physical layer. OSI offers a directory of standards that are not only necessary for communication but also important for maintaining bibliographic standards.

Packet Switching

A data network as defined by the CCITT X.25 standard, whereby a virtual call is established but individual packets of data may be separately routed across the network.

Personal Computer (PC)

A microprocessor based unit with a central memory typically ranging between 64 KB and 1 MB. PCs having 8 or 16 or 32 BPW are available in the market.

Protocol

A rule of conduct, a procedure for ordering the exchange of formated information packets between correspondents. Protocol are interpreted through hardware and software.

Pert

Program evaluation and review technique. A time event network analysis system in which the various events in a programme or project are identified, with the planned time for each, and are placed in a network showing the relationships of each event to other events.

Page

In virtual storage systems, a fixed length block of instruction, data, or both, that can be transferred between real storage and external page storage; typically about 4 K bytes. A program will be divided into pages in order to minimize the total amount of main memory storage allocation to the program at any one time. The pages will normally be stored on a fast direct access store and can be moved into main memory by operating system or hardware whenever the instructions of that subdivision need to be performed.

Pager

It is a one-way communication device. One can only receive messages through it. These one-way messages are very short, and pass on very limited information. To contact the sender, one will have to use the nearest phone available. Every paging service operates on a specific frequency. One has to first subscribe to a paging service and then buy a compatible pager.

Pacing

In virtual storage systems, the process of transferring pages between real storage and external page storage. If a page is not transferred from auxiliary storage until it is actually needed, then paging is said to be done by demand.

Parallel Processing

Processing more than one program at a time on a parallel basis, where more than one processor is active at one time, as distinguished from multiprocessing where only one processor is active on one program at a time.

Powerful

Software is considered powerful if it is efficient and provides a wide range of options. In user software, it refers to the user's ability to put these options into action without too much effort. In system software, it denotes the ability to generate complex commands with a minimum of instructions. Hardware is considered powerful if it is faster, larger, and more versatile than comparable machines.

Quantization

The process of approximation of signal by discrete levels is known as amplitude quantization. The sample is then converted into a code group by means of an encoder.

Relay

A system which performs an intermediate function in the communication between two or more end systems, e.g., a node in a public switched network.

Redundancy

A repetition of information or the insertion of information which is not new.

Rs-232-C

A technical specification published by the Electronic Industries Association establishing the interface requirements between modems and terminals or computer.

Repeater

A device inserted at intervals along a circuit to boast, amplify and/or regenerate the signal being transmitted. A repeater is needed because the quality and strength of the signal decays over distance.

Remote Area Business Message Network (RAMBN)

It was established in 1991 by the Department of Telecommunications. This is a satellite based network with a star configuration and has a master earth station at Sikandrabad near Delhi. This network is used to exchange of messages among closed\ user groups.

Synergetic

A combination of data elements such that more information is apparent from the combination than from the elements treated independently.

Security

The general subject of making sure the computerized data and program files of the company cannot be accessed, obtained or modified by unauthorized personnel, and cannot be fouled up by the computer or its programs. Security is implemented by special software, special hardware, and the computer's operating procedure.

Software

A term coined to contrast computer program from the hardware of a computer system. Software programs are stored sets of instructions stored in the hardware. They govern the operation of a computer system and make the hardware run. Software is a key determining factor in getting more computer power per dollar. Software is used to define the processor programs, library routines, manuals and other services program supplied by a computer manufacturer to facilitate the use of a computer. In addition, it may refer to other programs specially developed to fit the users need and also to all the documents associated with a computer.

State-Of-The-Art

The most current research and up to date technology in specific field of knowledge.

Sampling

Sampling process converts a continuous signal into a train of pulses. Sampling of data is one of the fundamental operations in digital systems. In a digital system only certain discrete values of amplitudes of the sample are allowed. Any sample which falls between the two allowed levels is converted into a sample of amplitude level nearest to the actual value of the signal.

Sampling Theorem

It states that no loss of information occurs if the signal is sampled at a rate which is at least twice as fast as the signal's highest frequency content. The sampling frequency is determined by the highest frequency content of the signal.

S Band

Frequencies in the 2.5 GHz range, used for community reception from satellites.

Spread Spectrum Technique

A means of spreading a transmitted signal over extra-bandwidth to permit redundancy in transmission and reception without interference from other signals using similar frequencies.

Scientific and Industrial Research Network (SIRNET)

It is a computer communication network initially started for CSIR Laboratories. The SIRNET electronic mail mode is at INSDOC. It is connected to Education and Research Network (ERNET) set up by the Department of Electronic (DOE). Through ERNET, SIRNET has access to Unix User Network, an international network. Also it has access to JANET, CSNET and BINET. The software used for SIRNET is Basic Networking Software with standard UNIX package to communicate with other UNIX systems.

Standardization

To promote fast and fault free communication from a source to a user or a user to source, it is important that the conversion of information into signals and signals into information is achieved in efficient way. It is important that international standards must be maintained for switching/packet switching or transmission equipment or protocols.

Telemetering

The transmission of data from a point of observation to a recording point, often by radio.

Transducer

A device which converts one form of energy into another.

Transponder

A device which transmits a signal upon receiving another signal. A microwave receiver, amplifier, and transmitter in a satellite that amplifies and changes the frequency of a signal from an earth station and retransmits it to earth.

Transmitter

The device that sends the telecommunications signal through a wire or cable or through the air.

Tag

A character or a digit or a series of characters or digits which are attached to a field or a record as a means to identify or to signal the computer of what is coming next.

Tele Tax

The international service for text interchange which provides a rapid exchange of text via the telephone network and other public data networks.

Terminal

A device for entering data into or receiving data from a computer system or computer network. A point in a communication network at which data can either enter or leave.

Thesaurus

A terminology list to control access points in a file. Generally used with respect to control of subject terms for use in information retrieval systems.

User Friendly

Refers to software and hardware systems that are supposedly easy for a user to learn without requiring a great deal of specialized knowledge or training.

Uplink

An earth station used to transmit to a satellite; the transmission from the earth to the satellite.

Video-Text

The generic name for a system that transmits alpha-numeric and graphic information for display on a video monitor.

Vsat

Very small aperture terminal.

Value Added Services

They include facilities such as roaming, teleconferencing, closed user group facility, short message service facility, voice mail, call barring, call forwarding, call hold and call waiting, call number identification presentation or restriction, bill on demand with prior request, advice of charge on handset display screen and many more.

Vikram

It is a packed switched public data network of the DOT. The network management centre is in Delhi, and switching nodes at Bombay, Calcutta, Madras, Bangalore, Hyderabad, Ahmedabad and Pune with 12 remote access points all connected by leased or dial up lines.

Virtual Terminal

One of the protocols being developed for the OSI application layer for terminal access to computer.

White Noise

Random energy containing all frequency components in equal proportions within the bandwidth, phases are random.

Winchester Disk

Rigid, non-removable, magnetic oxide coated, random access disk sealed in a filtered enclosure along with the read/ write heads and head actuator. Heads fly only about 20 micro-inch from disk surface, allowing very dense data storage. Capacity ranges from 5 Mb (325 to 16,000 pages) for the 5¼ inch disk and from 6.5 to 635 Mb (1625 to 15,8750 pages) for 8 inch disk, calculated at 4000 characters per single spaced page.

Window

An isolated portion of a Cathode ray tube screen that is used to display information independently from the rest of the screen display.

Word Processing

The transformation of ideas and information into a readable form of communication through the management of procedures, equipment and personnel.

Word Star

A popular word processing software package developed by MICRO PRO International.

X.25

Interface between the data terminal equipment (DTE) and circuit terminating equipment for terminals operating in the packet mode and connect to public data network by a dedicated circuit.

X.400

Message handling systems: system model service elements.

Yardstick

Standards of performance for evaluating devices or processes.

Zenith

A point directly overhead.

Bibliography

1. Abramson, N., "Packet Switching with Satellite," Proc. NCC, pp. 695-702, 1973.
2. Archer, E.J., "Identification of Visual Patterns as a Function of Information Load," J.Exp. Psychol, 48, 313, 1954.
3. Baron, R.L. and Piccirilli, A.T., "Digital Logic and Computer Operations," McGraw Hill Book Company, New York, 1967.
4. Booth, T.L., "Digital Network and Computer Systems," John Wiley & Sons, Inc., New York, 1971.
5. Bartee, T.C., "Digital Computer Fundamentals," John F.Rider, Publisher, Inc., N.Y., 1964.
6. Baran, P., "On Distributed Communication Networks," IEEE Trans. Commun. Syst., Vol. CS-12, pp. 1-9, Mar., 1964.
7. Binde, R., "A Dynamic Packet Switching System for Satellite Broadcast Channels," Proc. ICC, p. 41, 1975.
8. Boorstyn, R.R. and Frank, H., "Large Scale Network Topological Optimization," IEEE Trans. Commun., Vol. CoM -25, pp. 29-47, Jan., 1977.
9. Boulter, B.A., "A New Active Device Suitable for use in Digital Circuits," Electron. Eng., Vol. 35, No. 420, pp. 86-91, Feb. 1963.
10. Brewett, J.P. and J.H., Rubel, "Video Delay Lines," Proc. IRE., Vol. 35, pp. 1580-84, Dec., 1947.
11. Balakrishan, A.V., "A Note on the Sampling Principle for Continuous Signals," IT 3, 143, Jun., 1957.
12. Barnard, G.A., "The Theory of Information," J.Roy Statist, Soc., 13 B, 46, 1951.

13. Blachman, N.M., "A Generalisation of Mutual Information," Proc. I.R.E., 49, 1331, Aug., 1961.
14. Blachman, N.M., "Noise and its effect on communication," McGraw Hill, 1966.
15. Blazic Borka Jerman, "Scientific Communication through Computer Networks," Science and Development, 30 (2), pp. 29-32, Apr.- Jun. 1991.
16. Bawden, David, "Choosing an automated system," Aslib Information, 18(9), pp. 272-74, Sep., 1990.
17. Chen, Y., "Digital Computer Design Fundamental," McGraw Hill Book Company, New York, 1962.
18. Cadzow, J.A. and Martens H.R., "Discrete Time and computer control systems," Prentice Hall Inc., Englewood Cliffs, N.J., 1970.
19. Cadzow, J.A., "Discrete time systems," Prentice Hall Inc., Englewood Cliffs, N.J., 1973.
20. Cooper, W.D., "Electronic instrumentation and measurement techniques," Prentice Hall Inc., Englewood Chiff, N.J., 1970.
21. Casey R.G., "Allocation of copies of files in an information network," Proc. SJCC, pp. 617-25, 1972.
22. Clark, D.D., Pogran, K.T. and Reed, D.P., "An introduction to local area networks," Proc. IEEE, Vol. 66, pp. 1497-1517, Nov., 1978.
23. Codd, E.F., "A relation model of data for large shared data banks," Commun. ACM, Vol. 13, pp. 377-87, 1970.
24. Campbel, L.L., "Information theory and the separability of signals with overlapping spectra," IT 7, 193, 1961.
25. Cathod Ray, "Information theory," Wireless word, 58, 365, 1952.
26. Chang, T.T. and Lawton, J.G., "On the comparison of communication channels", IT 10, 97, Jan., 1964.
27. Cherry, C., "The communication of information," Endeavour, 23, 13, Jan., 1964.
28. Cawkell, A.E., "Electronic information delivery systems," Critique 1 (1) pp. 1-12, Jul./Aug., 1988.

29. Cronin Blaise, "The competitive campus: Networking and higher education," Libri 39 (3), pp. 173-84, Sep., 1989.

30. Director, S.W. and Rohrer, R.A., "Introduction to system theory," McGraw Hill Book Company, N.Y., 1972.

31. Dalal, Y. and Metcalfe, R., "Reverse path forwarding of broadcast packets," Commun. ACM, Vol. 21, pp. 1040-48, 1978.

32. Davies, D.W., "The control of congestion in packet switching networks," IEEE Trans. Commun., Vol. COM-20, pp. 546-50, Jun., 1972.

33. Donnelle, J.E., "Components of a network operating system," Comput. Networks, Vol. 3, pp. 389-99, Dec., 1979.

34. Davies, I.L., "On determining the presence of signal in noise," Proc. IEE, 99, pt. 3, 45, Mar., 1952.

35. Donaghue, Hugh P., "Implication of trans-border data flows to library networks," IFLA Journal, 9(1), 1983, pp. 34-38.

36. Ecker, J.P., "A survey of digital computer memory systems," Proc. IRE, Vol. 41, pp. 1393-1406, Oct., 1953.

37. Flores, I., "Computer design," Prentice Hall, Englewood Cliffs, N.J., 1967.

38. Field, J.A., "Efficient computer—computer communication," Proc. IEE, Vol. 123, pp. 756-60, Aug., 1976.

39. Fleming, H.C. and Hutchison, R.M. Jr., "Low speed data transmission on the switched telecommunication network," Bell syst. Tech. J., pp. 1385-1406, Apr., 1971.

40. Frank, H. and Chou, W., "Topological optimization of computer networks," Proc. IEEE, Vol. 60, p. 1385, Nov., 1972.

41. Fraser, A.G., "Delay and error control in a packet switched network," Proc. ICC, pp. 22.4-121 to 22.4 -125, 1977.

42. Fidel, Raya and Grandall, Michael, "The AACR 2 as a design Scheme for bibliographic databases," Library quarterly 58(2) pp. 123-42, Apr., 1988.

43. Gerla, M. and Kleinrock, L., "Topological design of distributed computer networks," IEEE Trans. Commun. Vol. Com-25, pp. 48-60, Jan., 1977.

44. Green, P.E., "An introduction to network architectures and protocols," IEEE Trans. Commun, Vol. Com-28, pp. 413-24, Apr., 1980.

45. Gabor, D., "Theory of communication," J. IEE, 93, pt. 3, 429, 1946.

46. Gates, Yuri, "User needs and technology options for electronic document delivery," Aslib Proceedings 35(4) pp. 195-203, Apr., 1983.

47. Ghosh, Bhabani Kumar, "National information network in developing countries with special reference to India," Herald of Library Science, 18(1-2), pp. 105-12, Jan-Apr., 1979.

48. Gupta, R.C., "Computerised indexing through CDS/ISIS software package," Lucknow Librarian, 21(4), pp. 153-58, Oct-Dec., 1989.

49. Hill, F.J. and Peterson, G.R., "Digital systems: Hardware organisation and design," John Wiley & Sons. hInc., 1973.

50. Heath, F.G., "Digital computer design," Oliver and Boyd, Edinburgh, 1969.

51. Huffman, D., "A method for the construction of minimum redundancy codes," Proc. IRE, Vol. 40, pp. 1098-1101, Sep., 1952.

52. Hakimi, S.L., "Simultaneous flows through a communication network," CT 9, 169, 1962.

53. Harman, W.W., "Principles of statistical theory of communication," McGraw Hill, 1963.

54. Hopkinson, Alan, "The UNESCO common communication Format : Progress to data," International Cataloguing and bibliographic control, p. 27, Apr.-Jun., 1988.

55. Iyengar, Vasundhara S., "Computer networking: USIS experience," Iaslic Bulletin, 33(4), pp. 129-34, Dec., 1988.

56. Jensen, E.D., "The Honeywell Experimental Distributed Processor—An Overview," Computer, Vol 11, Jan., 1978. pp. 28-38,

57. Johnson, W.C., "Transmission lines and networks," McGraw Hill Book Company, New York, 1980.

58. Jain, S.L., "Computerisation of information work," IASLIC Bulletin 32(3), pp. 125-27, 1987.

59. Jelinek, F., "Loss in information transmission through two way channels," Inf. and control, 6, 337, 1963.

60. Korn, G.A., "Minicomputers for engineers and scientists," McGraw Hill Book Company, New York, 1973.

61. Khan, R.E., "The organization of computer resources into a packet radio network," IEEE Trans. Commun., Vol. Com-25, pp. 169-79, Jan. 1977.

62. Kleinrock, L., "Analytic and simulation methods in computer network design," Proc. SJCC, pp. 569-79, 1970.

63. Kleinrock, L. and Yemini, Y, "An optimal adaptive scheme for multiple access broadcast communication," Proc. ICC, pp. 7.2.1 to 7.2.5, 1978.

64. Kasahar, Y., "Representation of communication channel capacities by means of Electrical networks," J. Inst. Elec. Comm. Engrs., Japan, 37, 791, Nov., 1954.

65. Khinchin, A.I., "Mathematical foundations of information theory," Dover, 1957.

66. London, K.R., "Introduction to computers," Affiliated East West Press Pvt. Ltd., New Delhi, 1971.

67. Ledley, R.S., "Digital computers and control engineering," McGraw Hill Book Company, New York, 1960.

68. Landau, H.J. and Pollak, H.O., "The dimension of the space of essentially time and band-limited signals," B.S.T.J., 41, 1295, Jul., 1962.

69. Linden, D.A., "A discussion of sampling theorems," Proc. IRE, 47, 1219, 1959.

70. Lahini, Abhifit and Sunder Singh, "Bibliographic databases and networks: Indian Scenario," NISSAT Newsletter, 8(2), Apr-Jun., pp. 3-16, 1989.

71. Mc Cracken, D.D., "Digital computer programming," John Wiley & Sons., Inc. New York, 1964.

72. Millman, J. and Halkias, C.C., "Integrated electronics: analog and digital circuits and systems," McGraw Hill Kogakusha Ltd., Tokyo, 1972.

73. Mahmond, S. and Riordan, J.S., "Optimal allocation of resources in distributed information networks," ACM Trans. on Database Syst., Vol. 1, Mar., pp. 66-78, 1976.

74. Martin, J., "Communications satellite systems," Englewood Cliffs, N.J., Prentice Hall, 1978.

75. Merkle, R.C., "Secure communications over insecure channels," Commun. ACM, Vol. 21, pp. 294-99, April, 1978.

76. Morris, R., "Information and satellite technology," Aslib Proceedings 32(2), pp. 71-76, Feb., 1983.

77. Mertz, P., "Information theory impact on modern communication," Trans. AIEE, 76, Pt I, 431, 1957.

78. Muroga, S., "On the capacity of a discrete channel," J. Phys. Sco. Japan, 8, 484, 1953.

79. Martin, Susan K., "Information technology and libraries toward the year 2000." College and Research Libraries 50(4), pp. 397-405, Jul., 1989.

80. Martin, W.J., "The network market-place and its implications," Aslib Proceedings 42(6), pp. 165-67, Jun., 1990.

81 Morris, Anne and Barnacle, Stephen, "The human side of library automation," The Electronic Library 7(2), pp. 84-92, Apr., 1989.

82. Moholt Pat, "The influence of technology on networking," Special Libraries, 80(2), Sping, pp. 82-84, 1989.

83. Nieuwenhuysen, Paul, "Computerised storage and retrieval of structured text information: CDS/ISIS version 2.3," Program 25(1), Jan., pp. 1-8, 1991.

84. Natarajan, M. and Kaliyaperumal, R., "Impact of new information technology and document provision and supply," ILA Bulletin 24(4), Jan-Mar., pp. 214-220, 1991.

85. Nyquist, H., "Certain factors affecting telegraph speed," BSTJ, 3, 324, 1924.

86. Naylor, Bernard, "Harmony through networking," Library Association information technology group Newsletter (20), pp. 16-28, Oct. 1989.

87. Phister, M., "Logical design of digital computers," John Wills, New York, 1958.

88. Peterson, W.W. and Brown, D.T., "Cyclic codes for error detection," Proc. IRE, Vol. 49, Jan., pp. 228-235, 1961.

89. Pouzin, L., "Packet networks, issues and choices," Proc. IFIP Congr. 77, pp. 515-21, 1977.

90. Pandian, M. Paul and Ravichandra Rao, I.K., "An automated serial control system: A module," Library science with a slant to documentation and information studies, 26(4) pp. 285-326, Dec., 1989.

91. Project Ernet, NISSAT Newsletter 9 (4) pp. 6-10, Oct.-Dec., 1990.

92. Rajaraman, V., "Principles of computer programming," Prentice Hall of India Pvt. Ltd., New Delhi, 1969.

93. Ragazzini, J.B. and Franklin, G.F., "Sampled data control system," McGraw Hill Company, New York, 1958.

94. Roberts, L., "Extensions of packet communication Technology to a hand held personal terminal," Proc. SJCC, pp. 295-98, 1972.

95. Ramsden, Hilary and Remsden Stephen, "The use of information technology by information services," The Aslib information technology survey, London, Aslib, p. 49, 1990.

96. Rea, W.T., "The communication engineers needs in information theory," Trans. AIEE, 75, pt. I, 805, 1956.

97. Roddem, T., "Narrow band pulse communication," Wireless world, 56, 202, Jun., 1950.

98. Raitt, D.I., "Recent development in telecommunication and their impact on information services," Aslib Proceedings 34(1), pp. 54-66, Jan., 1982.

99. Scott, N.R., "Electronic computer technology," McGraw Hill Book Company, New York, 1970.

100. Schwartz, M., Bennet, W.R. and Stein, S., "Communication systems and techniques," McGraw Hill Book Company, New York, 1966.

101. Schicker, P. and Duenki, A., "The virtual terminal definition," Comput. Networks, Vol. 2, pp. 429-41, Dec., 1978.

102. Selfridge, O.G. and Schwartz, R.T., "Telephone technology and privacy," Technology Review, Vol. 82, pp. 56-65, May, 1980.

103. Shoch, J.F., "Packet fragmentation in inter-network protocols," Comput. Networks, Vol. 3, pp. 3-8, 1979,

104. Shoch, J.F. and Stewart, L., "Interconnecting local networks via the packet radio network," Proc. Sixth Data Commun. Symp., pp. 153-58, 1979.

105. Sunshine, C.A., "Interconnection of computer networks," Comput. networks, Vol. 1, pp. 175-95, Jan. 1977.

106. Sugarman, R., "Sampling oscilloscope for statistically varying pulses," Rev. Sci. Instr., Vol. 28, No. 11, pp. 933-38, Nov., 1957.

107. Schwartz, L.S., "Information capacity of communication networks," Proc. NEC, 15, 414, 1959.

108. Shannon, C.E., "A mathematical theory of communication," BSTJ, 27, 379 and 623, Jul., Oct., 1948.

109. Shannon, C.E., "Communication in the presence of noise," Proc. IRE, 37, 10, 1949.

110. Shannon, C.E., "Channels with side information at the transmitter," IBMJ., 2, 289, 1958.

111. "SIRNET electronics Mail system," NISSAT Newsletter 10(1), pp. 3-6, Jan-Mar. 1991.

112. Smith, H. Christini, editor, "Open system interconnection: The communications technology of the 1990's" Papers from the perconference seminar held at London, Aug. 12-14, 1987, Munchen, K.G. Saur, 1988.

113. Stonier, Tom, "Intelligence networks: overview, purpose and policies in the contex of global social change," Aslib Proceedings, 38(9), pp. 269-74, Sept. 1986.

114. Tou, J., "Digital and sampled data control systems,." McGraw Hill Book Company, New York, 1959.

115. Taub, H. and Schilling, D.L., "Principles of communication system," McGraw Hill Book Company, New York, 1971.

116. Treleaven, P.C., "Exploiting program concurrency in computing systems," Computer, Vol. 12, pp. 42-49, Jan., 1979.

117. Trevor, J.B., "Artificial delay line design," Electronics, Vol. 18, pp. 135-37, Jun., 1945

118. Tuck, Bill, "Network updata," Aslib Proceeding 41(5), pp. 191-96, May, 1989.

119. Tuller, W.G., "Theoretical limits on the rate of transmission of information," Proc. IRE, 37, 468 (49).

120. UNESCO and International Council of Scientific Union: Synopsis of the feasibility study on a world science information system, Paris, UNESCO, p. 27, 1971.

121. Woollons, D.J., "Introduction to digital computers design," McGraw Hill Book Company, U.K., 1972.

122. Ward, S.A. and Terman, C.J., "An approach to personal computing," Compcon, Spring, pp. 460-65, 1980.

123. Wittie, L.D., "A distributed operating system for a reconfigurable network computer," Proc. First Int. Conf. on Distrib. Syst. IEEE, pp. 669-77, 1979.

124. Walton, Robert, "Managing technology," Library Journal 115(5), pp. 667-68, March 15, 1990.

125. Woods, L.B., et.al."Networking: yesterday, today & tomorrow," Resource sharing and information network, 6(1), pp. 5-16, 1990.

126. Zamanakos, A.S., "Bits of information," Trans. AIEE, 77, pt. 1, 197, 1958.

Index